THE SAN FRANCISCO 49ERS

THE FIRST FIFTY YEARS

———

BY GLENN DICKEY

WITH PHOTOGRAPHS BY MICHAEL ZAGARIS

Turner Publishing, Inc.

ATLANTA

LIBRARY OF CONGRESS CATALOGING-IN-PUBLICATION DATA

Dickey, Glenn.
The San Francisco 49ers: the first fifty years/by Glenn Dickey; photographs by Michael Zagaris.—1st ed.
p. cm.
ISBN 1-57036-199-1 (hardcover)
ISBN 1-57036-258-0 (paperback)
1. San Francisco 49ers (Football team)—History.
2. San Francisco 49ers (Football team)—Pictorial works.
I. Zagaris, Michael.   II. Title.
GV956.S3D52   1995
796.332'64'0979461—dc20
95-11327
CIP

Published by Turner Publishing, Inc.
A Subsidiary of Turner Broadcasting System, Inc.
1050 Techwood Drive, NW
Atlanta, Georgia 30318

Distributed by Andrews and McMeel
A Universal Press Syndicate Company
4900 Main Street
Kansas City, Missouri 64112

First Edition
10 9 8 7 6 5 4 3 2 1

Printed in the U.S.A.

TO NANCY AND SCOTT,

WHO MAKE MY LIFE WORTHWHILE.

G. D.

TO ARI, FOR ALL HIS HELP AND LOVE

BOTH ON AND OFF THE FIELD,

AND TO MR. D., WHO MADE IT ALL POSSIBLE.

M. Z.

YOU GET IT FROM SOMEWHERE

It was a record-setting crowd that massed at Candlestick Park, but turnstile counts can't convey the magnitude of that afternoon and early evening. Measured in the expenditure of unbridled hope and naked emotion, no other Bay Area football game ever came close. ¶ As the sixty thousand-plus privileged partisans gazed through crystal-clear January air to the field below, you almost could see their thoughts riding above the stadium like an advertisement scrolling across a blimp: Would the 49ers' thirty-sixth season, despite its unforeseen triumphs and euphoric sense of momentum, suffer the same fate as the previous thirty-five? Was San Francisco destined to remain a city of beauty and culture and progress but not championship football? ¶ The 49ers had been good during those thirty-five years since 1946, and they had been bad, too. More often, they had been frustratingly average. They had never won a conference or league title; no other NFL franchise could trace its roots back so far and make the same dubious claim. ¶ Now, here were the 49ers at the swirling tail of the 1981 NFC Championship Game, 89 yards from Super Bowl salvation and less than five minutes from abrupt banishment. The Dallas Cowboys — perhaps the most adulated and reviled sports franchise east of the Pecos, and the team that bumped San Francisco from the playoffs three consecutive years in the early 1970s — had taken a 27-21 lead a minute into the fourth

(Left) Dwight Clark makes The Catch against Dallas in the 1981 NFC Championship Game.

quarter, and they were threatening to brand that figure into the Candlestick scoreboard and into the hearts of the 49er faithful for eternity. ¶ Joe Montana, then the 49ers' twenty-five-year-old quarterback, still was at a point in his professional career when radio talk-show callers could, in all seriousness, weigh his abilities against those of, say, Steve Bartkowski or Lynn Dickey. His teammates, however, already knew Montana was a different breed. "He'd won a national championship in college [at Notre Dame], so this was no big deal to him,"tackle Keith Fahnhorst said later. "I'd never won a damn thing."

It was an imposing opponent Montana faced when he looked downfield toward the distant allure of the enemy end zone. The 1981 season had marked the Cowboys' fifteenth trip to the playoffs in sixteen years. They had former Super Bowl co-MVPs (Harvey Martin and Randy White) glaring at Montana from the defensive line, and over the preceding decade they had authored a lengthy chronology of Hail Marys and death-defying victories.

The 49ers, in contrast, were enjoying their first playoff run in nine seasons and their first winning record in five. Two seasons earlier, the team finished an abysmal 2-14. Twenty-nine of the forty-five players on San Francisco's roster had joined the team during the last two years. Thirteen rookies dotted the depth chart.

Recently acquired defensive end Fred Dean made his presence felt against the Cowboys.

Perhaps they were too young to perceive their peril. Maybe a more experienced team would have succumbed to bad associations and common sense. But the only historical facts that concerned the 49ers were these: They strung together a 13-3 regular-season record, the NFL's best in 1981; they had brutalized the Cowboys 45-14 on this same field in October; and they outgained—in their opinions, had outplayed—Dallas thus far in the rematch.

So far it had been a remarkable game, a topsy-turvy affair that already had seen five lead changes. The 49ers, executing the revolutionary possession-passing offense of coach Bill Walsh, moved forcefully against Dallas's defense but turned over the ball six times. From that standpoint, they were lucky to be in the game.

As the huddle broke, San Francisco center Randy Cross remembered his horoscope for the day: "You feel positive and highly revved-up about a dream you've been pursuing."

Walsh was feeling positive himself because, though they were starting at their own 11-yard line, the 49ers still owned three time outs to complement the 4:54 that showed on the game clock. Montana was happy, too, as he spotted the Cowboys in a Nickel package with six defensive backs. The Cowboys, conscious of the 49ers' vapid ground game (no back playing for San Francisco in the championship game rushed for more than 330 yards during the season), were daring them to run the ball.

Walsh, in wired communication with offensive line coach Bobb McKittrick on the field and quarterbacks coach Sam Wyche in the press box, stuck to the 49ers' strength and called for a swing pass to halfback Lenvil Elliott. It fell incomplete. Dallas girded itself for another pass, but Walsh ordered a draw and Elliott picked up 6 yards. It was third-and-4, the first critical play on a drive that would be full of them. Montana passed to wide receiver Freddie Solomon, who scooped up the low throw at the sideline for a first down at the 23-yard line.

Then Walsh went on the offensive. The 49ers sent Elliott, a little-used veteran subbing for injured starter Ricky Patton, around right end for 11 yards, then around left end for 7 more. "You really have to credit Lenvil Elliott," Cross said. "With him, we got our Bob back." It was a reference to Bob-18 and Bob-19, San Francisco's right-side and left-side sweeps. The Cowboys were surprised, and thrown a little off-balance. Elliott was not the foremost of Dallas's worries, but he was inflicting some Texas-sized damage.

The 49ers had moved the ball to their 41-yard line, easing out of a tight corner and into more spacious terrain. The Cowboys were being devoured in small nibbles, and the city by the bay was rocking in living rooms and taverns from the airport to the Presidio. Two plays later, Dallas was flagged for jumping offside, and San Francisco had another first down, at its 46-yard line.

Quarterback Joe Montana began building his reputation as a San Francisco legend with the victory over Dallas.

Montana passed to Earl Cooper, a lethal pass catcher out of the backfield, for 5 yards. When referee Jim Tunney signaled the two-minute warning, the 49ers were in Dallas territory.

Cross celebrated by vomiting on the Candlestick turf, the result of a stomach virus. He wasn't the only ailing 49er; several had battled the same virus during the week (wide receiver Dwight Clark shed seven pounds), and linebacker Keena Turner had chicken pox.

The Cowboys were not only seething with malevolence, they were tired also. Sensing they were ripe for a little trickery, Walsh called for a reverse to Solomon, who zipped around the left side for 14 yards. Montana went to work, teaming with wide receiver Clark for 10 yards on an out pattern, then hitting Solomon for another 12. Montana called a time out to ponder — along with Walsh and his staff — first down at Dallas's 13-yard line.

The next play almost became the one to be replayed for years on northern California VCRs. Solomon broke free in the left corner of the end zone, but Montana, the quarterback who never flinched, sent the pass sailing over his head.

Walsh was visibly pained on San Francisco's sideline — but he wasn't out of ideas. He sent Elliott sweeping again, and the veteran picked up 7 yards on the left side. The 49ers burned another time out. With 58 seconds remaining they were perched on the Cowboys' 6-yard line, facing third-and-3.

Walsh called for a pass play, knowing that his team had two chances to get it done: if Montana were pressured or his receivers covered, he could throw the ball away and go for broke on fourth down. "Sprint Right Option" was the plan. The formation flanked Solomon inside Clark on the right side. Clark was to clear out underneath, springing Solomon on a path to the right corner of the end zone. If Solomon wasn't open, Clark was supposed to move right-to-left in the end zone, then stop sharply and double back in the opposite direction. The 49ers had worked on the play, its primary and secondary options, ad nauseum, especially Montana and Clark, who had logged dozens of hours of pitch-and-catch as extracurricular practice.

The crowd stood as one, sixty thousand knotted stomachs and constricted throats, as Montana shouted his signals. Montana took the snap and drifted to his right. The quarterback immediately found himself endangered, hounded by defensive tackle Larry Bethea and blitzing linebacker D. D. Lewis, but especially by Ed "Too Tall" Jones, the Cowboys' 6-foot, 8-inch defensive tackle. Montana was in retreat, bearing down on the right sideline. Solomon had slipped, and he had no idea if Clark was open. "I couldn't see anyone except Too Tall Jones," Montana said.

Montana jumped off his back foot — normally the first scene in a sequence that leads to disaster — and launched the ball through the end zone. After the game, the grumbling Jones insisted Montana was trying to throw the ball away. Walsh admitted he already was thinking about going to the sweep on the next play.

A yard in front of the end line, Clark had a half-step on Dallas' rookie cornerback Everson Walls. They had been two of the game's standout performers, Clark with 7 receptions for 114 yards, Walls with 2 interceptions and a fumble recovery. But that corner of the end zone no longer had room for two stars.

Later in the game, Eric Wright (21) made the game-saving tackle on a pass to Drew Pearson.

Even in retrospect, even knowing that Clark leaped into the air and caught that whizzing spiral, it doesn't seem possible. In the best of health, Clark never was considered an athletic giant by NFL standards. He was a tenth-round draft choice who carved his path to success with the tools of hard labor: sure hands, precise routes, and wise decisions. Just for a moment, however, Dwight Clark became Clark Kent's better half. "You get it from somewhere," Clark said. "How does the mother pick up the car that has her baby trapped? You just get it from somewhere." With one mighty bound, Clark picked up the vehicle that had pinned the 49ers for thirty-five seasons and heaved it aside like an aluminum can.

If a 49ers fan — in fact, if any student of the game — closes his eyes for a second, he can see the image as if he'd been staring into the lens of a slide projector for too long. There is Clark, body fully extended, back arched, every molecule in his body directed skyward. There is Walls in a desperate attempt to disrupt the impending act, the look on his face registering not rage, dismay, or fear, but utter surprise. Clark's fingers envelop the ball so tenuously that you want to see the next frame just to make sure he came down with it. When he watched a replay later, Montana, who had been flat on his back during the pivotal moment, gasped. "I knew it was high, but…Dwight must have jumped three feet to get that. He can't jump that high."

Cross's wife, Patricia, had noted that the 49ers always won when the game clock stopped at her husband's jersey number, 51, in the fourth quarter. When Clark came down with Montana's pass, Randy shot a glance at the clock. It read :51.

The touchdown wasn't the final word, though. There were a few postscripts beneath

Clark's signature. First was Ray Wersching's extra point, which gave the 49ers the 28-27 lead they had been pursuing for most of the fourth quarter. And, befitting one of the best games in NFL history, the Cowboys didn't go quietly. In fact, they sent a shiver through Candlestick Park that could have been measured on the Richter scale. On the first play of Dallas's last-chance possession, Pro Bowl wide receiver Drew Pearson took a pass over the middle from Danny White and was a step from a 75-yard counter-miracle when cornerback Eric Wright reached out with one hand to drag him down.

Jim Stuckey (75), bearing down on Danny White in this photo, recovered White's fumble in the closing seconds of the game, and the 49ers were in the Super Bowl for the first time.

Still, the Cowboys were in San Francisco territory, and they needed only a field goal to win. They would proceed no farther. Lawrence Pillers pummeled White on the next play, and Pillers's counterpart at defensive end, Jim Stuckey, fell on the fumble and clutched it as if he were protecting a family heirloom from Kublai Khan's horse soldiers.

Most of those final thrills have become obscured in the shadow of Clark's leaping reception. There have been hundreds of thousands of catches throughout NFL history ... but only one was The Catch.

Has one play ever reversed the fortunes of a franchise so dramatically? Buoyed by The Catch, San Francisco defeated Cincinnati 26-21 in Super Bowl XVI two weeks later. Over the next thirteen seasons, the 49ers would add four Super Bowl victories, ten NFC West titles, and a legacy of excellence that would define the era in pro football.

At Super Bowl XXIX in Miami, not a single player remained in San Francisco from the 1981 squad. It was Jerry Rice, perhaps the greatest wide receiver of all time, making the crucial catches, not Dwight Clark; it was Steve Young piloting the offense, not Joe Montana; it was Tim McDonald menacing opposing receivers, not Ronnie Lott. And pulling all the strings was coach George Seifert, a Walsh protégé.

The only constants in the shifting sands of a decade and a half were a crazed and ever-widening fan base and the devoted stewardship of owner Edward DeBartolo Jr. DeBartolo is the owner that every coach dreams of—involved enough to make the necessary acquisitions, wise enough to stay out of the way on game day. DeBartolo's love of the game has, as much as anything, kept the 49ers aloft while other NFL teams have bobbed up and down on the turbulent seas of free agency, injuries, and complacency.

Still, it all comes back to The Catch. "Who knows what would have happened to the 49ers if we'd lost that game?" Cross wondered in retrospect. "That win made it possible for us to get to the Super Bowl not just that time but in years to come." "It changed all of our lives," Montana said years later.

And it is no overstatement to say it changed the course of modern NFL history. When Dwight Clark urged his muscles and bones to overstep their bounds for that one second in January 1982, it may have looked like a small step from distant vantage points, but it truly was a giant leap for the San Francisco 49ers.

World War II was a newsreel of misery and devastation for many of Europe's great capitals. When the final armistice was signed, citizens across Europe were sweeping ash from the streets and finishing the half-done demolition jobs on thousand-year-old monuments in Berlin, Paris, and Warsaw. ⌘ San Francisco, perched on the "safe" side of the world, was launched into its heyday. The northern California city's population jumped by 25 percent during the four years of American conflict. Soldiers, sailors, and airmen had been assigned to San Francisco from all over the United States, and thousands were so enchanted by the area that they made it their peacetime home. ⌘ There were plenty of reasons for

(Above) The first home game in 49ers history was on September 1, 1946, against the Chicago Rockets. Parker Hall's touchdown pass to Alyn Beals (53) keyed a 34-14 rout. (Pages 16–17) Hugh McElhenny bursts through the Bears' defense in 1958; (page 18) Leo Nomellini; (page 19) Norm Standlee (72) and Gail Bruce (54) team to stop a New York Yankees ball carrier; (pages 20–21) Joe Perry; (opposite) Market Street, San Francisco, 1945.

enchantment. San Francisco long had been considered an American gem, a city of East Coast architecture, California climate, and a unique, home-grown culture. It was one part Gold Rush, one part cutting-edge metropolis, one part bohemia.

Writers from Jack London to Mark Twain praised its innate beauty and brawling spirit, and tourists came from everywhere to ride the cable cars, eat sourdough bread, and watch the monstrous fog swallow the Golden Gate Bridge.

Indeed it could have been asked in 1946, what do other major American cities have that San Francisco does not? There was an answer: professional sports. The sports business, perhaps even more than others, was dominated by an east coast mentality that perceived the West as a giant national park, a huge, picturesque object of entertainment.

That prejudice dogged San Francisco, Los

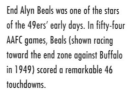

End Alyn Beals was one of the stars of the 49ers' early days. In fifty-four AAFC games, Beals (shown racing toward the end zone against Buffalo in 1949) scored a remarkable 46 touchdowns.

Angeles, and Seattle like an unjust prison sentence. Old money and old industry were less than keen to welcome the Pacific coast into its chummy circle of friends. It took a different sort of stroke to redraw the map. It took a new league.

THE NEW LEAGUE

San Francisco had a thriving Triple-A baseball franchise, the Seals, which had produced many major leaguers, including Joe DiMaggio, and which would set a minor league attendance record in 1946. The Bay Area had five schools playing on the highest level of intercollegiate football—California, Stanford, the University of San Francisco, St. Mary's, and Santa Clara.

San Franciscans argued that the city didn't need major-league sports to be considered major league. Even so, the fact was indisputable: in the world of

professional sports, the city was behind towns of comparable size such as Cincinnati and St. Louis, which otherwise had few of the advantages enjoyed by San Francisco.

Tony Morabito would change that by creating the San Francisco 49ers, a new team in a new league, the All-America Football Conference. "San Francisco was always a good football town on Sunday," said Al Ruffo, who was both friend and attorney for Morabito, "but it was college ball. St. Mary's, USF, and Santa Clara used to play big games at Kezar Stadium. One day, Tony asked me, 'What do you think of a professional football team in San Francisco?' I told him I thought it could be great."

Morabito first attempted to get a franchise in the National Football League. Ruffo remembers a meeting in Chicago in 1943, when that city was headquarters for the NFL and Elmer Layden was the league's commissioner. Morabito and Ruffo met with Layden and five owners, including NFL pioneer George Halas, Washington Redskins owner George Preston Marshall, and Philadelphia owner Bert Bell, who later would become the NFL commissioner. "Tony said he'd submit financial statements," Ruffo said. "Tony and Al Sorrell owned not only a lumber yard but also a very large piece of property a little farther south of Army Street, and that's where he wanted to build a training camp with a dormitory, so the players who were not married could live there and practice. We said we could do it financially, but at the end of the conference, Elmer Layden said, 'Well, sonny, why don't you get a football first?'" The NFL rejected Morabito's bid.

Morabito was livid—no surprise for a man whose emotional temperature frequently ran a couple of degrees under the boiling point. Fortunately for the future of pro football in San Francisco, though, he had an alternative. Earlier that year, *Chicago Tribune* sports editor Arch Ward, the originator of baseball's All-Star game and football's Pro Bowl, had come up with the idea of a new professional football league. Ward's friend, *San Francisco Chronicle* sports editor Bill Leiser, suggested Morabito as the owner of the San Francisco franchise. "That was really the only choice we had because we thought reapplying to the NFL would be futile," Ruffo said.

FATHER FIGURE

Tony Morabito loved owning the 49ers, and he had great affection for his players. Morabito would come to practice every day and watch while sitting on a tackling dummy on the sidelines. He never tried to tell his coaches what to do, but he talked encouragingly to players when they came off the field.

"He loved the players," team executive Lou Spadia said. "I remember one day a player came off the field and said, 'That's a beautiful coat. I'd love to have a coat like that.' Tony took off the coat and gave it to him."

There wasn't much money in pro football at the time—the 49ers didn't even break even until 1957—but players knew that Tony would do the best he could for them. Morabito had a handshake agreement with Joe Perry that Joe would get a $5,000 bonus if he rushed for 1,000 yards. Perry got the money two years in a row, 1953 and 1954, when he became the first player in NFL history to rush for 1,000 yards in consecutive years.

There were no drawn-out negotiations. After being drafted in the first round by the 49ers in 1957, John Brodie met Morabito in the club's offices, located on Market Street in San Francisco. Brodie's fiancée, Sue, who soon became his wife, waited in a double-parked car while Brodie "negotiated." It took only ten minutes for Brodie and Morabito to agree on a $16,000 contract.

Sometimes, it didn't take that long. "I was like a son to Tony," tackle Bob St. Clair said. "I didn't even negotiate my contract. I just signed a blank contract and he filled in the terms.

"One time, I decided I should negotiate. I told him, 'You've got an all-pro offensive tackle and an all-pro defensive tackle [Leo Nomellini]. I want as much as Leo gets.'" Morabito said no, and St. Clair threatened to go to Canada. After some more thrust and parry, Morabito said, "You don't understand. You're getting more than Nomellini."

So much for negotiating.

When players learned at halftime of a 1957 game with the Chicago Bears that Morabito had been stricken with a heart attack, they played the second half in an emotional fervor. Nomellini had tears streaming down his face.

Coach Frankie Albert learned during the third quarter that Morabito had died. After the game, which the 49ers won, Albert was told Morabito would have been happy that his team had won. "If he was going to live," Albert said, "it would have made me happy to lose by a hundred points."

So on June 3, 1944, Morabito and Ruffo met in St. Louis with Ward and others who were interested in creating a new league. At the meeting it was agreed that the new league would have franchises in New York, Chicago, San Francisco, Los Angeles, Buffalo, and Cleveland. (By the time league play began, franchises had been added in Brooklyn and Miami.) The All-America Football Conference was born. The proposed start date of 1945 was impossibly optimistic, considering that the country was involved in the biggest war the world had ever known. The first season would actually kick off in 1946.

AN ENTHUSIASTIC OWNER

It would be nice to report that the 49ers were an instant success, but in fact they ran third in 1946 behind the college game and the Catholic Church. The Catholic colleges had first call on Kezar Stadium for their big Sunday games. "That first year, we had to play two games on Saturday, and we drew fewer than ten thousand fans for them," said Lou Spadia, who began his thirty-two-year link with the 49ers in the front office that season. The colleges started their Sunday games at 2:30 P.M. so they wouldn't interfere with noon Mass. Not being in a position to offend anybody, the 49ers did the same. It was hardly an auspicious beginning, but Morabito was not deterred by the many early problems.

Morabito had risen from an $80-a-month job as a truck driver to partnership in Consolidated Companies, which owned lumber yards and built homes. But unlike many self-made men, he regarded money as a commodity which should be spent. "Tony loved to live first class," Spadia said. "He didn't like guys who put on airs—he never joined a country club— but he loved to eat in good restaurants. When we went on the road, he always knew where he was going to eat every night, and he kept some restaurants in business, too. We always went first class, stayed in the best hotels."

Usually, it fell to the public-relations man to make reservations for Morabito at good restaurants, and also to make sure the hotel was a good one.

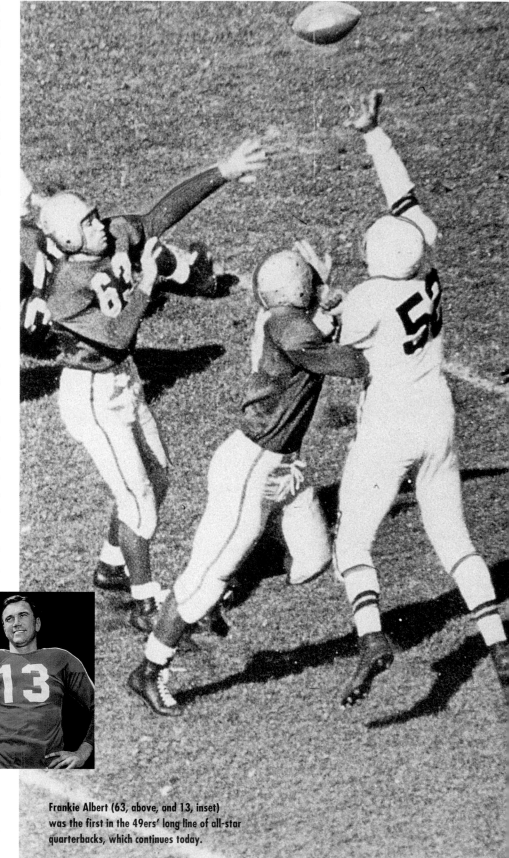

Frankie Albert (63, above, and 13, inset) was the first in the 49ers' long line of all-star quarterbacks, which continues today.

Local legend Lawrence T. (Buck) Shaw gave the new franchise instant credibility.

Spadia remembers one time when it didn't work out. "Tony was on the road with his wife, and when they checked into their room, the bed hadn't been changed and the room was dirty. He called up [public relations man] Dan McGuire and bawled him out. When Dan got off the phone, he told me to come with him. We went down to housekeeping, where Dan put on an apron, and I got a dust mop. We went up to Tony's room and his wife let us in. We started sweeping and dusting, and when Tony saw us, he just fell down laughing."

Morabito had a good sense of humor, but humor was just one of the stops on a wide emotional spectrum. He was a lusty man who could laugh with you, cry with you, and, most of all, argue with you. "I never agreed with him on anything, and that was the thing he liked," said Ruffo, who first met Morabito when both men were undergraduates at Santa Clara in the late 1920s. "I would always take the opposite side. We argued like the dickens all the time, but he enjoyed that. It was a challenge. We never got angry at each other."

Spadia remembers another side of Morabito. "He was very loyal. He never forgot a friend. I remember one time we were walking down the street, and a guy driving a garbage truck yelled out to him. It turned out he was a high school classmate of Tony's. Tony jumped on the truck and rode a block with him."

Morabito was also crazy about football. He played in high school, at St. Ignatius in San Francisco, but was forced to stop after breaking his shoulder. That and his lack of size—he was only about 5-feet, 5-inches tall—prevented him from playing at Santa Clara, but he became an ardent backer of the sport, contributing time and money to the Santa Clara boosters after his graduation.

It took that kind of enthusiasm to become the owner of the 49ers, because pro football was a marginal operation even for NFL clubs at that point, let alone for a new league. During World War II, the NFL had continued to play, but on a reduced level; the Philadelphia and Pittsburgh franchises, for example, combined to form a team known as the Steagles.

Morabito's first move was to hire a coach, Lawrence T. (Buck) Shaw, who had coached

Morabito's alma mater, Santa Clara. The hiring may have been sentimental, but it also was smart, because Shaw had an excellent offensive mind.

INSTANT CREDIBILITY

Shaw also gave the new club credibility because of his link to a storied football past. He had been a star tackle on the Knute Rockne-coached Notre Dame teams of the early 1920s, playing two years with George Gipp, and had been a high-profile coach at Santa Clara before the war. "Buck Shaw was a very salable item for the 49ers," said former San Francisco Chronicle sports editor Art Rosenbaum. "To get that kind of coach in 1946 was very important."

Hiring Shaw put the stamp of "major league" on the 49ers from the start, a fact that became more important as time went on. The 49ers always have always enjoyed a special place in San Francisco and the entire Bay Area, because they were its first major-league team, and the only one to begin in the city.

Shaw's salary was $25,000—very good money then. Two years later, Morabito gave Shaw a choice: he could have a salary of $25,000 a year or $15,000 and 25 percent of the club. Shaw took the $25,000. "He did what any sane man would have done at that time," Spadia said, "because twenty-five percent of nothing was nothing. Still, it would have been a little like getting Coca-Cola stock at the very start."

Getting players wasn't a problem. "Morabito concentrated on local schools, especially Stanford and Santa Clara, and on players who had played on the pre-flight teams in the area during the war," Spadia said. Quarterback Frankie Albert and full-back Norm Standlee, for instance, were from Stanford. "We wanted to get the entire backfield from Stanford's 1940 Rose Bowl team," Ruffo said, "but Hugh Gallarneau was under contract to the Chicago Bears and Pete Kmetovic was the property of the Philadelphia Eagles." Touchdown-producing receiver Alyn Beals came from Santa Clara. Star halfback John Strzykalski was from Milwaukee but played at St. Mary's Pre-Flight. ("His wife loved it out here," Spadia said. "Green Bay tried to sign John, but she didn't want to go back to Wisconsin.") "It was like a reunion," Albert later recalled, "because so many of us

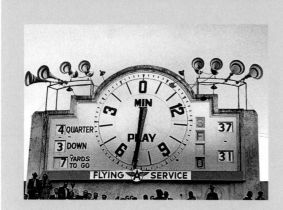

THE 49ERS' FIRST HOME

Kezar Stadium was an unusual facility. It was built on a narrow strip of land bordering Golden Gate Park, which gave it a picturesque setting but also limited the number of seats which could be built on the sidelines—only 19,000 of the 59,000-plus were between the goal lines. All the seats were benches, and only seventeen inches were allowed for each seat.

When the 49ers attracted sellout crowds, Kezar was very uncomfortable because fans were shoe-horned into the seats, with knees in their backs from fans behind them. Team executive Lou Spadia commissioned a study on the possibility of installing chair seats, but the idea was abandoned because it would have cut the seating capacity to 37,000.

There also was virtually no parking at Kezar—only three hundred slots for "official" use, which meant press, politicians, and friends of politicians, the third group being the largest.

Still, Kezar had its charm. Because the best weather months in San Francisco are September and October, the early-season games at Kezar were especially pleasant; on the sunny side, young men often took off their shirts to soak up the sun. Fans would picnic in the park before coming to the game, and they acclimated to the lack of parking in different ways.

"People would park out in the avenues or in the park," former *San Francisco Chronicle* sports editor Art Rosenbaum remembered. "If you got to Kezar an hour before the game, you could see people walking across the park. It was a very special scene.

"A lot of people would park right behind Kezar or in other places nearby a day before the game and have a friend drive them home. The day of the game, they'd get a ride to the park or take the streetcar, and then they'd drive home after the game."

had played against each other during the war."

Every starter on that first 49ers team played either college ball or for a military team in the area. For the record, here's how the offense lined up, with schools or military teams in parentheses, for the 49ers' first game, a preseason match in San Diego against the Los Angeles Dons: center, Gerry Conlee (St. Mary's); guards, Dick Bassi (Santa Clara) and Eddie Forrest (Santa Clara); tackles, John Woudenberg (St. Mary's Pre-Flight) and Bob Bryant (Monterey Pre-Flight); ends, Alyn Beals (Santa Clara) and Bob Titchenal (San Jose State); quarterback, Frankie Albert (Stanford); halfbacks, Len Eshmont (Monterey Pre-Flight) and John Strzykalski (St. Mary's Pre-Flight); fullback, Norm Standlee (Stanford).

The defense? Just turn them around, because players played both ways in 1946. "Frank Albert was our best defensive back," Spadia said. "I remember Frank one day saving a touchdown by tackling [halfback] Buddy Young, who was a great runner."

There were only thirty-three players and three coaches: Shaw and his two assistants, Ruffo and Jim Lawson. Lawson had coached under T-formation pioneer Clark Shaughnessy at Stanford.

Ruffo, a man of incredible energy who still practices law at eighty-six, was an assistant coach, legal counsel for Morabito, a lawyer in San Jose, and, as head of the City Council in San Jose, that town's top government official.

John Strzykalski's bruising running endeared him to 49ers fans but also earned him eight broken noses in seven years in pro football.

EARLY DAYS

This was the start of a process that has evolved into the sophisticated operation of today's NFL, and everything about the 49ers in the opening years seems crude by today's standards. Commercial airplane travel, for instance, was in its infancy, so on short trips the 49ers traveled by bus or train. They always had one three-game swing through the East, and they'd stay between games to save money. If they played in Buffalo and then in Baltimore, they'd take buses to a hotel in the Baltimore area the day after the Buffalo game. Shaw took note of the kinds of players he had when he planned those trips.

"We'd have two buses," Spadia said. "One was the 'Good Apple' bus that had the coaches and players who didn't drink beer. I was always on that bus. We'd arrive about one o'clock in the afternoon. The 'Bad Apple' bus would stop for six-packs and salami along the way, and it would roll in maybe about 4:30 P.M. That was supposed to be the players' day off, and Buck was realistic. He always had beer in the dressing room after the games. These were guys who were all twenty-five, twenty-six, or older, and who had been in the service. You weren't going to tell them they couldn't drink beer."

Besides, at that time, players were playing for the love of the game, not the money. "That first year, our top salary was $10,000 [Frankie Albert]," Spadia said, "and we had some salaries around $2,800. Bruno Banducci, who'd been an all-pro guard at Philadelphia, was getting $5,000. Of course, $5,000 could buy a house then.

"There were no endorsements, either. Guys would retire a lot earlier than they do now, because if they were doing well in their careers away from the field, it didn't make a lot of sense to keep playing football. Alyn Beals was an example. I don't think Alyn ever made more than about $4,500. He made more than that in the offseason with his liquor store, so he finally stuck with that."

Albert agreed. "If a guy wasn't getting as much playing time as he wanted, he'd quit, because he knew he could make as much driving a truck," he said. "Schoolteachers were making as much as most players. We knew that because a lot of guys who quit went into high school coaching and teaching."

SUITED TO THE T

There's never been a better match than Frankie Albert and the T-formation.

As a college sophomore at Stanford in 1939, Albert was a nondescript tailback in the Single-Wing formation for a team that went 1-7-1. Then Clark Shaughnessy brought the T to Stanford, and his 1940 team, with Albert at the controls, was undefeated, beating Nebraska in the Rose Bowl.

In 1946, the 49ers' first head coach, Buck Shaw, brought in Jim Lawson, who had been an assistant at Stanford, to help install the T-formation.

Shaw liked to have his quarterback throw to the backs. The backfields of the time all had three running backs, but Shaw often had one of them go in motion. That caught teams off guard—they didn't know how to defend against the extra receiver.

But no matter how innovative he could be, Shaw's offense was only as good as the quarterback running it, and Albert was a master. Albert had flair, and he ran the T in a manner unique to him. He was an accurate, though not strong-armed, passer and a good runner, but it was his daring that made him so effective.

There may have been better quarterbacks, but few as exciting as Frankie Albert.

"All of us had to have offseason jobs," said Pro Football Hall of Fame fullback Joe Perry, who joined the 49ers in 1948. "I was a mailman, worked in construction, sold cars."

There was another big difference: size. "Norm Standlee, at 245 pounds, was our biggest player," Albert said. "For awhile, Dutch Elston was our center, and he was hardly bigger than me, 190 to 165."

Games were not even broadcast at the start of the first season. "The concept of rights fees was unknown," Spadia said. "Tony thought he would have to pay to get the games on the radio." Morabito was told he could get money, but it wasn't until the season was a couple of games old that he came up with a sponsor, Tarantino's Restaurant on Fisherman's Wharf, which paid $5,000 for the rest of the season.

The radio broadcasts became very important to the 49ers success, building a following for the team throughout northern California. In that pre-television era, fans listened to games and created their own mental images of the players. Soon they started coming to the games to see how their images corresponded to reality. On game day, the Golden Gate Bridge and Bay Bridge would be filled by cars, trucks, and vans carrying fans from as far as two hundred miles away.

The 49ers worked to become part of the community, starting with their nickname, which referred to the 1849 Gold Rush. The first 49ers logo, taken from a local advertisement, showed a drunken miner celebrating with two pistols, one of which was aimed just over his head. In the ad, there was a saloon in the background—appropriate given San Francisco's reputation as a town of hard drinkers—but that was excised from the logo.

Uniform colors were also tied to local history. "Tony wanted red jerseys and gold pants, as a connection to the Gold Rush," Ruffo said, "but Buck's wife wanted silver pants because he was known as 'The Silver Fox.' So, we had silver pants that first year. But the second year, Tony decided to go to the gold pants he'd always wanted."

Tickets were a bargain that first season, and season tickets were discounted. Seats on the 50-yard line were three dollars, but a season-ticket buyer got seven games for the price of six—eighteen dollars.

JOE THE JET

Joe Perry is the 49ers' leading career rusher with 7,344 yards, and he took punishment for every yard. Perry's career began before players wore facemasks, and in a 1951 game against the Los Angeles Rams he came back to the huddle mumbling and holding his mouth after being slammed by a Larry Brink forearm.

"What's the matter, Joe?" quarterback Frankie Albert asked. Wordlessly, Perry held out tooth fragments he was holding in his palm. "Well, Joe, those are no good, throw them away," said Albert, who then called Perry's number on the next play. Perry bolted up the middle for a touchdown.

Perry had to be tough because he was the only black player on the 49ers and one of few in the NFL in his early years. He had no trouble with his teammates. "Guys from the South were my greatest friends," he said. "Y. A. Tittle, Jimmy Cason. We were like family. We ran together all the time."

Opposing players weren't as friendly, though, and some of them looked for Perry to give him an extra lick. Perry never backed down. "He'd come back to the huddle bleeding," Albert remembered, "and he'd say to me, 'Shorty, run that same play, because this time I'm going to get him.'"

Teams often employed a "shadow" against the 49ers—one player who was responsible for Perry on every play. That started in the All-America Football Conference.

The strategy was adopted by NFL teams as well. The Chicago Bears used linebacker George Connor. Perry remembers a play in which he was a decoy, but Connor whacked him and broke his rib. "Is that you, George?" Perry asked. "Yeah," Connor growled, "and I'm going to be here all day."

Perry recognized that as part of the game, a very physical one in those days, and he didn't complain. He says, in fact, that he and Connor became friends in later years.

With some teams and players, though, it went beyond rough play. In Baltimore a defensive player yelled at Perry, "Come back here, nigger, and I'll kill you." Perry yelled back, "I'm coming. Better bring your whole family."

Off the field, there were times when Perry couldn't stay with the rest of the team or eat with them. "In Baltimore," he said, "I stayed at the same hotel as the rest of the team, but when I came down to the dining room, I was told I couldn't eat there. I just started turning over tables. I went crazy. They kicked the whole team out of the hotel."

They should have known better than to mess with Joe Perry.

A similar discount applied to 30-yard line seats—two dollars by the game but twelve dollars for the season. Even so, the club sold just 1,100 season tickets. Most fans opted for seats from the 10-yard line to the end zone, which were just one dollar.

There were some good crowds in those early days—thirty-four thousand attended the first pre-season game—but they weren't frequent enough. According to Ruffo, the team lost $144,000 that first year. "Tony never took a dime in salary out of the operation or it would have been more," he said.

Originally, Morabito co-owned the team with Al Sorrell and Ernest Turre, his partners in Consolidated Companies. Sorrell and Turre wanted out, though, after the first two seasons, so Morabito assumed sole ownership of the club.

For the newspapers, college football was still the big story. The *Chronicle* gave the 49ers decent coverage, but not the *Examiner*. "Tony made a deal with the *Examiner* to let them sponsor one exhibition game," Spadia said. "The *Examiner* would share in the revenues for their charities, and in return they'd promote the game. But after that, we'd be back in the obituaries."

Morabito had such a volatile personality that his relationship with newspapermen fluctuated constantly, usually depending on what they had written most recently, but he had a long-standing feud with *Examiner* sports editor Curley Grieve that started because of this deal. The *Chronicle*'s Bill Leiser, who helped Morabito get the franchise, was bothered by the fact that Morabito had made this arrangement with the *Examiner*. Morabito told Leiser he would not renew when the three-year-deal expired, and Grieve never forgave him. "Grieve was a guy who could carry a grudge," Spadia said. "I remember one game we drew about thirty-eight thousand fans, and the *Examiner* didn't carry a line about it the next day."

The *Examiner*'s Prescott Sullivan, who wrote a humorous column but one that could have a bite to it, often needled Morabito in print. Morabito had a habit, during the game, of going down to the tunnel that led to the dressing room so he could greet the players as they came off the field. Sullivan wrote that he did it because he was so cheap, he wanted to catch footballs kicked over the goal posts before they could go into the stands. "Sully wrote it tongue in cheek, but that's not the way Tony took it," Spadia said.

Morabito retaliated by barring the *Examiner*'s beat writer, Bob Brachman, from any area under the 49ers' control. "He even wanted to keep Brachman out of the press box, but that was under control of the city," Spadia said. "When we went on the road, I was road secretary, so it was my job to keep him out of areas. He couldn't come into the players' cars on the train, for instance."

Until the day he died, Morabito never again spoke to Grieve. Other disagreements with newspapers and their writers were of shorter duration, but no less heated. "Morabito had a short fuse," Art Rosenbaum said. "He had a bad list. It was kind of a badge of honor to be on it, and some guys made it all the time." Rosenbaum, former sports editor for the *San Francisco Chronicle* and the kindest of men, even made it a couple of times.

The *Chronicle* had a serious dispute with the 49ers' owner in the early fifties. Beat reporter Bruce Lee had been banned from the 49ers' practices because of a story that Morabito claimed had broken a confidence. "Because Kezar was a public facility, Lee couldn't be banned from that, so the *Chronicle* covered the games but gave the 49ers only very short stories during the week," Rosenbaum said. "We got a lot of criticism from readers because of that, but eventually Lou Spadia came to the *Chronicle* offices and made peace, and we went back to covering the 49ers as if nothing had happened."

That was the vindictive side of Morabito, but those working for him, such as Spadia, knew a much warmer side. "I'd never met him before I came to the team, and he wasn't the one who hired me— John Blackenger was," Spadia says. "But Tony treated me like a son." No doubt when Morabito looked at Spadia, he did indeed see the son he never had, because many of the attributes Spadia ascribes to his benefactor—including hard-working

and loyal—can be used in his own description.

After his first heart attack in 1953, Morabito was told by his doctor to sell the team. "He talked to Clint Murchison [who later would become the owner of the expansion Dallas Cowboys] about buying the team," Ruffo said. "I drew up a contract for $460,000, and I asked Tony what he wanted me to do. He didn't say anything for a few days, and then he told me, 'Forget it. If I'm going to die, I'd rather do it owning the football team.'"

After a second heart attack in 1955, Morabito changed his mind and sold 45 percent of the club to his friends, including some who worked for him. Ruffo got five percent. So did Spadia. By this time, the book value of the franchise was $600,000, so five percent was worth $30,000. "Of course, I didn't have $30,000," Spadia said, "so he told me I could pay it off from future profits [from his share of the club]. There weren't any profits then, but in 1957, we sold out almost every game, and I was able to pay for it in a couple of years."

The 49ers' financial success came after Morabito's death. Another heart attack killed him during a 1957 game.

It bothers Spadia that Morabito has not been inducted into the Pro Football Hall of Fame in Canton, Ohio. Even without that kind of honor, though, Morabito's legacy has long survived him. Without his commitment, the 49ers certainly wouldn't have stayed in business long enough to join the NFL in 1950. "He was nuts to think this would work," Spadia said, "but he had a dream."

FROM FORMER COLTS LINEMAN ART DONOVAN, ON HIS ELECTION TO THE PRO FOOTBALL HALL OF FAME:

"I KNOW ONE PLAYER WHO HAS TO BE LAUGHING WHEN HE READS THAT I MADE THE HALL OF FAME—A GUARD BY THE NAME OF BRUNO BANDUCCI, WHO PLAYED FOR THE SAN FRANCISCO 49ERS AND BLOCKED ME ALL OVER THE FIELD."

THE NAME OF THE GAME WAS OFFENSE

The early 49ers set a pattern from which the team seldom deviated for its first quarter-century: great offense, mediocre defense.

"Buck Shaw ran an offense a lot like Bill Walsh's," Lou Spadia said. "He'd send Norm Standlee out in the flat and throw the ball to him, and Standlee was like a runaway freight train. Unfortunately, Buck never cared anything about

Forty Niners

FORTY NINERS vs. BROOKLYN DODGERS
SEPTEMBER 22, 1946

25c

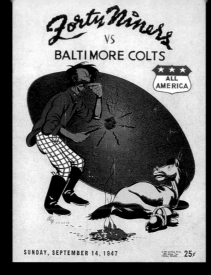

Forty Niners
VS
BALTIMORE COLTS

ALL AMERICA

SUNDAY, SEPTEMBER 14, 1947

25¢

FORTY NINERS

SAN FRANCISCO

BUFFALO BILLS OCTOBER 16, 1949 - KEZAR STADIUM

25c

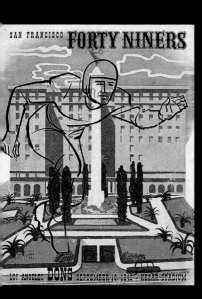

SAN FRANCISCO FORTY NINERS

LOS ANGELES DONS SEPTEMBER 18, 1949 - KEZAR STADIUM

25c

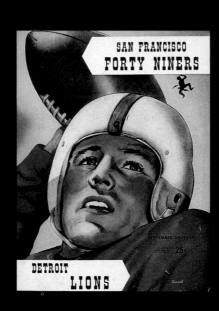

SAN FRANCISCO
FORTY NINERS

DETROIT LIONS

25c

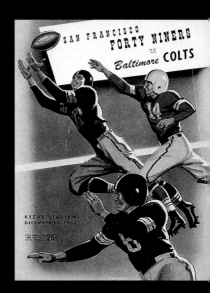

SAN FRANCISCO FORTY NINERS
vs
Baltimore COLTS

KEZAR STADIUM
DECEMBER 13, 1953

25c

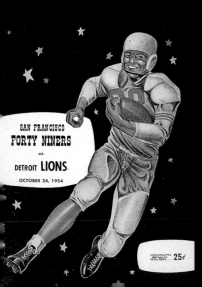

SAN FRANCISCO
FORTY NINERS
vs.
DETROIT LIONS

OCTOBER 24, 1954

25¢

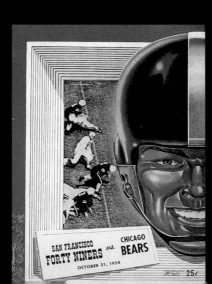

SAN FRANCISCO
FORTY NINERS vs. CHICAGO BEARS
OCTOBER 31, 1954

25c

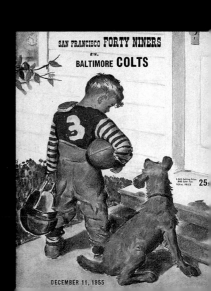

SAN FRANCISCO FORTY NINERS
vs.
BALTIMORE COLTS

DECEMBER 11, 1955

25c

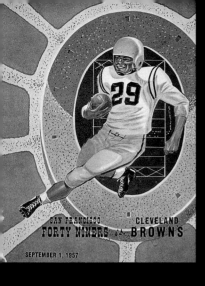

SAN FRANCISCO
FORTY NINERS vs. CLEVELAND BROWNS

SEPTEMBER 1, 1957

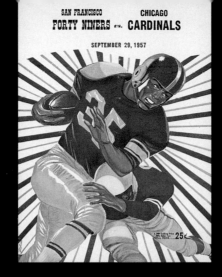

SAN FRANCISCO
FORTY NINERS vs. CHICAGO CARDINALS

SEPTEMBER 29, 1957

25¢

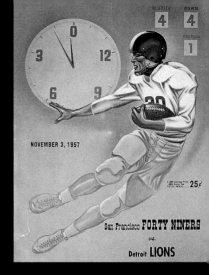

QUARTER 4 DOWN 4
YDS TO GO 1

NOVEMBER 3, 1957

25¢

San Francisco FORTY NINERS
vs.
Detroit LIONS

SAN FRANCISCO
FORTY NINERS vs. PHILADELPHIA EAGLES

SEPTEMBER 21, 1958

25¢

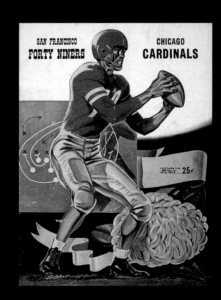

SAN FRANCISCO
FORTY NINERS vs. CHICAGO CARDINALS

25¢

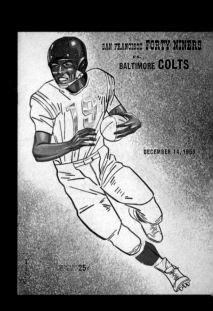

SAN FRANCISCO FORTY NINERS
vs. BALTIMORE COLTS

DECEMBER 14, 1958

25¢

San Francisco FORTY NINERS
GREEN BAY PACKERS

25¢

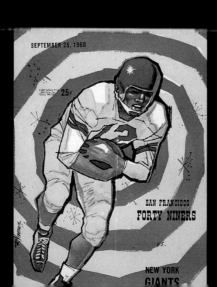

SEPTEMBER 25, 1960

25¢

SAN FRANCISCO
FORTY NINERS
vs.
NEW YORK GIANTS

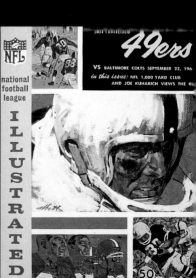

NFL
national football league
ILLUSTRATED

San Francisco
49ers
VS BALTIMORE COLTS SEPTEMBER 22, 196
in this issue: NFL 1,000 YARD CLUB
AND JOE KUHARICH VIEWS THE R

50¢

defense, and he never looked for players who could play good defense."

But Shaw was revered by his players. "He was a real gentleman," said kicker Joe Vetrano, who felt his former coach belongs in the Pro Football Hall of Fame. "You never heard anybody say a bad word about Buck Shaw."

Certainly not the quarterbacks. "Buck was a perfect quarterback coach," said Y. A. Tittle. "He would work hard with you during the week to make sure you were prepared, and then in the game, he'd leave you alone. If you threw an interception or called a dumb play, he never second-guessed you."

Shaw had his flaws. Al Ruffo remembered, for instance, that he didn't see the need for a real scouting system. "We did our first scouting by calling up college coaches," Ruffo said. "It was Tony Morabito who decided we needed a scouting system, and he put in a good one, with scouts all over the country."

Assistants did the hands-on coaching. "Buck wasn't one to get in and coach the guys hitting the

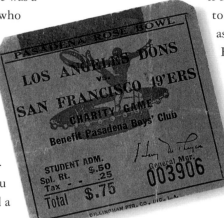

As with everything else, the price of football has gone up. Six bits got you into this charity game between the 49ers and Los Angeles Dons in 1948.

blocking dummy," Ruffo said. "He'd leave that up to his assistants. He would never give a guy hell if he made a mistake. So I had to supply the fire to motivate the players. He needed that kind of assistant. When I left the 49ers, they brought in Eddie Erdelatz, and he was that kind of fiery guy, too.

"Buck was a wonderful man. He was a terrific technician. He would run the plays over and over, and he would see the reactions of defensive players, then make adjustments. If a play didn't cause a reaction by the defense, he'd throw it out, because he figured it was no good, which was smart."

Shaw was an impressive figure on the sidelines, a dignified man who always seemed in charge. "He had such an aura about him," said Billy Wilson, who played for Shaw in the early fifties. "He was always immaculately dressed, wearing a gray suit, with a tie and a hat, and not a hair out of place. He'd carry a program on the sidelines so that when he knelt down, he could put the program under his knee."

Shaw was very much aware of his image and appearance. "I heard him curse in private, but in

THEY'RE NUMBER ONE

Tackle Leo Nomellini was the 49ers' first draft choice as a member of the National Football League. It was a wise selection: Nomellini went on to play fourteen seasons for the team and was inducted into the Pro Football Hall of Fame in 1969. Other top draft picks proved fortuitous — and some did not. The 49ers' first-round draft picks since 1950 (if the club had no first-round selection, the first player drafted is listed with the round in parentheses):

Year Player, College, Position	Year Player, College, Position	Year Player, College, Position	Year Player, College, Position
1950 Leo Nomellini, Minnesota, T-DT	1961 Jimmy Johnson, UCLA, WR-CB	1971 Tim Anderson, Ohio State, S	1984 Todd Shell, Brigham Young, LB
1951 Y. A. Tittle, Louisiana State, QB	Bernie Casey, Bowling Green, WR	1972 Terry Beasley, Auburn, WR	1985 Jerry Rice, Mississippi Valley State, WR
1952 Hugh McElhenny, Washington, HB	Bill Kilmer, UCLA, QB	1973 Mike Holmes, Texas Southern, DB	1986 Larry Roberts, Alabama, DE (2)
1953 Harry Babcock, Georgia, E	1962 Lance Alworth, Arkansas, WR	1974 Wilbur Jackson, Alabama, RB	1987 Harris Barton, North Carolina, T
Tom Stolhandske, Texas, DE	1963 Kermit Alexander, UCLA, DB	Bill Sandifer, UCLA, DT	Terrence Flagler, Clemson, RB
1954 Bernie Faloney, Maryland, QB	1964 Dave Parks, Texas Tech, WR-TE	1975 Jimmy Webb, Mississippi State, DT	1988 Danny Stubbs, Miami, DE (2)
1955 Dickie Moegle, Rice, DB	1965 Ken Willard, North Carolina, RB	1976 Randy Cross, UCLA, C-G (2)	1989 Keith DeLong, Tennessee, LB
1956 Earl Morrall, Michigan State, QB	George Donnelly, Illinois, DB	1977 Elmo Boyd, Eastern Kentucky, WR (3)	1990 Dexter Carter, Florida State, RB
1957 John Brodie, Stanford, QB	1966 Stan Hindman, Mississippi, DE-DT	1978 Ken MacAfee, Notre Dame, TE	1991 Ted Washington, Louisville, NT-DE
1958 Jim Pace, Michigan, HB	1967 Steve Spurrier, Florida, QB	Dan Bunz, Cal State-Long Beach, LB	1992 Dana Hall, Washington, S
Charlie Krueger, Texas A&M, DT	Cas Banaszek, Northwestern, T	1979 James Owens, UCLA, WR-RB (2)	1993 Dana Stubblefield, Kansas, DT
1959 Dave Baker, Oklahoma, DB	1968 Forrest Blue, Auburn, C	1980 Earl Cooper, Rice, RB	Todd Kelly, Tennessee, DE
Dan James, Ohio State, C	1969 Ted Kwalick, Penn State, TE	Jim Stuckey, Clemson, DE	1994 Bryant Young, Notre Dame, DT
1960 Monty Stickles, Notre Dame, TE	Gene Washington, Stanford, WR	1981 Ronnie Lott, Southern California, DB	William Floyd, Florida State, RB
	1970 Cedrick Hardman, North Texas State, DE	1982 Bubba Paris, Michigan, T (2)	1995 J. J. Stokes, UCLA, WR
	Bruce Taylor, Boston U., CB	1983 Roger Craig, Nebraska, RB (2)	

public, he would never say anything more than 'son of a buck,'" Rosenbaum said.

He was also vain. "Several times we went out to dinner, and we'd look at the menu," Spadia remembers. "I'd make my selection and then Buck would say, 'That sounds good to me. I'll have the same.' After awhile I realized that he couldn't read the menu without glasses, but he didn't want to put them on."

Shaw, who coached nine years (1946–54), eventually was fired because Morabito felt he wasn't enough of a disciplinarian, but one player, Pro Football Hall of Fame tackle Bob St. Clair, felt Shaw had no choice. "Football was really a part-time job at that time, because there was no money," St. Clair said. "You played because of the fun of it, so if a coach gave you a hard time, and if you felt it was no longer fun, you would just get out of there."

The mists of time have obscured much of the memory of some of the best players from those teams, players such as Alyn Beals. Beals was a wide receiver (or end, as receivers were called then) who was neither particularly big nor fast. All he did was score touchdowns.

In the 49ers' fifty-four regular-season games in the All-America Football Conference, Beals scored 46 touchdowns. Even more remarkably, they came on just 177 catches, so he scored on roughly 26 percent of his catches. (By contrast, current 49ers wide receiver Jerry Rice, who has caught more touchdown passes than any other player in NFL history, scores on about 16 percent of his catches.)

"He was like Fred Biletnikoff," Rosenbaum said. "He could pick the ball out of the air. There would be three or four sets of hands there, but he would be the one who got it. He had terrific coordination. And Kezar was like a second home to him, because he'd practiced there when he played at Poly [Polytechnical High School, just behind Kezar]."

"Beals was like a cat," said Wilson, a rookie end in 1951, Beals's last season. "He wasn't very big and couldn't block anybody, but he was so quick, they couldn't cover him."

Another largely forgotten star of that time was halfback John Strzykalski. "He was the heart of our team," quarterback Frankie Albert said. "He could catch the ball, which was very important. We'd put

Bob St. Clair was a mammoth tackle who played twelve years for the 49ers (1953–64) and later was inducted into the Pro Football Hall of Fame.

him or Len Eshmont in motion, and other teams wouldn't put anyone out there, so we'd just swing the ball out to one of them, and they'd have a lot of running room. And jeez, he was tough."

In the pros at that time, players who were tackled could get up and run again until they were finally pinned to the ground. Spadia recalled one time when Strzykalski got up three times to add yardage to his run before being virtually buried by the other team.

The beating Strzykalski took curtailed his time as a premier back. Though he played through 1952 with the 49ers, he had only two years, 1947 and

1948, when he was an essential part of the offense. He ran for 906 yards (averaging 6.3 yards per carry) and caught 15 passes for 258 yards in 1947, then ran for 915 yards (a 6.5 average) and caught 26 passes for 485 yards in 1948.

Norm Standlee was both a bruising runner at fullback and a punishing linebacker on defense, and so highly respected by the players that he was nicknamed "Big Chief." But he was not quite the player he'd been with the Chicago Bears before the war, when he was compared to Bronko Nagurski and Jim Thorpe. Standlee fought in the Army in Burma during World War II. His military years had stripped him of his speed.

The key to the 49ers' offense was Albert, an imaginative play-caller who loved to gamble. He was a great all-around player. He played excellent defense, was an accurate passer and a running threat if he saw an opening, and was an outstanding punter who averaged 48.2 yards per punt in 1949.

Because he was the team's punter, Albert could gamble even on fourth down. "He'd run for first downs three times a game," said Y. A. Tittle, who followed Albert as the 49ers' quarterback. "People didn't realize that he could kick the ball at any time. So, what he would do sometimes would be to start running with the ball and, if he saw he couldn't make the first down, kick the ball instead. He could kick it thirty-five yards on the dead run, and I mean, the dead run."

One time, in a 1948 game against the New York Yankees, Albert punted 46 yards to New York's 12-yard line as he was being chased by Yankee defensive linemen. That season was his best with the 49ers. He threw 29 touchdown passes in 14 games and was named the league's co-most valuable player with Cleveland quarterback Otto Graham.

Albert's daring made the 49ers the most exciting team in the AAFC. "He never thought about the scientific part of the game," Tittle said. "He went on impulse. He'd come off the field after scoring a touchdown, and I'd ask him, 'What defense were they in?' and he'd say, 'I don't know. I never looked.' It didn't make any difference to him because he felt he could beat any defense — and he was right."

"He was a great leader, a guy players really

THE SOURCE

Hardy Brown, a 49ers linebacker in the 1950s, was known for his brutal style of hitting runners and receivers with his shoulder instead of tackling them. Often he would knock opponents out of the game.

Brown also had a strange sense of humor, which he showed after a 1952 loss to the Rams in Los Angeles, when he was talking to *Los Angeles Times* writer Dick Hyland.

There were two hours before the flight back to San Francisco, and 49ers coach Buck Shaw told players they didn't have to go on the team bus to the airport. Some of the players headed for a local bar.

Hyland cornered Brown in the bar to try to get a story. Brown said, "Now, if you don't write this, I'll tell you a secret: We've got a lot of dissension on this team. This team's all shattered."

The next day, the headlines screamed of the 49ers' supposed dissension. "Buck was so mad, he could have killed Hardy," Gordy Soltau said.

Hardy Brown (right, while with Chicago) was famous for his shoulder tackles.

wanted to play with and for," Spadia said. "He would do some crazy things. I remember playing the Bears in 1952. Without discussing it with [coach] Buck [Shaw] or anybody, he moved [tackle] Leo Nomellini to fullback and gave him the ball. The players thought it was great. I don't think Buck thought it was."

Nomellini thought it was great, too — with reservations. "We had talked about it, but we never worked on it in practice. We said we'd do it sometime when we were way ahead [the 49ers won this particular game 40-16]. The problem was, he moved Joe Arenas into my spot at tackle. Joe was only 180 pounds. How was he going to block somebody who was 250 pounds? We only ran it this one time because I fumbled. I had run for five yards when Don Kent of the Bears just ripped the ball out of my grasp. So, from that point on, they said, the hell with it."

The game was fun for Frankie Albert and for his teammates, who still laugh about his antics. "In 1949, I was in a competition with Harvey Johnson [of the New York Yankees] to become the first kicker to kick one hundred straight PATs [points after touchdown]," Joe Vetrano said. "I had ninety-nine, Johnson had ninety-eight. We scored, and I was getting ready to go for the conversion. I took a step forward and looked down, and the ball was gone! Albert [the holder] stood up and threw a pass to Alyn Beals for the PAT."

Albert, of course, knew that Vetrano would have more chances. Vetrano went on to convert an AAFC-record 107 consecutive extra points, one of which was a dropkick. He also set AAFC records with nine extra points in one game (a 63-40 win over the Brooklyn Dodgers in 1948) and by scoring in fifty-six consecutive games.

Tittle believes strongly that Albert should be in the Pro Football Hall of Fame, not just for his play but for his contributions to the game. "I think he really sold football to the Bay Area, more than anybody else," Tittle said. "I'm not sure pro football would have survived in San Francisco without Frankie Albert.

"He was everything a T-formation quarterback was supposed to be in those days. He was clever, he was quick-witted, he had tremendous leadership.

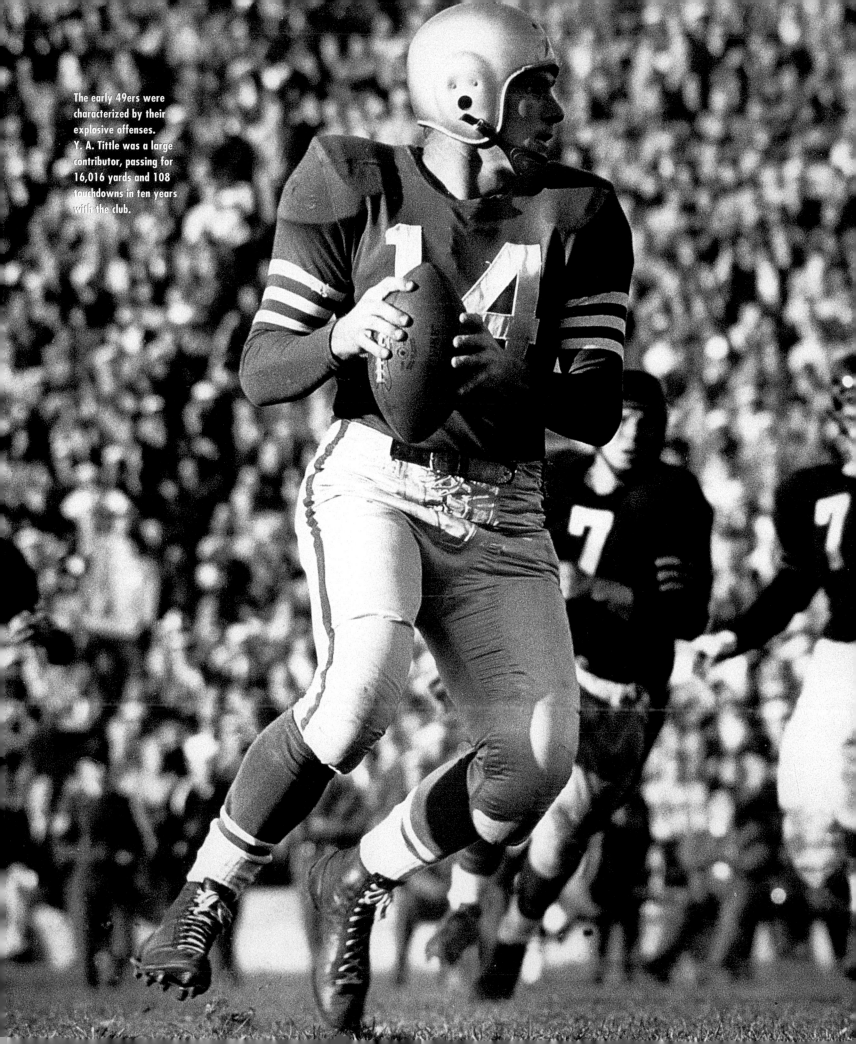

The early 49ers were characterized by their explosive offenses. Y. A. Tittle was a large contributor, passing for 16,016 yards and 108 touchdowns in ten years with the club.

Outtakes from publicity photos, 1950s-style.

He was a winner. He was perhaps the greatest influence on my career. Playing behind Frank my first year with the 49ers, seeing how he was in the huddle, watching him, how he made football fun… That was a great experience for me."

ANOTHER OFFENSIVE THREAT

As good as the 49ers were offensively the first two seasons, they took a big step up in their final two years in the AAFC, averaging about 35 points a game in each of those years and scoring a remarkable 69 touchdowns in 1948. The difference? Future Hall of Fame fullback Joe Perry, who joined the team in 1948 after finishing a four-year hitch with the Navy at Alameda (California) Naval Air Station.

"He added so much speed to our club," Albert said. "When you were the quarterback turning around to hand the ball off, you had to do it very quickly." In fact, when Perry first joined the 49ers, there were times when he started so quickly that Albert couldn't get the ball to him.

Later, that was a problem for Tittle, too. "I used to kid him that he was a Southern boy, slow walking, slow talking," laughed Perry. "He wasn't used to our bang-bang way of doing things." For his part, Tittle jokingly would accuse Perry of being in motion on every play. "Perry was the fastest off the ball I've ever seen," Tittle said. "He could fly from that stance of his. The running game was different then. Now, tailbacks like Emmitt Smith and Barry Sanders sit back seven yards and pick their spots. Back then, running backs lined up three-and-a-half yards behind the line of scrimmage and would just pop. The hole was either there or it wasn't."

There was another important part of Perry's play that went unnoticed, except by his teammates and others with the 49ers: his mental alertness. "He knew not only his assignments but what everybody else on the offense was supposed to do," Spadia said. "Sometimes, Albert would forget how a play was supposed to go, and Perry would remind him."

Their great offense was never quite enough for the 49ers, though. Cleveland dominated the AAFC, always leaving the 49ers behind, though the 49ers had excellent regular-season records of 9-5, 8-4-2, 12-2, and 9-3. It was no disgrace losing to the Browns, who were probably the best team in pro football at the time, but it was frustrating.

Paul Brown ran a very sophisticated operation in Cleveland, from a superb scouting system to a perfectly organized team. He had skimmed off much of the best talent from the service teams and had Otto Graham as his quarterback.

"Graham may have been the best quarterback of all," said Gordy Soltau, who starred at end for the 49ers in the 1950s. "Certainly, he was the best of his time. He was a great athlete. He was an All-America basketball player in college and he played with the [National Basketball League's] Rochester Royals in 1946. He won the championship with the Royals and that fall won a championship with the Browns."

"Otto Graham was, in my judgment, the best quarterback of all time," said Ruffo, who saw Graham at the start of his great career. "He could run, he could pass. He could throw long. He threw everything like a bullet. The Browns executed so well. You might have known what they were going to do, but you couldn't stop them."

Most of all, Cleveland had Brown, who was so completely the franchise that the team was named after him. "Paul Brown had the most modern system of teaching football of any coach in the business," said Soltau, who went through a Cleveland training camp in 1950 before being traded to the 49ers. "Nothing was left to your imagination. He spelled out every assignment you had to carry out, and you learned it. You had a leather binder they picked up every day. The first five pages were the Paul Brown theory of football. He had a coach for every position; the 49ers had two assistants. Practices were one hour, ten minutes. Most coaches kept players on the field for two or three hours. Brown had more brainwork, more classroom time. Everything was geared to reaching a point of perfection."

Sound familiar? It should to 49ers fans. Bill Walsh brought the same kind of preparation, attention to detail, and devotion to perfection to the 49ers in 1979. Earlier in his career, Walsh had been an assistant to Brown, and he has always credited Brown with being a big influence on his coaching philosophy.

Because the 49ers played in the same division as the Browns, they were shut out of postseason play during their first three years. In 1949, the final AAFC season, the league could field only seven teams (Brooklyn was absorbed into the New York franchise), so there were no divisions. Once again, the 49ers finished second to the Browns, but this time the playoffs included the top four teams. The 49ers beat New York 17-7 and Cleveland beat Buffalo 31-21, so the 49ers and Browns met in the last AAFC Championship Game.

"During the season," Vetrano said, "we had played in a game that drew 72,000 people in Cleveland. So we were anticipating another big crowd there. But there was a blizzard the day of the game, and there'd been a rail strike, so there were only about 17,000 [actually 22,550] people there. When we looked up at the stands and saw so few people, our hearts sank." Cleveland won the game 21-7.

Vetrano kept the check stub from his player's share of that game, so he had an exact record as well as a telling comparison with the present-day game. "We got $172.61, with $21.70 taken out for

FROM BEARS COACH GEORGE HALAS, ON HUGH McELHENNY'S 94-YARD PUNT RETURN FOR A TOUCHDOWN IN A GAME IN 1952:

"THAT WAS THE DAMNEDEST RUN I'VE EVER SEEN IN FOOTBALL."

withholding," he said. "They had given us watches, but they charged us $5.70 for them, so our total payoff was $145.21."

And so, the All-America Football Conference came to an end. Three teams—Baltimore, Cleveland, and San Francisco—were absorbed into the National Football League for the 1950 season.

A BAD START

For the Browns, it was a chance to prove they were the best team in pro football. They went 10-2 in the regular season and then beat the Los Angeles Rams 30-28 for the NFL championship.

The 49ers plunged to 3-9. What happened?

"That was a tough year for the 49ers," said Gordy Soltau, who was a rookie in 1950. "We didn't have the size the rest of the league had. Billy Johnson at center was 215 pounds, and our tackles were about 215, too. Frankie Albert had to run for his life. Of course, he was good at it. He was a fabulous scrambler and a great gamesman. He loved to outsmart the defenses. We ran a lot of screen passes because we didn't have a line that could blow people away, so we had to try to fool them."

Soltau had played at the University of Minnesota with Leo Nomellini, a two-time All-America selection, and the two became teammates on the 49ers. Nomellini was the 49ers' top draft pick in 1950, but Soltau's route was circuitous. He had been drafted by the Green Bay Packers, who then traded him to Cleveland before he'd played a game for them. Before training camp ended, the Browns traded him to the 49ers, who were seeking both an end and a kicker to replace Vetrano, who had been released.

At 3-9, the 1950 season was the worst the 49ers would experience in their first seventeen seasons, but there was a consolation prize: it gave them the chance to draft future Hall of Fame quarterback Y. A. Tittle.

Tittle had played for Baltimore in the AAFC (after being traded there from Cleveland), but Baltimore was absorbed into the NFL in 1950.

A LONG STORY

Hugh McElhenny's 89-yard touchdown run against the Dallas Texans in 1952 still stands as the longest run from scrimmage in 49ers' history. McElhenny owns the second- (86 yards) and third-longest (82 yards) runs, too. The 49ers' longest...

Run from Scrimmage	89 yards	Hugh McElhenny	October 5, 1952, at Dallas Texans
Forward Pass	97 yards	Steve Young (to John Taylor)	November 3, 1991, at Atlanta
Punt Return	95 yards	John Taylor	November 21, 1988, vs. Washington
Kickoff Return	105 yards	Abe Woodson	November 8, 1959, at L.A. Rams
Interception Return	94 yards	Alvin Randolph	December 11, 1966, vs. Chicago
Fumble Return	99 yards	Don Griffin	December 23, 1991, vs. Chicago
Field Goal	56 yards	Mike Cofer	October 14, 1990, at Atlanta
Punt	86 yards	Larry Barnes	September 29, 1957, vs. Chi. Cardinals

After a disastrous 1-11 season, the Colts folded and their players were put into the draft pool with the college players. The 49ers, who had the second pick in the first round, grabbed Tittle. (Tittle thus earned the distinction of being a first-round draft pick three times: He was selected by the Detroit Lions of the NFL and the Browns of the AAFC in 1948, and by the 49ers in 1951.) Tittle played very little that first season because Albert was still the quarterback, and the 49ers bounced back to post a 7-4-1 record in 1951. Albert's continuing effectiveness was partly intuitive, but it also resulted from his knowledge of opposing players.

"Frank wasn't so much concerned about what defense a team was in as who was in the defense," Soltau said. "In those days, you got to know the other teams very, very well, because there weren't any substitutions unless you were injured and got

Hugh McElhenny's flashy running style earned him the nickname "The King." He joined the 49ers in 1952 and rushed for 604 yards while averaging 7 yards per carry as a rookie.

carried off the field. If you played against the Rams, you knew you were going to play against the same eleven guys all day, and when you played them again, you were going to see the same guys.

"So you looked more where these guys were than what defense they were in. You knew if you were going to run here, you had to block Larry Brink. You knew Andy Robustelli was going to be here, and Don Paul was going to be there. You really had a lot of knowledge about the guys. Whether you could do anything about it, well, that was up to you."

There was another significant addition through the draft that year: linebacker Hardy Brown. A twenty-first round pick, Brown was a real steal. He had an unusual style, knocking down runners and receivers with a shoulder block rather than a tackle, but it was effective. He literally knocked players out

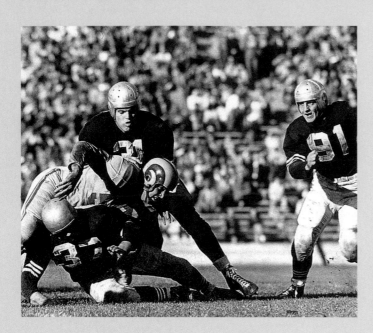

MUTUAL (DIS)AFFECTION

From the time the 49ers joined the NFL in 1950 until the Rams moved to St. Louis following the 1994 season, the rivalry between San Francisco and Los Angeles was fueled by the dislike the residents of the two cities had for each other.

The rivalry was one-sided at first (Los Angeles won five of the first six games). The Rams, who played in the 1950 and 1951 title games, had the glamorous players — Bob Waterfield, Norm Van Brocklin, Elroy Hirsch, and Tom Fears. They had the glamorous women, too — Waterfield was married to actress Jane Russell, and Glenn Davis was engaged first to Elizabeth Taylor, and then to Terry Moore.

Gordy Soltau remembers the first game he played in the Los Angeles Coliseum, a 28-21 loss to the Rams in 1950. The temperature exceeded 100 degrees. It was so hot that the 49ers didn't go to the dressing room at halftime, but sat instead in a shaded corner with cold towels. The fans were heckling them, so Frankie Albert threw an orange into the stands. Soon, the fans were pelting the 49ers with oranges.

"After the game," Soltau said, "here we are coming up the tunnel. We look like we've been dragged through a wringer, and the Rams come up and all these lovelies grab them and they go off into the sunset."

After that, beating the Rams was a priority for the 49ers. One of their most satisfying wins was their first, a 44-17 triumph in 1951 at Kezar Stadium in which Soltau scored 26 points on 3 touchdowns, a field goal, and 5 extra points.

"That was the last game for Glenn Davis," he said. "Hardy Brown hit him with a shoulder, and that was it. On the last play of the game, Hardy hit their big fullback, Dick Hoerner, and everybody poured onto the field. When Hoerner finally got to the locker room, he found out he'd broken his arm."

The next year, the hitting was fierce in a preseason game the 49ers won 17-7. Players were leaving the game with serious injuries.

"At halftime," Soltau said, "[Rams owner] Dan Reeves and Tony Morabito visited the two dressing rooms and made a joint announcement: 'Hey now, you guys, we want you to play strong, competitive football, but will you quit trying to kill each other? We can't afford to have our teams knocked out in training camp.'"

of games. "Hardy put a lot of pressure on offensive teams, and it brought the defensive team up because he made it known we weren't a lot of pansies, that we could hit with anybody," Soltau said.

At that time, the draft lasted thirty rounds. The year before, the 49ers had also made an excellent late pick, getting Billy Wilson, who would set club receiving records that lasted until the 1980s. Wilson was drafted after his junior year but went back to school for another year before joining the 49ers in 1951.

"Pro football was not that big at that time," Wilson remembers. "I had never even seen a professional game. I hardly knew any 49ers except for Frankie Albert and Norm Standlee, and I knew them because I'd seen them play at Stanford. With the Knothole Gang, for a quarter, we would take a train to Stanford, see the game, and come back on the train to San Jose."

Wilson was a shy, unassuming man who was so good that people took him for granted. In his ten-year career, Wilson caught 407 passes for 5,902 yards, club records at the time. "With the emphasis on passing today, he'd probably catch a hundred balls in a season," Tittle said. "I never saw him drop a ball, not in practice, not in a game."

Wilson, now a scout with the 49ers, remembers a much different game. "We didn't have a tight end, and we always had three running backs. If a back was flanked to my side, I had to do what a tight end does now — block the linebacker or cut off the defensive end. Not a lot of fun for a guy who weighed 184 pounds."

Soltau remembers other differences in pro football in his time. "Because there were fewer players, you were more involved with every play, every down, both in practice and in the game. Today, there are so many specialists, particularly on defense. We didn't have that luxury. If you had a third end, he had to be able to play someplace else. In practice, you were all there all the time, so you got to know each other a lot better than players do now.

"We were on the road a lot. As a West Coast team, we had two or three trips a year to the East where we stayed. We didn't have a lot of money, so we couldn't go anywhere. We played poker, bridge, cribbage."

In that era, the game was tougher, more a test of strength than finesse. The rules were more liberal, permitting the defense to do things that are forbidden now. There were fewer officials, too, so players didn't have to worry as much about being penalized for foul plays.

McELHENNY ARRIVES

The next year, 1952, started even better for the 49ers when they drafted University of Washington running back Hugh McElhenny in the first round.

Those who were fortunate enough to see McElhenny play for the 49ers all agree: he was the best running back ever. His teammates nicknamed him "The King," and he made the Pro Football Hall of Fame in his first year of eligibility.

McElhenny still holds the 49ers' club record for longest run from scrimmage (89 yards). But statistics only hint at the kind of excitement he created. Injuries often kept him out of the lineup or reduced the number of times he could carry the ball. Joe Perry contributed more statistically, because a tire iron to his head wouldn't have kept Perry out of the lineup.

McElhenny was hit by everything but that tire iron. The rule permitting a back to get up and run after being tackled still was in effect, and the term "gang tackling" took on an entirely different meaning with McElhenny. "He was so dangerous, the defense couldn't take any chances, so everybody just piled on him," Soltau remembered. "He would have gotten killed if they hadn't changed that rule."

But when McElhenny was healthy and running free, he was beautiful to watch. He had the speed of a sprinter, having run the hurdles in junior college, and nobody ever had McElhenny's moves. At full speed he would cut left or right, or sometimes both, in rapid succession and leave tacklers sprawled in his wake. Other backs might slide out of a tackler's grasp, but McElhenny would leave them grasping air.

He had great peripheral vision, and even when his speed left him, his moves and vision made him dangerous. The run that's most often talked about, in fact, came when he was past his prime—and against the 49ers. Playing with the expansion Minnesota Vikings in 1961, McElhenny ran 39

End Billy Wilson had never seen a professional football game before he was drafted by the 49ers. He caught on fast, setting club records for receptions (407) and yards (5,902) in a ten-year career.

yards, measured in the usual terms, but probably covered twice that territory in reality as he weaved back and forth, eluding nine attempted tackles. "Matt Hazeltine missed me twice," McElhenny remembers.

"I remember runs where there'd be a guy coming up from behind him and all of a sudden, McElhenny would make a little move and the guy would miss him," former 49ers' broadcaster Bob Fouts said. "Somehow, he just had the sense that a guy was there.

"After Tittle was traded to New York, the 49ers played a game there against the Giants. After the game, Tittle was surrounded by reporters. By that time, McElhenny was with the Giants, too. Nobody wanted to talk to McElhenny because he was no longer the runner he'd been, but I thought as I looked at him, if he had played in New York instead of San Francisco at the start of his career, nobody would have ever heard of Frank Gifford."

Even before joining the 49ers, McElhenny was a legend. One story said he had found his way from Compton Junior College in southern California to Seattle by following a trail of $20 bills. Albert introduced him to the 49ers as a man who had to take a pay cut to play professional ball. There also were whispers that McElhenny had personality conflicts with coaches and teammates.

Albert wasn't concerned about McElhenny's reputation, especially after seeing him play in an all-star game in Honolulu. Frank called Tony Morabito that night — in his exuberance forgetting the time difference that made it 2 A.M. in San Francisco — and told Morabito, "We've got to get this guy!"

Morabito concurred, and the 49ers drafted McElhenny in the first round. The fact that McElhenny, with his unquestioned ability, lasted until the ninth pick made some think his reputation had hurt him, but in fact the draft was one of incredible college talent. The picks ahead of McElhenny included Bill Wade, Ollie Matson, Babe Parilli, Ed Modzelewski, Les Richter, and Frank Gifford.

In his first preseason game with the 49ers, McElhenny told Albert, "Give me the ball."

"You don't know the plays," Albert said.

"Draw up one for me," McElhenny said.

Albert told him to look for a pitchout. McElhenny took the pitch and ran 42 yards for a touchdown.

The game that really made McElhenny's reputation came on October 19, 1952, against the Bears in Chicago. Since they had come into the NFL, the

The 49ers boasted some outstanding runners in the forties and fifties. One of them was J. D. Smith (24), who rushed for 1,016 yards and scored 10 touchdowns in 1959.

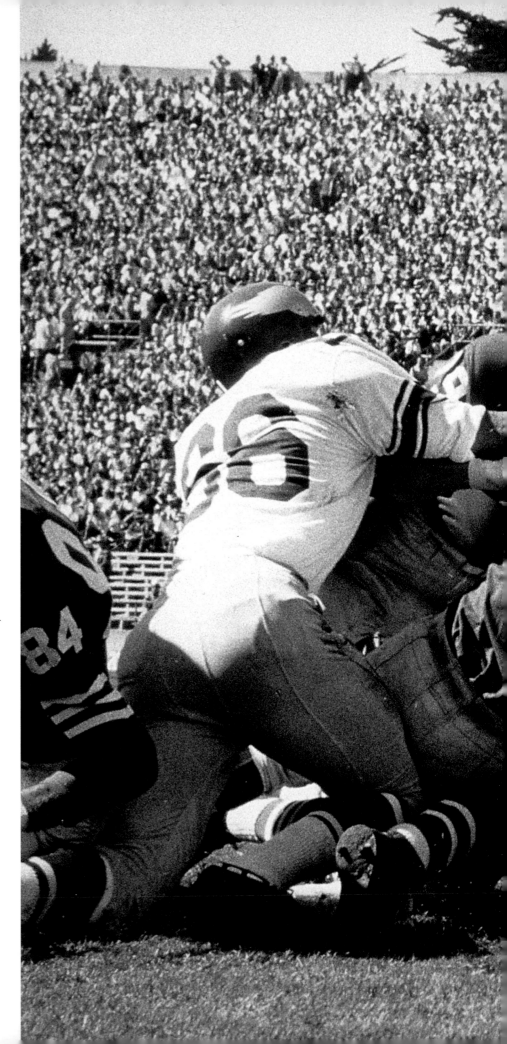

Gordy Soltau (above) and Leo Nomellini joined the 49ers as rookies in 1950, but the team struggled to a 3-9 record in its first year in the National Football League.

McElhenny also ran for 114 yards on just 12 carries to pace the 49ers' 40-16 rout. Chicago assistant Clark Shaughnessy, the same coach who had installed the T-formation for the Bears and Stanford, called McElhenny a combination of breakaway back George McAfee and powerhouse Bronko Nagurski, the two best running backs in Bears' history.

Though Albert sold pro football to the Bay Area, McElhenny took the 49ers a step further, to the level where attendance of fifty thousand per game became the norm. "Before McElhenny, there was still doubt as to whether the franchise could survive in San Francisco," Lou Spadia said, "but he created so much excitement. He brought in new fans, people who had never thought of coming to our games before."

GOOD-BYE TO FRANKIE

As one hero emerged, another was fading. From the beginning, Frankie Albert and the 49ers had been synonymous, but nothing is forever in professional sports. As the 1952 season unfolded, it became obvious that Albert's skills were diminishing. Fortunately, it also was obvious to Albert, who would make a gracious farewell that would enable him to return later as a coach and part-owner.

It is not unusual for star quarterbacks to play into their late thirties and even forties, but Albert was a different type of quarterback, one who relied on his quickness and deception far more than mere arm strength. At thirty-two, Albert had lost some of his quickness and perhaps some of his love for the game. The game was changing, too, as the Los Angeles Rams in particular were showing how devastating the long passing game could be, with Norm Van Brocklin and Bob Waterfield throwing to fleet receivers such as Elroy "Crazy Legs" Hirsch and Bob Boyd, as well as to Tom Fears, their outstanding possession receiver. That definitely was not Albert's kind of game. Y. A. Tittle, the nominal backup (Albert and Tittle split playing time almost equally in 1952) was much better suited to that type of play.

Now Albert says, "Tittle chased me to Canada," where Albert signed a contract for 1953, but the

49ers had been told, "You don't belong in the NFL until you can beat the Bears." They hadn't yet, but the Bears, trailing 14-9 in this game, made the mistake of punting to McElhenny. He fielded the ball on the 6-yard line, though he was not aware of it. "I thought I was around the twenty," he said later. "If I'd known where I was, I'd have let it bounce into the end zone."

Instead, he took the ball and weaved his way 94 yards down the field into the end zone, as the other 49ers watched in awe.

remark is made with good humor, because the two respected each other during their playing careers and have remained friends ever since.

As the season drew to a close, Albert announced that he would be retiring — the Canadian offer had not yet come — and a special ceremony was held before the final game for him and running back John Strzykalski, who also was retiring.

The game ended in the first half for Strzykalski, who suffered the eighth broken nose of his career on an off-tackle play.

Albert, though, went out in style. He ran the bootleg, quick-kicked, and completed 16 of 26 passes, 1 for a touchdown, as the 49ers beat Green Bay 24-14. He even threw a block that helped spring McElhenny on a run. "That was the first block I've thrown in two years," he said after the game. "I'm glad they didn't see me coming."

Tittle was the quarterback for the 1953 season, which included a game against the Rams that not only is a highlight of that rivalry but also is among the most exciting games in franchise history.

"The Rams were leading twenty to nothing just before the half," Soltau remembers. "Then, on fourth down, Norm Van Brocklin went back to punt but threw instead to Dick "Night Train" Lane, who was wide open — but Lane dropped the ball. That gave us our chance, and it kind of made us mad, too, because it was like Van Brocklin was trying to rub it in, not just beat us."

The 49ers got the ball on the Los Angeles 28-yard line and trimmed the deficit to 20-7 at half-time on Tittle's touchdown pass to Billy Wilson. They scored again on a Joe Perry run early in the third quarter to pull within six points. The Rams countered with a 90-yard touchdown drive, but the next time Los Angeles had the ball, Van Brocklin fumbled and the 49ers' Lowell Wagner recovered. Perry scored another touchdown, and the Rams led 27-21 entering the fourth quarter.

In the final quarter, the 49ers went ahead for the first time on a 4-yard touchdown run by rookie halfback Bill Mixon, but the Rams regained the lead at 30-28 when Ben Agajanian kicked a field goal with about three minutes left. After Agajanian kicked off into the end zone, the 49ers started from their 20-yard line. The Rams were in a deep zone, so

Hugh McElhenney

Joe Perry

John Henry Johnson

Y. A. Tittle

PRE-INFLATION DOLLARS

The 49ers have always been blessed with great offensive players, and never more so than in the mid-1950s, when they had the "Million-Dollar Backfield."

Every member of that backfield — quarterback Y. A. Tittle, fullback Joe Perry, and halfbacks Hugh McElhenny and John Henry Johnson — is in the Pro Football Hall of Fame.

Tittle, one of the finest pure passers in the history of the NFL, was a tough man, physically and mentally, who would stand in the pocket and wait until the last split-second for a receiver to get open, knowing he would get hammered when he released the ball.

Perry was known as "The Jet" because of his incredibly fast start, so fast that he sometimes went by Tittle before Y. A. could hand off the ball. Perry is still the leading ground-gainer in 49ers history (7,344 yards), though that total doesn't include his two years in the All-America Football Conference.

McElhenny, who some people consider the finest running back ever, would cut so sharply that tacklers would be left grabbing nothing but air. He compared his running style to a man running through an alley at night, dodging shadows.

Johnson was overshadowed by his more famous teammates, but he was a powerful and fast runner — Tittle said that when the 49ers ran 50-yard sprints in practice, Johnson beat everybody. He would clash with tacklers head-on and, when he was brought down, dare them to hit him harder.

What was it like to play in that backfield? "Everybody came back to the huddle saying, 'Give me the ball, give me the ball,'" Perry remembers. "I don't know how Y. A. kept everybody happy, but he did."

To get the most out of that talent, Tittle often used McElhenny as a man in motion and threw to him — a forerunner of some of today's formations with two running backs and a flanker.

Unhappily, injuries often kept the 49ers from having all four players in the backfield at the same time. McElhenny, in particular, was plagued by injuries throughout his career.

The "Million-Dollar" label was hung on the backfield as a symbol of a value that was almost incomprehensible at the time. Inflation has since set in, and each of the players would make well over that in a year if they were playing today.

R. C. Owens's trademark was the "Alley-Oop" catch. He leaped high over Detroit defensive back Jim David to grab this touchdown catch in the 49ers' conference playoff loss to the Lions in 1957.

stadium, and when I looked up, all I could see was sun. Y. A. always has said the kick was no good, but he 'called it' for the referee."

The 49ers won 31-30.

CHAMPIONSHIP FRUSTRATION

Always a bridesmaid, never a bride," says Leo Nomellini, issuing a complaint that is echoed by many of the early 49ers. Several times, the 49ers had very good teams, but not quite good enough to win a championship. In fact, only once in the first eleven years of the franchise did the 49ers reach the playoffs.

The 49ers came oh-so-close. In 1951, for instance, their 7-4-1 record was just a half game worse than the Rams' 8-4, which was good enough for the Western Conference title. In 1953 they were an excellent 9-3, but still a game behind Detroit's 10-2. (In those days, only the winners of the two conferences met in postseason play, unless there was a tie for first.)

No year in that stretch was as frustrating as 1954, however. That was the year of the "Million-Dollar-Backfield" of Tittle, McElhenny, Perry, and John Henry Johnson, all members of the Pro Football Hall of Fame.

There probably has never been a backfield that good — when the components were healthy. That was the problem, though. Tittle was hurt early in the 1954 season but still played as the 49ers won four and tied one in their first five games. McElhenny was at his absolute peak the first five games of the season, gaining 515 yards on just 64 rushes, an incredible eight yards a carry. But against Chicago in week 6, he separated his shoulder and was lost for the year. Though Perry went on to gain 1,049 yards, the first back ever to gain more than 1,000 yards in consecutive seasons (remember that this was a twelve-game season), the loss of McElhenny doomed the 49ers, who won only three of their last seven games.

It also doomed Buck Shaw. Morabito blamed the disappointing season more on the "country club" atmosphere under Shaw than the loss of McElhenny. He did not renew Shaw's contract, in effect firing the popular coach.

It was a devastating blow to Shaw, whose overall

Tittle flipped a short pass to McElhenny, who began one of his magical runs. He got help immediately from Leo Nomellini, who leveled Rams' tackle Bud McFadin to break McElhenny loose in the secondary.

Defensive backs Woodley Lewis and "Night Train" Lane converged on McElhenny but grabbed only air as the 49ers' back pivoted and cut to the right sideline, with the Rams in pursuit. At the Rams' 9-yard line, Lewis finally caught McElhenny and brought him down.

Now Tittle had two concerns — to score and to use up time so the Rams would not have time to score themselves. Three running plays and a 5-yard penalty later, Soltau lined up for a field-goal attempt.

To this day, nobody knows whether Soltau's 13-yard kick with five seconds left was good. Tittle jumped up as soon as the ball was kicked, throwing his arms in the air as if signaling a successful kick and blocking the view of the official, who nonetheless signaled field goal, too. "I couldn't see the ball," Soltau said. "The sun was just over the rim of the

FROM AN OFFICIAL TO Y. A. TITTLE,
DURING A GAME AGAINST GREEN BAY
IN THE MID-1950S:

"HEY, Y. A., WHEN
ARE YOU GOING TO
THROW ONE OF
THOSE BIG ALLEY-
OOPS? I NEVER HAVE
SEEN THE THING."

FROM TITTLE TO THE OFFICIAL:

"HOW ABOUT THE
NEXT PLAY?"
(HE DID).

NO HOLDS BARRED

Bob St. Clair was a terrific offensive tackle who eventually was voted into the Pro Football Hall of Fame. He also was a genuine character known for his habit of eating raw meat. "I started that when I was a kid," St. Clair said. "My grandmother would slice up meat, and I'd grab a piece and eat it like that. I never ate it cooked."

When he discovered later that others alternately were amazed and repulsed by his eating habits, St. Clair had some fun. "In training camp, I'd pick up some raw liver and cover it with a paper napkin, and then I'd go over to where the rookies were sitting. I'd take it out and start eating it, and there'd be blood running down my chin. They'd look at me, decide they weren't hungry, and leave the table."

In training camp, St. Clair and some of his teammates would sometimes hunt deer. He'd clean the catch and cut it up. "I'd hold up the liver and say, 'This is how you see if the deer was healthy. If the liver has spots on it, you don't want to eat the deer because he was probably sick. But if it looks good like this...' Then I'd take a bite out of it and ask if anybody else wanted a bite. Nobody ever did."

St. Clair grew up in San Francisco's Mission District and went to Polytechnic High and USF, both of whom played games at Kezar Stadium, home of the 49ers when St. Clair played. As a junior, St. Clair played on an undefeated team at USF, but the Dons weren't invited to a bowl game, and the school dropped football. St. Clair transferred to Tulsa because the Missouri Valley Conference was the only major conference that did not require transfers to sit out a year.

He furthered his reputation at Tulsa by winning his only Golden Gloves boxing match, though he had no boxing experience. At 6-feet, 9-inches, he towered over his opponent and realized early in the match that his opponent was frightened. "I just came right at him," St. Clair said, "backing him up in the corner. I grabbed him with one hand and whacked him with the other. I hit him as he was going down and, when he went down, I got down on one knee and hit him on the top of his head. Somebody grabbed me from behind, and I threw my arm back to knock him off. It was the referee! People were booing and booing, but the referee finally raised my hand as the winner.

"I'll tell you one thing: That sure put me in solid with my football teammates. They loved me after that."

record was an excellent 72-40-4. "When he was fired, he was really, really, really downcast, and very resentful," Art Rosenbaum remembers. "He said in all of his life, starting with his first job as an assistant at the University of Nevada, he had never been fired. He was too much of a gentlemen ever to say it, but I know he got a great deal of satisfaction a few years later when he went back to Philadelphia and won an NFL title [in 1960]."

It was the end of an era. The two men who had symbolized the 49ers when they first started play were Shaw and Albert, and both were gone. To replace Shaw, Morabito hired Norman (Red) Strader, who had coached earlier at St. Mary's, and who was expected to be a disciplinarian.

"Buck was very loose, very soft on the discipline," Al Ruffo said. "He never had bed checks, never threatened anybody. Tony thought it was too loose, so he brought in Strader. I told Tony that Strader was so tough on little things, he'd have the squad in an uproar. The players wouldn't play for him."

Broadcaster Bob Fouts remembered one of those little things: "One day in training camp, it was really hot, and Frankie Albert [then an assistant coach] yelled at Strader, 'Hey, Red, how about a little water out here?' Strader just sputtered. Water on the practice field? You'd have thought Albert was talking Communist theory or something."

Strader was clearly one of those coaches who functions best as an assistant. There was no pattern to what the 49ers did that season. "He must have brought one hundred players to training camp, looking at everybody to find players who could help," Fouts said. Not enough of them could. The 49ers were 4-8 in 1955, and Morabito told Ruffo, "You were right." After that year, Strader was gone.

Although pro football was becoming more of a business, it still was more relaxed than it is today because the big money was still far in the future.

"We didn't work out in the offseason because we had to get jobs," remembered Bruce Bosley, who started his thirteen-year career with the 49ers as a defensive end in 1956, before moving to the offensive line. "So the first couple of days of training camp, there were a lot of guys throwing up because they weren't in shape.

"Even during the season, football wasn't really a

full-time job. We didn't lift weights because the feeling then was that lifting weights made you muscle-bound and slowed you down. We didn't have the meetings that they have today. We'd practice two or three hours in the afternoon, and that would be it." Bosley never lost the feeling that football was more a game than a business, and he thoroughly enjoyed his years with the 49ers.

"When we went on those two- and three-week road trips, it was almost like a vacation," he said. "We'd have the games on Sunday, of course, and the practices, but after practice we'd have all that time to hang out together. It was just great fun."

From his spot in the booth, Fouts agreed. "It seemed to be more fun then," he said. "I think we [the broadcasters] were closer to the team than the guys are now. We traveled with them, and I used to sit in on the team meetings. I'd sit in with the offense one day, the defense the next. I mostly wanted to find out what the other team was expected to do. Nobody ever objected to me being there. Monty Stickles used to sit in the back of the

Above, Y. A. Tittle. Below, the board of stockholders in 1957. Standing (left to right): Lawrence Purcell, Al Ruffo, Franklin Mieuli, James Ginella. Seated (left to right): Vic Morabito, Tony Morabito, Dr. William O'Grady.

room and say, 'Pssst. There's a spy in here.' But that was Monty's way of having fun."

Fouts's main contribution to 49ers' lore was the term "red dog" for a blitz. Listeners would hear Fouts screaming, "Here comes the red dog!" with the approximate intensity you'd expect if he'd been warning of a Russian invasion off the coast. "That expression came from [coach Howard] Red Hickey," Fouts said. "When he was with the Rams [in the early 1950s], he'd watch the linebackers and if he saw one coming, he'd yell, 'Red dog, red dog!' I used to watch the quarterback with one eye and the linebackers with another because if the linebacker started coming, it changed the whole play."

The 49ers used the blitz more than most teams in a vain attempt to compensate for their defensive weaknesses—and for a time were victimized themselves with alarming regularity. Offensive sequences constantly were disrupted by blitzes from other teams.

Then it turned around. With John Brodie at quarterback, the 49ers started picking up blitzes with ease, leaving Brodie free to throw to receivers left open by the risky defense. Word got around the league that the 49ers couldn't be blitzed because Brodie always spotted it coming and switched his call.

After Brodie's retirement, he explained the 49ers' secret. Before going out for a pass, running backs hesitated for one count to check the linebacker on that side. If the linebacker was coming, the back stayed in to block. If the linebacker stayed put, the back went out for a pass. Because teams seldom used defensive backs or even middle linebackers to blitz, Brodie could account for the two possible trouble spots with that simple plan.

The new coach replacing Strader in 1956 was Albert, who had spent one year on the staff as an assistant. Morabito thought Albert would restore some fire to the club, and he also was aware that Albert's name

would bring the 49ers more attention and, presumably, increased ticket sales.

The reaction to Albert's hiring by the press and among fans was positive, but Ruffo again had his doubts. "Albert was too close to the players," he said. "When he was an assistant coach and they went out on a binge, he went with them. And he became a part-owner, too. I told Tony that it was going to be hard. But he was very close to Frank."

Watching from the broadcast booth, Fouts saw a regrettable change in Albert. "He had always been a happy-go-lucky guy, but when he became a coach, that all changed," he said. "He really felt the pressure. He got bags under his eyes.

"As a player, Albert really coached the team on the field. Buck Shaw basically let him run practice. There were many times when he'd yell out to Albert, 'Let's run such-and-such a play,' and Albert would yell back, 'Nah, we've already run that today.' When Albert became the coach, Red Hickey was running the offense. One day he said to Hickey, 'Let's run that play again,' and Hickey said, 'Nah, we've already run that enough.' It had come full circle."

From the start, some reporters were saying that players were unhappy with Albert's criticism. When the 49ers lost their last three preseason games in 1956 (after winning their first three), there was a report that Albert would quit, the implication being that otherwise he might be fired before the 49ers even played a regular-season game!

That was just wild speculation by a reporter, however—hardly unusual at the time. "You didn't have the sophistication in the media that you have now," says Brodie, then a senior at Stanford who soon would be in the middle of many controversies as a 49er. "Now, both on TV and in the newspapers, you have guys who really understand the game. At that time, reporters were more like fans, and they didn't know anything. I don't think some of them wanted to know."

The criticism of Albert increased when the 49ers lost six of their first seven regular-season games. Tittle thought he understood Albert's problem. "Frank didn't coach with the same assuredness he'd had as a player," he said. "As a player, he did what felt right, but as a coach, he looked for rules and reasons."

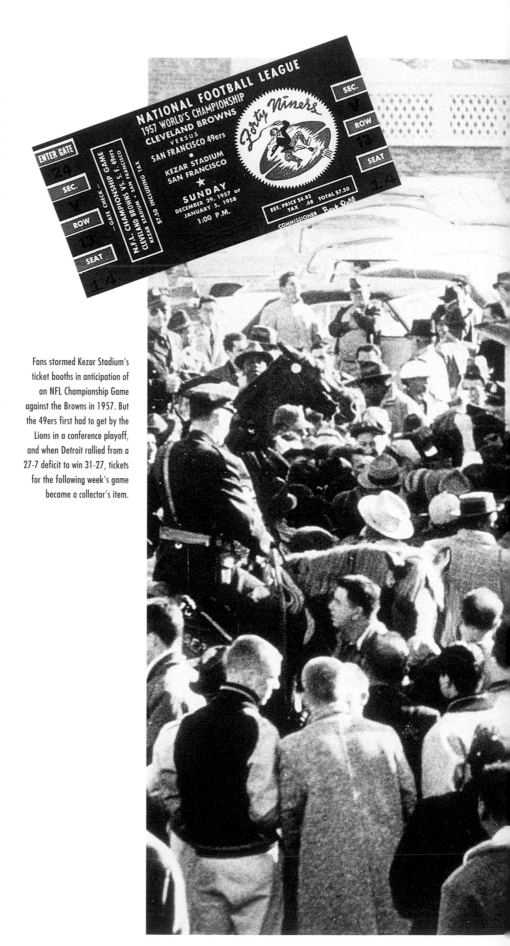

Fans stormed Kezar Stadium's ticket booths in anticipation of an NFL Championship Game against the Browns in 1957. But the 49ers first had to get by the Lions in a conference playoff, and when Detroit rallied from a 27-7 deficit to win 31-27, tickets for the following week's game became a collector's item.

With future Hall of Fame quarterback Bobby Layne out with an injury, Kyle Rote (18) led the Lions to a come-from-behind victory over the 49ers in a conference playoff game in 1957.

One thing that specifically affected Tittle was Albert's insistence on calling plays from the sidelines, a practice which is customary now but wasn't done by anybody but Paul Brown at that time. "We all grew up with the quarterback calling the play," Tittle said. "That was a big part of being a quarterback. Quarterbacks were leaders. A guy like Bobby Layne couldn't throw the ball all that well, but players believed in him. Even if you called the wrong play, you made it work sometimes because the players believed it would work.

"When Frank tried calling the plays, it didn't work at all. Then, in the second half of the season, he went back to letting me call the plays, and we won four [and tied one] of our last five games."

Their second-half rally set the stage for 1957, the closest the 49ers would get to a championship until 1970.

THE ALLEY-OOP

It was a preseason game against the New York Giants at Kezar Stadium in 1957 that started it. Near the end of the game, Y. A. Tittle threw a high, looping pass into the end zone and a tall rookie receiver named R. C. Owens leaped into the air and caught it for a touchdown.

"I was trying to throw the ball away," Tittle said. "I just threw it up in the air, and R. C. came down with it. It was just a lucky catch."

Not so to Owens, who came up to Tittle on the

sideline and said, "I can catch that pass every time."

The Alley-Oop was born.

"He couldn't catch it every time, of course," Tittle said, "but he could catch it maybe one out of three times. And when you've got third-and-twenty-seven—well, I don't know many passes you can count on for a first down or a touchdown in that situation."

Before that play, nobody knew much about Owens, except for his brief stint as a basketball player. After playing at the College of Idaho, he took a break in the summer of 1956 to spend a week at the 49ers' training camp but then went back to basketball, touring Europe with the Seattle Buchan Bakers.

By 1957, Owens was back with the 49ers in training camp, but his basketball training still was his main qualification. R. C. never was fast by receiver standards, but he could outjump any defensive back.

In practice, he and Tittle worked on the pass, which became known as the Alley-Oop, though nobody is certain why. Owens told Tittle not to throw a perfect spiral when he threw the Alley-Oop, but to put a little wobble on it. "I always felt that gave me a chance to catch the front end or the back end," Owens said. "That doesn't make much sense, but it did to me."

Teams now throw a "Hail Mary" pass as a desperation move at the end of games, but that type of pass is significantly different from the Alley-Oop.

"For the 'Hail Mary,' teams will put four receivers on one side of the field and hope for a deflection," Tittle said. "We'd just put R.C. alone on one side of the field. He'd be double- or triple-teamed, but we had the confidence he could come up with the ball."

Owens's basketball training was important for a reason other than his leaping ability. "As a rebounder, you're looking for the ball coming down and maybe you make a move to make another player think it's coming down in one spot and you go to another."

"The defender is taught to stay between the receiver and the goal line, so we always threw the ball short," Tittle said. "It was up to R. C. to figure out how to get it. We didn't even have a number for the

MOUNTAIN HIGH

Bruce Bosley, who played thirteen seasons for the 49ers as a guard and center, grew up in the mountains of West Virginia and went to the University of West Virginia. When he was drafted by the 49ers in 1956, he didn't even know there was such a thing as pro football. "What's the 49ers?" he asked Mountaineers' coach Art Lewis.

Lewis told Bosley he could probably make $5,000 a year playing pro football. "I thought that was all the money in the world," Bosley said. "There were homes being built in my hometown for $6,000. I thought, 'You mean, I could almost pay for a whole house in one year?'"

49ers scout Jack White offered him $7,000. Bosley was flabbergasted. He could only say, "I'll have to think about that." White, who thought Bosley had to be convinced, told him the 49ers would also pay him a signing bonus of $1,500.

Bosley happily accepted.

play. In the huddle, I'd just say Alley-Oop on two."

The play became very popular with the fans, as writers spent much of their game stories describing the unusual touchdowns.

"The Alley-Oop pass was a nice part of the game," Tittle said. "It gave people a lot of excitement because everybody knew what was going to happen. You knew the play was between the quarterback and R. C. Owens. So everybody stood up and watched."

The Alley-Oop could be a distraction, Owens remembers. "One time against Green Bay, a referee told Y. A. he wanted to see the Alley-Oop because he'd heard so much about it, so Y. A. told him when he was going to throw it," Owens said. "Well, he faded back to pass and he just got annihilated. He got up and said to the referee, 'Did you see what those guys did to me?' And the referee said, 'No, I was looking for the Alley-Oop pass.'"

When it worked, though, it was spectacular, and never more so than against the Detroit Lions at Kezar on November 3, 1957.

The game was topsy-turvy from the start. The Lions scored the first 10 points, the 49ers the next 28. Then Tobin Rote, substituting for injured Bobby Layne, brought the Lions roaring back to take the lead at 31-28 with just 1:25 left.

Tittle completed four passes to move the 49ers to the Detroit 41 with 10 seconds remaining. There was no suspense in anticipation of the next play — and not a lot of hope for 49ers fans either, because San Francisco was operating against the best defensive backfield in the league—"Chris's Crew," named for Jack Christiansen, later to be a 49ers head coach.

Owens loped downfield with characteristically deceptive strides and swung into the right corner of the end zone, with Christiansen in back of him and Jim David in front. Tittle looped the ball downfield, and Owens jumped, snaring the ball with his large hands as Christiansen and David watched in frustration and then fell to their knees, pounding the turf with their hands. The 49ers had won, and the reputation of the Alley-Oop was made.

The joy of that victory was in marked contrast to the week before, when the 49ers were playing the Chicago Bears at Kezar. The 49ers were trailing 17-7 at halftime when players were told that owner Tony Morabito had suffered a heart attack while watching the game. He was taken to St. Mary's Hospital.

Neither the fans at the stadium nor the radio audience knew that Morabito had been stricken. Franklin Mieuli, a very close friend of Morabito who owned 10 percent of the team, was the producer of the radio broadcast. He told announcer Bob Fouts not to go on the air with the news that Morabito had been taken to the hospital, and Fouts didn't know until after the game that Morabito had died.

After learning of Morabito's heart attack, the 49ers took the field for the second half in an emotional frenzy. In the third quarter, Albert got a note from Dr. Bill O'Grady: "Tony's gone." Albert told his players, who played with even more fervor after that. The football they played in that second half wasn't pretty, but it was effective, and they came back to beat the Bears 21-17, with an 11-yard pass from Tittle to Billy Wilson that gave the 49ers their winning touchdown.

Another chapter in 49ers' history was closed. The man whose vision had brought the 49ers into existence didn't live long enough to see the finish of their most exciting season.

A BIG DRAWING CARD

An earlier victory in Chicago was also noteworthy. The game was won on an Alley-Oop pass, but it should have been disallowed. Owens was bumped out of bounds on his way down the sideline, which made him an ineligible receiver, but he came back in bounds and actually caught the ball on his knees in the end zone.

Chicago Bears coach George Halas, having seen Owens go out of bounds, was livid.

"He couldn't believe that was happening to him, especially in Chicago, where he had everything going his way," Fouts said. "We always went into Chicago fearing the worst. A referee who worked quite a few of the Bears games actually put

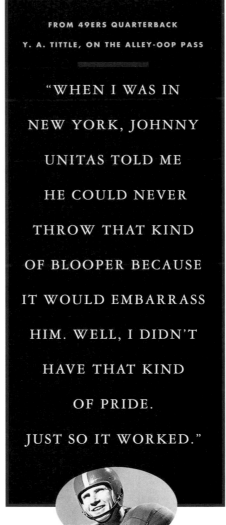

FROM 49ERS QUARTERBACK
Y. A. TITTLE, ON THE ALLEY-OOP PASS

"WHEN I WAS IN NEW YORK, JOHNNY UNITAS TOLD ME HE COULD NEVER THROW THAT KIND OF BLOOPER BECAUSE IT WOULD EMBARRASS HIM. WELL, I DIDN'T HAVE THAT KIND OF PRIDE. JUST SO IT WORKED."

out their highlights show after the season, and his wife sat with Halas's wife in a box. We didn't expect to get many breaks, but we did that time."

The dramatic last-minute victories made the 49ers their fans' darlings and a big hit around the league. At home, they sold out four games. In Detroit, they attracted a Lions' record 56,915 fans. In Los Angeles, it was a league record—102,368.

Tittle, the NFL player of the year that season, and Owens were the big stories in the 49ers' success, but others had their moments of glory, too, including rookie quarterback John Brodie and, of course, Hugh McElhenny.

In consecutive years, the 49ers made a quarterback their first draft pick. Earl Morrall had been the first pick in the regular draft in 1956 (the NFL had a "bonus pick" at the time who was taken before the regular draft began, and Pittsburgh had selected defensive back Gary Glick).

Brodie was the second pick in the 1957 draft, behind Heisman Trophy winner Paul Hornung, who went to Green Bay. Being picked second in that draft was a great honor. Players drafted after Brodie that year included Jim Brown (Cleveland), Jim Parker (Baltimore), Jon Arnett and Del Shofner (Los Angeles), and Len Dawson (Pittsburgh). Hornung, Brown, Parker, and Dawson are in the Pro Football Hall of Fame.

Obviously, the 49ers thought highly of Brodie, but that didn't mean he was in their immediate plans: Tittle was smack in his prime.

"The existing viewpoint was that no quarterback should play before three years," Brodie remembers, "and the existing viewpoint was correct. There was so much more to playing quarterback in those days because you had to call plays. That meant you really had to know your teammates, not only how fast they could run but what they could do in critical situations.

"That didn't mean that I thought I should sit. The first day I came to camp, I said to Earl, 'Who do you think is the best player in the league?' Earl said, 'That bald-headed guy [Tittle] over there, and if you think you're going to play….' Well, I figured I had a step up on Earl because at least I thought I should be playing."

Brodie was right in one regard: he was ahead of Morrall, who was soon traded to the Pittsburgh Steelers for linebacker Marv Matuszak. Still, Brodie sat. In the first ten regular-season games he didn't take a snap from center, and he probably wouldn't have played at all that season except that Tittle was hurting.

"He pulled a muscle against the Giants," remembered Bruce Bosley, then playing right guard for the 49ers. "Sam Huff, who had been a teammate of mine at West Virginia, was playing middle linebacker. Sam would quickly go one direction or the other, depending on where he saw the play going. So, we had one play where I pulled to the right. Sam flew out of there, leaving the middle wide open, because he figured Y. A. wouldn't run. But he did, and he ran about twenty-five yards straight up the middle because nobody was there, and he pulled a muscle doing it."

Tittle was a very courageous player who took tremendous hits because he waited until the last possible moment for a receiver to get open, and he hid his injuries, including this one. "He was going in the bathroom to tape himself up because he didn't want people to know he was hurt," Brodie said. "He was having such a great year, he just didn't want to quit because he was hurt.

"In those days, you played hurt. I remember R. C. went in the training room one day and [assistant coach] Red Hickey said to him, 'You look like one big Red Badge of Courage with all those heat pads on you. If you get one more pad, you're not going to play.' Coaches didn't even want guys getting treatment in those days because, really, there wasn't much a trainer could do."

So Tittle kept playing, in more and more pain. In the next-to-last game of the season, against the Baltimore Colts at Kezar, the 49ers were trailing 13-10 in the fourth quarter of a game they needed to win to remain tied for first place in the Western Conference. McElhenny got them in position to win the game when he took a short pass from Tittle and went 43 yards to the Baltimore 15-yard line.

GENTLE GIANT

Leo Nomellini was a reluctant 49er at first, but he came to treasure his association with the team. In 1950, Nomellini was drafted by the Chicago Rockets of the All-America Football Conference and the Los Angeles Rams of the NFL. "I was going to the Rockets because they offered me $14,000, which was a lot of money in those days for four months work. I didn't even talk to the Rams, because I knew they wouldn't offer that much."

Then the AAFC folded. Nomellini's draft rights were assigned to the 49ers, who had been brought into the NFL, and they offered Nomellini $8,500, take it or leave it. Nomellini took it. "I wasn't happy about it at the time," he said, "but it worked out."

Nomellini played fourteen seasons for the 49ers and never missed a game. For five years (1951–55), he played both offense and defense, then decided to concentrate on defense. "I liked defense better," he said, "and looking at it, it seemed that defensive linemen got more attention than offensive linemen."

He has a point. Nobody remembers much about Leo Nomellini as an offensive lineman, but everybody remembers what a force he was on defense. He was a bull—in the offseason, he was a professional wrestler—and fast for his size (6-feet, 1-inch; 260 pounds). Nomellini claims to have run the 100-yard dash in 10.6 seconds at age eighteen, and he often ran down quarterbacks and sometimes even running backs behind the line.

Surprisingly, he did not even play football in high school. While he was in the Marine Corps, Nomellini talked to a Navy pilot who thought he should try football, and he wound up playing half a dozen games for a service team. The pilot wrote to his alma mater, the University of Minnesota, and when Leo was discharged, he found a letter from Minnesota coach Bernie Bierman waiting for him at his Chicago home. "I didn't even get an athletic scholarship," he said. "I went there on the GI Bill of Rights."

Nomellini played both ways in college, though the trend already was to two-platoon football, so it wasn't a surprise when he continued doing it with the 49ers, too. One year, he was All-NFL on both offense and defense. "I asked the 49ers for a $1,000 bonus," he said. "They offered me $500. I said I'd just keep wrestling, but when they offered $750, I reported. I wanted to play football."

Nomellini was inducted into the Pro Football Hall of Fame in 1969, his first year of eligibility.

Because of his injury, Tittle was an immobile target for the Colts' pass rushers. With about a minute-and-a-half left, he tried a second-down pass into the end zone which was incomplete. As soon as he threw it, he was swarmed under by Baltimore defensive linemen. He was writhing in pain on the grass before he was carried off.

Albert summoned Brodie, who laughed out loud when he heard his name. "Albert asked me why I was laughing," Brodie said. "I said, 'I haven't

Frankie Albert guided the 49ers on the field as their regular starting quarterback from 1946 to 1951. He returned in 1956 to lead them from the sidelines, beginning a three-year stint as head coach.

played all year and now I'm supposed to come in and win the game?'"

Brodie knew nothing about Baltimore's defense, nor even what his teammates could do. In the huddle, he looked around and asked for suggestions. Billy Wilson told him to throw it his way and Brodie did, but the pass was batted away. Now it was fourth down on the Baltimore 14-yard line, and Brodie was still asking for help. McElhenny spoke up. "Throw the damn thing into the left-hand corner of the end zone," he said. "I'll be there."

He was, and Brodie's throw was on target for the winning touchdown. The 49ers had pulled out another incredible victory, 17-13.

That was the end of Brodie's heroics. He started the next week against Green Bay, but Tittle came off the bench to throw a couple of touchdown passes in a 27-20 victory. So the 49ers finished the regular season tied with Detroit for the Western Conference title, setting up a playoff game at Kezar which still causes long-time 49ers fans to scratch their heads and say, "What happened?"

The 49ers had split their two games that year with the Lions, winning the dramatic game at Kezar described earlier and losing 31-10 on the road.

Detroit would win three NFL titles in the decade. The Lions were a wild bunch, with quarterback Bobby Layne the chief hell-raiser for a team that never saw a curfew they couldn't break. "They mostly came to the stadium that day in cabs, and it sure wasn't from the hotel," Owens remembers. "The team bus was half empty, but that was the way those guys were. Most of them probably couldn't have played a game on a full night's sleep."

The 49ers played a near-perfect first half. Tittle hit Owens on a 34-yard Alley-Oop for one score. McElhenny took a short pass and went 47 yards for another. Billy Wilson caught a touchdown pass from Tittle, and Gordy Soltau kicked a 25-yard field goal to give the 49ers a 24-7 halftime lead.

The dressing room walls were very thin at Kezar, and the Lions could hear the 49ers whooping it up at halftime. "It was like, 'We've got this game, we've got them,' as opposed to, 'Hey, we've got a lot of game left,'" Owens said. "We were conscious of having that game in our back pockets."

It certainly seemed that way early in the third quarter when McElhenny took a pitchout and zipped 71 yards to Detroit's 9-yard line. The Lions forced the 49ers to settle for a field goal, but with a 27-7 lead, the 49ers were not worrying.

In an amazing turnaround, though, the Lions scored two touchdowns in the third quarter and added another to take a 28-27 lead one minute into the fourth quarter. The 49ers had the ball four more times but turned it over each time, once on a Perry fumble and three times on Tittle interceptions. The Lions added a field goal to make the final score 31-27. They were Western Division champions.

So, what did happen? Owens talks about "getting out of our game plan," and Tittle agrees.

"We played it too close to the vest," Tittle said. "Detroit wasn't that explosive, though the Lions were a good team. Today you can't sit on a lead, because it's more wide open and you can score points faster. But at twenty-seven to seven in those days, you could almost coast in, and we tried to coast in and that was wrong.

"I take responsibility for that, because I was calling the plays. Like, third down and seven, you run the draw. But you'd get six yards and have to punt, where you might have gotten a first down by throwing the ball. We had a good running attack, so we thought we could run the ball, too, but we goofed."

Tittle called the plays, but his play-calling only reflected the thinking of the coaches.

"There was a lot of talk at halftime that we shouldn't take any chances," Wilson said. "We had just moved up and down the field in the first half. I thought we should keep doing the things that we'd done so well in the first half, but we didn't."

Coaches like to say that "we win as a team and we lose as a team," and this game certainly proved the second part of that. The 49ers' offense was shut down, and the defense broke down. "They executed well against our sieve-like defense," Owens said. "If we'd had a good defense, we would have won the championship."

Sad but true. The spectacular Alley-Oop victories had obscured the truth about the 49ers: they didn't have the defense to be a championship team.

ROLL CALL

When Tony Morabito started the 49ers' franchise, one of his first moves was to hire Lawrence T. (Buck) Shaw as coach. Shaw spent nine years with the club and won seventy-two games — more than any other coach until Bill Walsh. A complete list of 49ers' head coaches and their career records (including postseason):

1946–54	Lawrence (Buck) Shaw	72-40-4
1955	Norman (Red) Strader	4-8-0
1956–58	Frankie Albert	19-17-1
1959–63	Howard (Red) Hickey*	27-27-1
1963–67	Jack Christiansen	26-38-3
1968–75	Dick Nolan	56-56-5
1976	Monte Clark	8-6-0
1977	Ken Meyer	5-9-0
1978	Pete McCulley**	1-8-0
1978	Fred O'Connor	1-6-0
1979–88	Bill Walsh	102-63-1
1989–present	George Seifert	84-24-0

*Resigned after three games in 1963
**Released after nine games in 1978

In the regular season, they gave up 264 points—
22 points a game. They were, in fact, outscored for
the season because their offense produced 260
points. Clearly, those are not the statistics of a
championship team.

There are individual games which have a pro-
found influence on the future of a team, and this
game was one of them. It marked the start of the
49ers' decline and eventual plunge into a decade of
darkness, the ghastly 1960s.

"At halftime," Bruce Bosley said, "I was thinking about the $5,000 we'd get for winning the
game. After the game—well, I didn't recover until
Dwight Clark caught that pass [against Dallas in
the 1981 NFC Championship Game]. I felt that
a big weight had been lifted off my shoulders after
all those years."

The loss to Detroit was the beginning of the
end for Tittle as a 49er because he lost the confidence of Hickey, who was then the offensive backfield coach and later the head coach. As an
assistant, Hickey was basically what would be
called an offensive coordinator today, and he made
the decisions not only on the 49ers' game plans but
also on the starters.

"Red always blamed Tittle for losing the championship game," Brodie said. "I started nine games
in 1958—and Tittle had been the player of the year
the season before. Figure that out."

Fouts also noted Hickey's lack of confidence in
Tittle. "He said to me several times, 'You've got
second-and-five and Tittle goes back to pass, and
then it's third-and-fifteen,'" Fouts said. "Red just
hated the fact that Tittle would take the sack, but, of
course, Y. A. didn't want to throw the interception."

There also was a battle for control. "Now you
wouldn't have that, because all the control is on the
sidelines, with coaches sending in plays," Brodie
said. "But at that time, the control was all on the
field. Red was not going to relinquish his power,
and without that power you couldn't be a good
quarterback. I think in the back of his mind, Red
Hickey always knew he was going to replace Tittle.
He did not think Tittle was a great quarterback."

Brodie recalled an incident in training camp in
1958 that was an indication of things to come.

"We had been sitting, listening to Red talk,

before an intrasquad scrimmage," he said. "When
he finished, Tittle and I started throwing. Red
said to Tittle, 'Are you warm?' and Tittle said,
'No. We've been sitting, listening to you, Red.' So
Hickey turned to me and asked me if I was warm.
Well, of course I said, 'Yes, sir.' So he told me to go
in and play."

The playoff loss to the Lions also made inevitable the departure of Frankie Albert, who
resigned as coach at the end of the 1958 season.
Fouts believes Albert resigned because he knew
that he would otherwise be fired. "Albert always
collected mementos," Fouts said. "One day after
practice, he started giving away all the things he
had collected to the kids who had been watching
practice. I thought it was sad because I knew that
was his farewell."

The 1958 season was a disappointing one for
Albert. The 49ers went 6-6, but more than that, it
was the off-field abuse directed by unhappy fans
toward his wife that caused Albert to quit. "There
are no more stores where my wife can go without
being abused," he said. "You can only change mar-
kets and butcher shops so often."

What kind of coach was Albert? A definitive
answer is impossible because he only coached three
years; he kept the promise made at his press conference that he would never coach again. Tittle's analy-
sis, though, that Albert didn't coach with the same
confidence that he had as a player, probably hits
closest to the mark.

Albert was consumed by anxiety over the
game. "As a player, if people booed I could always
get them back on my side by bootlegging around
Len Ford for twenty yards," he said at the time.
"As a coach, I can't do a damn thing to release that
tension." He had to take sleeping pills the night
before a game.

Temperamentally, Albert seemed unsuited to
the coaching life, but things might have been different if the 49ers had won the playoff game against
the Lions, who went on to demolish the Cleveland
Browns 59-14 in the 1957 NFL Championship
Game. Albert might have gained the confidence he
needed to be a successful coach. We'll never know.

GOOD POINTS

Almost from the beginning, the 49ers have had a reputation as a free-wheeling, high-scoring franchise. In fact, the 49ers averaged nearly 30 points per game in their four years in the All-America Football Conference (1946–49). The highest-scoring 49ers teams (points per game) since the club joined the National Football League in 1950:

Year	Points Per Game	Regular-Season Record
1994	31.6	13-3*
1953	31.0	9-3
1987	30.6	13-2
1965	30.1	7-6-1
1984	29.7	15-1*
1993	29.6	10-6
1989	27.6	14-2*
1983	27.0	10-6
1992	26.9	14-2
1954	26.1	7-4-1

*Won Super Bowl

Frankie Albert's coaching career was highlighted by a playoff appearance in 1957, but the 49ers played below expectations in 1958, and the club's former quarterback resigned after a 6-6 season.

As a coach, Frankie Albert erred by being too soft on his players. Red Hickey, who succeeded Albert, was the opposite. Hickey had an iron hand on the controls. ⁋ Hickey came to the 49ers as an assistant from the Rams in 1955. "He seemed to have the idea that we were soft," end Gordy Soltau said. "Plus, [owner] Vic Morabito was quoted as saying, 'You guys are finally going to have somebody who will be tough on you,' so it was obvious he had the backing of management." ⁋ "He was a very hard man," R. C. Owens said. "I don't think he could coach today.... He knew the game, but he had a style that made it tough for a lot of players. If they made a mistake, the coach would be on top of them in front of the other players, and there were few guys who could play under those circumstances."

The sixties were not the best of times for the 49ers. (Above) A scene too often repeated: a tired defensive line (Clark Miller, 74; Roland Lakes, 60; and Dan Colchico, 86) has its back to the wall in a game against the Rams in 1963. Miller (right) shows the wear and tear. (Pages 66–67) Jack Christiansen (far right) exhorts his troops in 1963; (page 68) Charlie Krueger; (page 69) Len Rohde; (page 70) Bernie Casey; (page 71) Gene Washington; (opposite) Clark Miller.

NOTHING PERSONAL, BUT...

When he still was an assistant, Hickey approached Leo Nomellini in training camp in 1958 and told him, "Leo, nothing personal, but we've drafted this kid [Charlie Krueger] who we hope can beat you out, because if he can play better than you the 49ers will be a better team, because we'll be stronger and younger."

Krueger did become an outstanding defensive tackle for the 49ers, playing through 1973, but he didn't replace Nomellini, who lasted through the 1963 season.

Hickey also either traded, released, or forced into retirement many of the players who had been mainstays of the 49ers without replacing them with players of similar quality, which was probably a bigger problem than his coaching style. Soltau was one of the first to go. "Red told me I could come to training camp in fifty-nine, but I wasn't guaranteed a job," Soltau said. "I knew he thought I was just another slow, old end who he didn't want around." When CBS offered Soltau a broadcasting job, he accepted.

Hickey's player-cutting worked out for other teams, if not for the 49ers. In 1961, future Pro Football Hall of Fame running back Hugh McElhenny was left available for the expansion draft, and the Minnesota Vikings gladly took him.

Owens played out his option and went to Baltimore in 1962, sending shock waves around the league. There had been a gentlemen's agreement among owners that they would not sign players from other teams, but Carroll Rosenbloom, the owner of the Colts, violated it. After Rosenbloom signed Owens, the other owners passed a rule that forced a team signing a free agent to compensate the team losing the player. That became known as the Rozelle Rule (because commissioner Pete Rozelle decided the compensation).

Hickey didn't inherit a great team. As had been true of the 49ers throughout their history, they had a weak defense. From 1962 through 1969, in fact,

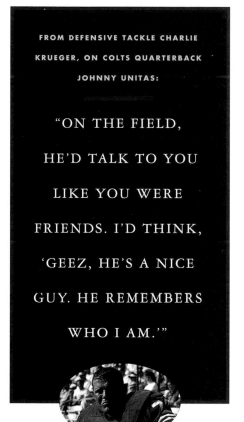

FROM DEFENSIVE TACKLE CHARLIE KRUEGER, ON COLTS QUARTERBACK JOHNNY UNITAS:

"ON THE FIELD, HE'D TALK TO YOU LIKE YOU WERE FRIENDS. I'D THINK, 'GEEZ, HE'S A NICE GUY. HE REMEMBERS WHO I AM.'"

the 49ers yielded at least 310 and as many as 402 points in a season, the latter an average of nearly 29 points per game.

The 49ers had problems even on offense. They had talented players but little idea how to utilize them. "We didn't have a system," quarterback John Brodie said. "Red would see something that worked for another team, and he'd put it into our game plans. I remember going into games where we were allowed to throw only one kind of pass." There was constant friction between Hickey and his quarterback, who was calling the plays on the field. "I can remember several games I told players, 'Don't worry about what's down here [on the game plan]. It's not going to get called,'" Brodie said.

Three games into the 1963 season, all losses, Hickey resigned.

THE SLIDE CONTINUES

Assistant coach Jack Christiansen replaced Hickey, but the 49ers' slide continued. There was one bright spot: the 49ers upset the Chicago Bears at home, the only loss the Bears suffered in 1963 on their way to the NFL championship. Otherwise, it was a dismal 2-12 season, the poorest in 49ers' history to that point.

Even worse, the 49ers, who always had been an exciting team even in defeat, suddenly were dull—they scored just 198 points all season. Christiansen couldn't be blamed for the 1963 debacle, or for a 4-10 record in 1964, but it must be said that he didn't help, either.

Christiansen was an outstanding player, a defensive back who was named to the Pro Football Hall of Fame in 1970 and an unquestioned leader in Detroit, where the defensive backfield was known as "Chris's Crew." As an assistant coach, he was close to the players, who respected his defensive knowledge. As a head coach, he didn't change. He remained a "players' coach," and that caused problems.

"Jack Christiansen was certainly a nice guy," tackle Len Rohde said, "but Jack wanted to be close to the guys. He'd sit down and have coffee and doughnuts with John Brodie, for instance. Well, if John didn't play well and Jack wanted to bench him, what was he going to do? He'd have to disassociate himself from a player, and the player would say, 'The guy was my buddy last week, and this week, he won't even talk to me.'"

OFFENSE-MINDED

The 49ers were respectable in 1965, finishing at 7-6-1. And they were exciting again. They scored 421 points, an average of 30 points per game. "We did that even though a lot of the time, we had to control the ball so we could keep our defense off the field," Brodie said. "Somebody said, 'Geez, we scored thirty points a game and we didn't even get to play us.'"

That was no joke. The 49ers' defense allowed 402 points that season. The most embarrassing loss was to the Chicago Bears 61-20, a game in which Gale Sayers scored six touchdowns. It was a game to remember, said defensive tackle Charlie Krueger. "When you look back over your shoulder at the scoreboard and it shows sixty-one points for the other team," he said, "that's as memorable as your best games."

Most of the time, though, the offense kept people's minds off the defense, and its improvement came for two reasons: Y. A. Tittle retired from the Giants as a player and joined the 49ers as an assistant coach, and the 49ers got some significant player help through trades and the draft.

"I'd played eight years," Brodie said, "and there were a lot of doubts about me. I wasn't a happy camper, and the city of San Francisco and the fans hadn't exactly endeared themselves to me. But when Tittle got here, he showed me how to play my way

TRADE DEFICIT

Y. A. Tittle for Lou Cordileone? An all-pro quarterback for a reserve defensive lineman? Considering that no money changed hands, as it did in some seemingly lopsided trades, this 1961 trade between the 49ers and the New York Giants might have been the worst in professional sports history.

Cordileone was incredulous when told of the deal. "Tittle for me?" he said. "Me and who else?"

There was a reason for it. Forty-Niners coach Red Hickey wanted to install the shotgun as his basic offense, and that system required that the quarterback be able to run. Tittle had been a tailback in college but injuries and age (he was thirty-four at the time of the trade) had taken away his running ability. When Tittle got the news, he thought about retiring. Bob Fouts, his friend and a 49ers broadcaster who did a radio show with him, had to convince him not to quit.

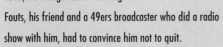

Lou Cordileone

Tittle had a thriving insurance business in Palo Alto, California, and he didn't want to leave.

"In those days, you played pro football to interact with the community," 49ers quarterback John Brodie said. "It sure wasn't for economic independence. What pro football did was get you started, helped you avoid the primary steps. People knew you, so it was easier to get going."

The trade, however, was the best thing that happened to Tittle because he went from a team that was defensively weak to one that was a defensive powerhouse. It took the pressure off him. With the 49ers, Tittle and Brodie would ask their defensive teammates before each game how many points they needed to score to win. The 49ers' defense being what it was, sometimes the answer was thirty-five.

The Giants' defense had a different approach. "I

Y. A. Tittle

don't care if you don't score a point, we're still going to win," middle linebacker Sam Huff told Tittle. "That's the way we've been doing it for ten years, and we'll still do it that way."

The first time Tittle threw an interception, Huff passed him on the way out to the field. "Don't worry about it," he said. "Just get ready—because we're going to get the ball back for you."

"From that point," Tittle said, "I just filled the air with footballs all season and never worried about it. In San Francisco, if I threw an interception, I was the reason we lost the game."

Tittle took the Giants to three consecutive NFL Championship Games (1961–63) and earned his ticket to the Pro Football Hall of Fame.

Cordileone? He played one season for the 49ers and retired.

out of it. He showed me how to drop properly, and he showed me how to simplify my play calls so I could do a lot of things from basic formations. We changed to the same kind of structure he'd had in New York, and we scored more points."

The 49ers also traded for running back John David Crow of the St. Louis Cardinals, a Heisman Trophy winner at Texas A&M. Brodie believes Tittle was instrumental in that trade. "John David was the single smartest football player I've ever known," Brodie said. "Tittle knew I needed that kind of player, a guy I could go to in tight spots. And Crow was a great leader. He taught me the value of leadership, so I could carry on when he left."

Wide receiver David Parks and linebacker Dave Wilcox were drafted in 1964, and fullback Ken Willard arrived in 1965. Wilcox was a great player for the 49ers, but one who received relatively little recognition. "Taking nothing away from Jimmy Johnson, who was a great defensive back, but I've always felt that he'd never have made the Hall of Fame if it hadn't been for Wilcox," Gordy Soltau said. "Wilcox shut down the run on that side, so Jimmy could roam free without having to worry about supporting against the run."

Bernie Casey had been a good receiver for the 49ers and led the club in receptions three consecutive years (1962–64), but Parks was a revelation. He played only four years for the team, leaving because of a contract dispute after the 1967 season, but up until that time, he was the best receiver in club history.

Parks had speed, receiving ability, and the ability to run after the catch. In his first season, he caught touchdown passes of 79, 80, and 83 yards, the latter a club record. In his second season, he caught 80 passes, 12 of them for touchdowns, in a 14-game season. He made the Pro Bowl three times.

With Parks's help, Brodie completed 62 percent of his passes and threw a club-record 30 touchdown passes in 1965. He averaged 9.14 yards per pass

Red Hickey ruled the 49ers with an iron hand beginning in 1959. He resigned three games into the 1963 season with a career record of 27-27-1.

attempt, another record. Despite Brodie's great season, though, Christiansen played musical chairs with his quarterbacks in 1966 and 1967.

QUARTERBACK CONTROVERSIES

The 49ers drafted George Mira in the second round in 1964. Mira was an intriguing player, with a slingshot of an arm. Though he was less than six feet tall, he could pass the ball 50 yards with ease, and he was an exciting quarterback who would scramble for good yardage when he couldn't find an open receiver.

Unfortunately, Mira never saw a defense he could read. He improvised everything, and there was no consistency—a brilliant play would be followed by a series of baffling ones. Christiansen wasted valuable time giving Mira his chance to fail.

It wasn't just Christiansen, however. General manager Jack White also lacked confidence in Brodie. "White always seemed to think that I was the reason we lost," Brodie said. After the 1966 season, White traded Casey and two other players to Atlanta for a draft choice, which he used to select quarterback Steve Spurrier, the Heisman Trophy winner from the University of Florida.

Spurrier, who has since become a successful college coach (he's now back at Florida), was a likable young man, so eager to succeed that it was hard not to root for him. He was bright, competitive, and an accurate passer, but he lacked a strong arm.

"Spurrier had one of the great minds in football," said wide receiver Gene Washington, who came to the 49ers as a first-round draft pick in 1969. "In instinct, savvy, and knowledge of the game, he was as good as anybody. But he didn't have the arm. If Steve had just a good arm, he'd have been a Hall of Fame quarterback." Spurrier shouldn't have been a number-one pick, but White selected him on the basis of his college success, not his pro potential.

White had been a scout for both the 49ers and New York Yankees. "His best recommendation was

In seventeen seasons with the 49ers (1957–73), John Brodie passed for 31,548 yards and 214 touchdowns. Many pro football observers believe he belongs in the Hall of Fame.

JOHN
BRODIE
S. F. 49'ERS
QUARTERBACK

Jack Christiansen was a successful player and assistant coach, but he couldn't stop the 49ers' slide in the mid-1960s. In four-plus seasons as head coach, Christiansen won only 26 of 67 games.

one we didn't take," Spadia said. "He begged us in 1957 to take Jim Brown."

By 1965, Spadia was president of the 49ers (Vic Morabito had died the previous year), but he was not a football man and didn't feel comfortable making football decisions. He asked White what it would take for him to work full time for the 49ers, not knowing that White wanted to get away from the Yankees. White said, "All you have to do is ask me."

White lasted as general manager, with mixed results, through the 1972 season. He and Spadia had a genuine affection for each other, but Spadia had some misgivings about him. "He was very opinionated, and once he made up his mind, there was no way you could change it," Spadia said. "He made some real mistakes on draft picks, but he could never admit a mistake."

One of the best examples was Cas Banaszek, the team's second first-round draft choice in 1967. Banaszek played tight end and linebacker at Northwestern, but he was ill-suited for both those positions and the 49ers. "I had no speed," he said, "but the 49ers didn't realize that because they hadn't timed me. They didn't even time me after the draft. They wanted me to play linebacker, to replace Matt Hazeltine, but that didn't work out, so they tried me at tight end. I was a good athlete who could catch the ball, and I could play in college because they didn't put anybody opposite me to stop me from going out. When I got to camp and Dave Wilcox lined up in front of me, that was a different matter.

Banaszek played in one preseason game as a tight end. When Brodie asked him in the huddle what he could do, Banaszek said, "I can't get out, and I can't get open. I'm playing the wrong position." Banaszek remembers, "They had to invent a medical term for me. They sent me up to Dr. Lloyd Milburn's office in the city and took X-rays. I'm sitting in the waiting room feeling fine when the technician comes out looking like somebody's died and tells me I've got 'loose ankles.'"

Eventually, Banaszek was shifted to offensive tackle and had a fine career, but not at all the one

the 49ers had envisioned when they drafted him.

The biggest problem for the 49ers, though, was the constant shuffling of quarterbacks, which caused seemingly endless debates in the press, among fans, and among the coaching staff. It became such a focal point that the first thing Dick Nolan did after he was hired to replace Christiansen in 1968 was to call Brodie into his office.

"He'd heard that I was a dissident, disrespectful, drank too much, did everything too much," Brodie said. "What he didn't understand was that I was committed to what I was doing. When he met me, what he saw wasn't what he had heard. When he asked if I wanted to be traded, I told him no, that I wanted to stay in San Francisco. He said he'd set up a competition in training camp for the quarterback job, and I said that was fine with me."

Brodie won the competition, of course, and it was his job without question for the next four seasons.

BUILDING A CHAMPION

Dick Nolan never would be confused with Knute Rockne. "He wasn't the kind of coach who was going to inspire you with locker-room speeches," tackle Len Rohde said. "The last two minutes before the game, Dick would say, 'Well, uh...' and look at his watch. 'We'd better get out there.'"

Still, noted middle linebacker Frank Nunley, "Nolan brought an enthusiasm with him that hadn't been there before. He also brought in some very good assistant coaches — such as Ed Hughes, who was his brother-in-law, Jim Shofner, and Paul Wiggin."

That enthusiasm was needed because the 49ers' franchise was moribund. "I played my college ball at Michigan," Nunley said, "where we had a stadium that seated 102,000. I think the smallest home crowd I played before there was more than 80,000. Then, the first game I played here, a preseason game in 1967, there were only 27,000 people. I looked up in the stands and my wife was sitting all alone in one section."

The change in coaches didn't seem to make any

FROM VIKINGS DEFENSIVE END JIM MARSHALL, WHO RETURNED A 1964 FUMBLE 66 YARDS THE WRONG WAY TO GIVE SAN FRANCISCO A SAFETY, ON HIS REACTION WHEN 49ERS GUARD BRUCE BOSLEY CAME OVER TO SHAKE HIS HAND:

"THAT WAS THE FIRST INKLING I HAD THAT SOMETHING HAD GONE WRONG."

difference at first. The 49ers were 7-6-1 in Nolan's first year and slipped to 4-8-2 in his second. The record in 1969 could have been better with a little luck: the 49ers lost four games by a touchdown or less that season. Brodie thought the loss of Tittle, who decided to devote all his time to his insurance business, was a big factor.

Tittle couldn't work full time as a coach because of his business, so he'd come in one day, look at films, and then put the game plan together in five or six hours. That annoyed other coaches, who told him they were working fourteen hours a day. "Yeah, I know," Tittle said. "What do you guys do all that time?"

"Obviously, that didn't please anybody," Brodie said, "so he was let go."

In 1970, Ed Hughes became the offensive coordinator and Hughes and Jim Shofner, who followed him, were able to get the 49ers back on track.

Defensively, too, the 49ers were using a different system, the Flex Defense that Nolan brought from Dallas. The Flex was designed to utilize linebackers and defensive linemen who were quick and agile but not very big. Their uncertainty while they were learning this defense masked the progress the 49ers were making, but ultimately the new defense—with better players—would make them a championship team. "It was a very disciplined defense," said Nunley, who became the starting middle linebacker when Ed Beard was injured in 1969. "Everybody had a specific assignment. It was totally different than the defenses today, where everybody is rushing the passer. At that time, the emphasis was on stopping the run.

"It really took three years for us to learn the Flex, because it was so complex. It was especially complex for me as the middle linebacker because I had to call all the defensive signals. One side of the Flex had a normal gap between linemen so teams usually wouldn't run at that. They'd run at the other side. So, if I thought I saw a run coming in that direction, I'd change the call so, though it looked like we were in the Flex, we wouldn't be on that side.

"I didn't always make the right calls. Sometimes, I'd call a defense that would wind up with a linebacker covering somebody like [speedy Dallas wide receiver] Bob Hayes. So we had some big

THE FAITHFUL

San Francisco fans now are proud to call themselves "The Faithful," but that slogan was started out of desperation by promotions director Dick Berg in 1969.

"We did everything we could to take the fans' minds off what they were actually seeing on the field," said Berg, mindful of the fact that the 49ers had a decade of mostly bad teams and were on their way to a 4-8-2 season in '69. "When I took players around to the booster clubs, they usually were from the earlier times—R. C. Owens, Gordy Soltau, Leo Nomellini.

"We started 'The Faithful' idea to tie in with the 'good old days' of the franchise.

"Then, we got lucky. The next year's team [1970] turned out to be a very good one, so for a change we could promote both the present and the past. Suddenly, the idea of being part of 'The Faithful,' fans who had been with the team since the beginning, was a very popular one. It was amazing how many times I heard from people who swore they'd been with the 49ers since the very first game."

plays against us, but generally it worked very well."

Meanwhile, the 49ers were having the best stretch of good drafts in their history. In 1967, they picked Nunley, Banaszek (an error that became a positive), and running back Doug Cunningham. In 1968, center Forrest Blue was the top pick, and the 49ers drafted linebacker Skip Vanderbundt and defensive lineman Tommy Hart with later picks.

In 1969, the 49ers got tight end Ted Kwalick and wide receiver Gene Washington with two picks in the first round, and linebacker Jim Sniadecki and defensive lineman Earl Edwards in later rounds. In 1970, they again had two first-round picks and again made two excellent choices, defensive lineman Cedrick Hardman and defensive back Bruce Taylor. Running backs John Isenbarger, Vic Washington, and Larry Schreiber, as well as wide receiver Preston Riley, were picked later.

Seven of those picks became defensive starters in addition to defensive back Mel Phillips, who had been selected in the 1966 draft. Plus, the 49ers already had three great defensive players—Jimmy Johnson at cornerback, Dave Wilcox at outside linebacker, and Charlie Krueger at defensive tackle. In 1969, they traded for free safety Roosevelt Taylor. For the first time in their history the 49ers were building a strong defense.

The offense was making strides, too. Brodie could have played the 1970 season in a rocking chair. His offensive line allowed only 8 sacks, an NFL record. "And two or three of those sacks came on blitzes that weren't picked up by backs," Len Rohde said. "The offensive line actually allowed only about five sacks. There are games when a quarterback gets sacked more than five times."

"We didn't have much of a running game," Gene Washington said. "We had Doug Cunningham, Larry Schreiber, Ken Willard. They were very average runners. So our offensive linemen just bunched up to keep everybody out, and we threw the ball. [Brodie attempted 378 passes in the 14-game season.] We knew that if we couldn't beat a team throwing the ball, we weren't going to beat them."

The running game, in fact, was almost unbelievably basic. "We had four plays," Banaszek said. "The sweep, blunt, and blunt counter, which were off-tackle runs, and a draw, where Brodie

would fake a pass and hand off to Willard."

Banaszek remembers that offensive line coach Ernie Zwahlen reminded them each week of their chance to set a record for least sacks allowed. "That was a great goal for us," he said. "We had a great closeness. We would all go out to dinner the night before a game, and Brodie would pay the bill."

Offensive linemen usually are the most anonymous members of the football team, and that line was no exception. Forrest Blue, an All-America in college and an all-pro in the NFL, was the only one who got much individual attention, much more

Dick Nolan guided the 49ers to their most successful stretch in their first three decades, building a team that won three consecutive division championships from 1970 to 1972.

than guards Woody Peoples and Randy Beisler or tackles Rohde and Banaszek. Brodie singles out Rohde as one of the best of his teammates, adding, "He was a super pass blocker, but he was so good, nobody ever paid any attention to him. He just did his job, game after game, season after season."

Rohde, like Banaszek, didn't start out at the position where he made his mark. Rohde had been tried at defensive end but was switched to offense when he was trapped repeatedly in a 1962 game against the Chicago Bears.

Rohde was in a funk for several weeks,

wondering where he could go when the 49ers released him, as he was certain they would. Then, before the seventh game of the season, against the Los Angeles Rams, tackle Bob St. Clair was injured. Though Rohde was the backup at both tackles, Hickey moved Leon Donohue, a reserve guard, into the starting lineup to replace St. Clair. Then, in the game, Donohue was injured. "I can remember [offensive line coach] Bill Johnson walking by me, looking up and down the bench for somebody to send in," Rohde said. "Well, there wasn't anyone else, so finally, he told me to get in there. I was up against Deacon Jones, and I played pretty well. They kept me in the lineup, and I kept doing all right, so I played the rest of the year. The next year, St. Clair

After twenty-five seasons in Kezar Stadium, the 49ers moved to newly enclosed Candlestick Park in 1971. A grass field replaced the artificial turf in 1979.

came back, so they shifted me to right tackle, and I played there for the rest of my career."

THE FIRST TITLE

Offensively and defensively, the 49ers were coming together as the 1970 season began— "I think we were the best team in football that year," Brodie said—and after nine games, they were 7-1-1.

"To me, the key was beating the Rams early in the season," Banaszek said. "During my career, we almost never beat the Rams [only four times in eleven years]. So when we beat them [20-6 in week 4], I think we realized for the first time that we could win. That's a great feeling."

But that season, the 49ers could beat the Rams only once. The Rams came north in the second game to win 30-13, one of only three losses suffered by the 49ers in the regular season.

That was the first year after the AFL-NFL merger, and the American and National Football Conferences were formed under the banner of the NFL. The 49ers were placed in the NFC West with Atlanta, New Orleans, and the Rams.

There was one constant: the Rams still were the team the 49ers had to beat. Going into the final game of the 1970 season, the 49ers had a one-game edge, but by the time they took the field in Oakland, that edge was down to half a game because the Rams had beaten the Giants in New York to finish their season at 9-4-1. A tie in the standings would give the division title to the Rams, who had the tie-breaker advantage because they'd scored more points in the two games with the 49ers, so the 49ers had to beat or tie the Raiders.

"That was the most memorable game of my career," Gene Washington said. "The Raiders were a very, very good team in those days, and to go over to Oakland and beat them was very tough."

The teams had vastly different images: the 49ers

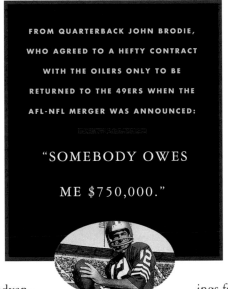

FROM QUARTERBACK JOHN BRODIE, WHO AGREED TO A HEFTY CONTRACT WITH THE OILERS ONLY TO BE RETURNED TO THE 49ERS WHEN THE AFL-NFL MERGER WAS ANNOUNCED:

"SOMEBODY OWES ME $750,000."

conservative, the Raiders, led by owner Al Davis, renegade. The Raiders were wildly individualistic, and they were determinedly public with their partying; whatever hell the 49ers raised generally was done privately. The Raiders were coached by John Madden, whose sideline antics were captured by the television cameras; the 49ers were coached by the very quiet Nolan. The Raiders went for the bomb on offense and gambled on defense; the 49ers played with discipline, both offensively and defensively.

Most expected the game to be emotional because it was the first time the teams ever played each other in the regular season. As it happened, though, the emotion was almost entirely on one side of the field. This was a game the 49ers had to win, but one that meant nothing in the standings for the Raiders, who had already clinched their division title.

"[Raiders linebacker] Bill Laskey and I were teammates at Michigan, and we talked before the game," Nunley said. "He told me they were going to whip our butts. But when one team has to win and the other doesn't, that's a tremendous advantage in football."

"We got the word that the Rams had won just

MERGER PAYS DIVIDENDS

In 1970, the AFL's merger with the NFL officially took effect, and the newly formed NFL was split into American and National Football Conferences. The 49ers were placed in the NFC West along with Atlanta, New Orleans, and the Los Angeles Rams, and won division titles each of the first three seasons under the new alignment. After a nine-year drought, the 49ers won the division again in 1981, and 10 more times between 1983 and 1994. Their 14 division titles since the merger is the most in the NFL. The number of division championships and playoff appearances for each NFL team in that span:

Team	Division Titles	Playoff Appearances	Team	Division Titles	Playoff Appearances	Team	Division Titles	Playoff Appearances
San Francisco	14	15	Buffalo	6	9	New England	2	6
Dallas	12	18	Washington	5	13	Arizona	2	3
Minnesota	12	16	Cincinnati	5	7	Tampa Bay*	2	3
Miami	11	15	Indianapolis	5	6	Atlanta	1	4
Pittsburgh	11	15	San Diego	5	6	Green Bay	1	4
L.A. Raiders	9	15	N.Y. Giants	3	7	New Orleans	1	4
L.A. Rams	8	14	Detroit	3	6	Seattle*	1	4
Denver	7	10	Houston	2	10	N.Y. Jets	0	5
Chicago	6	10	Philadelphia	2	8			
Cleveland	6	10	Kansas City	2	7	*Teams began play in 1976.		

BRODIE'S FAVORITE TARGET

Gene Washington was a great wide receiver, but fans can only guess what he would have done if he'd played his entire career with John Brodie at quarterback.

Washington, who had played at nearby Stanford, was an immediate star as a rookie in 1969, catching 51 passes and making the first of four consecutive Pro Bowl appearances. Not coincidentally, the 49ers soon had their first taste of real success—in Washington's second year, they began a stretch of three straight division championships.

Even then, though, they were frustrated by their hated rivals, the Los Angeles Rams. Of twenty-six games played between the two teams from 1968 to 1980, the 49ers won only three.

"Psychology is so important in football," Washington said. "The Rams always knew they could beat us. It didn't matter what we did. One game, I remember we knocked out the starting quarterback and Jerry Rhome came in. He couldn't throw the ball fifteen yards, but they still beat us."

Washington had grown up in southern California and played high school ball in Long Beach. To get Washington, an outstanding prep athlete, Stanford coach John Ralston promised him he'd play quarterback, and that's where he played as a sophomore. He was not a good college quarterback, though, and volunteered to switch to wide receiver as a junior.

"When I was growing up, I watched and rooted for teams like the Rams and USC," Washington said. "Then, when I came to Stanford, USC always beat us, and when I came to the 49ers, it seemed like the Rams were an extension of USC. It was really frustrating to play on a good team and go down there before friends and relatives and get beat."

In his first five seasons, with Brodie at quarterback, Washington was the premier deep threat in the NFC. He averaged 47 catches a season and 18 yards a catch.

When Brodie retired following the 1973 season, Washington's career figures were quite respectable. He set a club record—since surpassed—with 6,664 receiving yards and ranked second at the time only to Billy Wilson with 371 catches, but it's safe to say that his numbers suffered because the quarterbacks who followed Brodie can only charitably be called mediocre.

before we took the field," Washington said. "I've never seen a team so fired up. You could have heard the pregame prayer in the next county, we were so loud. I've never seen anything like that, the enthusiasm for going to battle."

Whether it was a lack of emotion or the rain—or both—the Raiders could not hang onto the ball all day, turning it over 9 times on 4 fumbles and 5 interceptions. The grateful 49ers, who had neither a fumble nor an interception, took a 24-7 halftime lead and coasted to a 38-7 victory to clinch their first division title. That 49ers team clearly was the best in franchise history to that point. Brodie won NFC player-of-the-year honors, and Bruce Taylor was named NFC rookie of the year.

ANOTHER FIRST: A PLAYOFF VICTORY

Though the victory over the Raiders was important because it clinched the division title, the most satisfying game may have been the next one, against the Vikings in Minnesota. The Vikings were favored, but Washington was confident. "The Vikings were a good defensive team," he said, "but they didn't compare at all to the Raiders, particularly the linebackers and defensive backs. "When we played against the Raiders, I'd line up [at wide receiver] on one side against Willie Brown, who would just pound you, and then I'd go to the other side against Nemiah Wilson, who was small but a great cover man. You just never got a break.

"The Vikings didn't have athletes like that. Playing against their secondary was a break. Their defensive line put a lot of pressure on the quarterback, but we knew that if Brodie had any time to throw, there was no way the Vikings could stop us."

The only problem for the 49ers was the weather. The temperature at game time was 10 degrees with a wind that made it the equivalent of several degrees below zero. "I'll never forget," Washington said, "the day of the game, we got off the bus and they'd piled up snow alongside the door of the locker room. It must have been fifteen feet high. Then the wind hit us, and we thought, 'We're going to play in this?'

"But when we got ready to go out, Brodie went out in his short sleeves, as if he were still in California, and I remember a couple of other guys did, too."

A psych job? Not really, laughed Brodie. "The

truth is, [trainer] Chico Norton forgot to pack our long-sleeved uniforms and we froze our asses off."

The 49ers had heaters by their bench, but Vikings coach Bud Grant refused to allow them for his players. "In old Metropolitan Stadium the benches were on the same side of the field," Rohde remembers. "By the end of the game, when Bud was down at one end of the field, a lot of the Vikings eased over to where our heaters were to get warm."

On the field, the 49ers were keeping the heat on, just as Brodie had expected. "We could score seventeen to twenty points against anybody," he said. "We knew they couldn't score very much, so if we scored seventeen to twenty, we could win. You play the game so much more patiently when you don't have to score thirty points."

The Vikings scored quickly when Paul Krause picked up Ken Willard's fumble on the 49ers' second play and returned it 22 yards for a touchdown, but the rest of the way, it was all 49ers.

Minnesota had been favored because many people thought the 49ers' passing game would suffer in the cold, but the frozen field also slowed the Vikings' "Purple People Eaters" pass rush of Alan Page, Carl Eller, Gary Larsen, and Jim Marshall. Brodie completed 16 of 32 passes for 201 yards and a touchdown and scored on a quarterback sneak. Bruce Gossett added the field goal that made the difference in the 17-14 victory.

"There was one play, a post-corner, where I broke first to the center of the field and then to the corner, and there was no way the cornerback could cover me," Washington said. "Brodie just waited for the right spot when he saw they were double-covering [tight end] Ted Kwalick and I was in single coverage, and then I beat them like a drum. They never did stop that play."

KEZAR'S FINALE

In the San Francisco Bay Area, there was talk of a possible "Bay Area Super Bowl," with the Raiders playing in the AFC title game in Baltimore and the 49ers hosting the Dallas Cowboys in the NFC Championship Game at Kezar Stadium.

This would be the last game at Kezar. The 49ers would move to Candlestick Park, remodeled

Steve Spurrier never fulfilled the promise of his Heisman Trophy–winning college career, but he proved to be a valuable asset in 1972 when he quarterbacked the 49ers for much of the season in place of injured John Brodie.

with additional seats for football, the next season. Candlestick certainly would be more comfortable for the fans, and the parking would be much better. The players, though, were a little sad about leaving Kezar.

"It wasn't exactly your perfect stadium," Rohde said. "You had to be one of the first players to take a shower after a game if you wanted any hot water, and the field could be like a swamp if it rained late in the year. But it had a grass field, which is a player's best friend, and it was home."

The 49ers were slight favorites over the Cowboys,

and Brodie felt they deserved to be. "We didn't think we had to score a lot of points. We figured if we could get twenty-one or maybe twenty-four points, we could win. We could have done that except for fluke things. There were about ten balls that were tipped. Willard lost one pass in the sun. Guys who made great catches in other games didn't make them in this one."

The game was decided by a touchdown, and in a game that close, there are always the "what-ifs" that Brodie remembers. Washington looked at it somewhat differently. "John remembers the details," he said, "but I think those plays were a symptom of a larger problem: Dallas was just better prepared for the game than we were. Maybe it was the coaching, or maybe it was just that they'd been in the playoffs before, and we hadn't. They were more comfortable.

"The Cowboys also were just too well-rounded for us. We could pass the ball, but they could do everything. We just couldn't stop their running attack. I can still see Duane Thomas [who gained 143 yards] running up and down the field. The 49ers hadn't had a back like that since Hugh McElhenny.

"The Cowboys were a great team and a great organization in those days. They had the 'Doomsday Defense' that was one of the best ever. They didn't make mistakes; you had to beat them. Mel Renfro was the best cornerback I ever played against. So you'd have to really slug it out to move downfield, and then they'd come back and run the ball down your throat."

Washington, in fact, got loose on a 42-yard pass play in the first quarter, taking the ball to Dallas's 10-yard line. But the 49ers couldn't score a touchdown, settling for a field goal and a 3-0 lead.

Defensively, there was an unforeseen problem. "Early in the first quarter," Nunley remembers, "their fullback, Walt Garrison, came up the middle and we had a terrific collision. We were both knocked out of the game for awhile. I came back, but I had a concussion, and I wasn't able to make the calls the way I should have. I just couldn't concentrate."

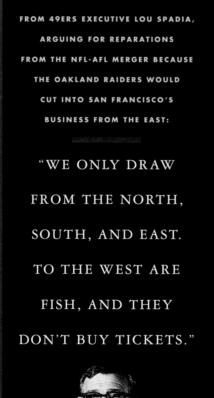

FROM 49ERS EXECUTIVE LOU SPADIA, ARGUING FOR REPARATIONS FROM THE NFL-AFL MERGER BECAUSE THE OAKLAND RAIDERS WOULD CUT INTO SAN FRANCISCO'S BUSINESS FROM THE EAST:

"WE ONLY DRAW FROM THE NORTH, SOUTH, AND EAST. TO THE WEST ARE FISH, AND THEY DON'T BUY TICKETS."

After the 49ers' field goal, the Cowboys scored 17 unanswered points, their two touchdowns following interceptions. The 49ers scored a late third-quarter touchdown on a Brodie pass to wide receiver Dick Witcher but lost 17-10.

DOWN TO THE WIRE AGAIN

The 49ers won their division again in 1971, even though they lost twice to the Rams. The losses to the Rams, along with others to Atlanta, New Orleans, and Kansas City, meant the 49ers had to win their final game of the season once again. And they did, beating Detroit 31-27, with the winning touchdown coming on a very unusual play—a 10-yard Brodie run on a quarterback draw.

In the first round of the playoffs, the 49ers beat former teammate Billy Kilmer and the Washington Redskins 24-20 on a rainy day at Candlestick Park. That brought on a championship game rematch with Dallas, this time at Texas Stadium.

It was almost a replay of the previous year's showdown, with Dallas's defense controlling the game and the 49ers' defense unable to stop the Cowboys' running attack. This time, Dallas held the 49ers to 1 first down in the first half en route to a 14-3 victory.

Time was running out on the 49ers. "We were still a very good football team," Washington said, "but in 1972, I knew that this would probably be our last shot at getting to the Super Bowl. Some of our key players were getting old, and we had no replacements. Brodie's career was winding down, and I knew Steve Spurrier couldn't replace him. Charlie Krueger was near the end. We didn't have a replacement when Dave Wilcox left, or Mel Phillips.

"We had some great players, but we didn't have the organization to sustain success. The Cowboys did, the Raiders did, the Steelers did later. The best example of a strong organization now is the 49ers, but that wasn't true then. We had to cut our number-one draft picks a couple of years in a row. You can't win that way."

Those number-one picks were defensive back Tim Anderson (1971) and wide receiver Terry Beasley (1972). Anderson was far too slow to play in the NFL, and the 49ers willingly let him go to Canada. Beasley was too small for the NFL of that day, when defensive backs and linebackers could knock down receivers without penalties. Cornerback Mike Holmes was the top pick in 1973. He lasted longer than Anderson and Beasley, but he wasn't very good, either.

Brodie, no fan of 49ers' management at that time, is convinced that the club's front office mixed up the scouting reports of Anderson and Jack Tatum, who were teammates at Ohio State. Lou Spadia, then the 49ers' president, concedes that possibility but thinks it is more likely that it was just a mistake by White, the club's general manager — and possibly Woody Hayes, who had coached Anderson and Tatum in college. "Jack [White] was close to Woody Hayes, and I think Woody thought more of Anderson than he did of Tatum," Spadia said.

It wasn't just that the 49ers made bad picks in the first round, either. From 1971 to 1973, they drafted only one player who became a standout, outside linebacker Willie Harper, a second-round selection in 1973. The 1972 draft brought them two fairly good defensive backs, Ralph McGill and Windlan Hall, and a punter, Tom Wittum. Nobody else from those drafts was a significant player for the team, though they had fifty-six picks in that period.

From the mid-sixties through 1970, the 49ers had excellent drafts and built the team that won three consecutive division titles. Then, from one of the very best drafting teams, they went to being one of the very worst. What happened?

In part, it was their draft position. The 49ers' success from 1970 to 1972 pushed them down to eighteenth and nineteenth in the league drafting order. In larger part, it was because the 49ers didn't take advantage of the computer system they had pioneered with the Dallas Cowboys and Los Angeles Rams. "Jack White didn't believe in the computer," Spadia said. "He was a very conservative guy and wasn't one to change."

The 49ers also suffered along with many other NFL/NFC teams because they virtually ignored

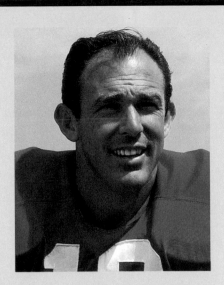

THE $750,000 QUARTERBACK

With the help of Al Davis, 49ers quarterback John Brodie changed the economic course of pro football in 1966.

Davis, the newly appointed AFL commissioner, encouraged AFL owners to raid NFL teams for quarterbacks. Brodie was high on the list, and at the Warwick Hotel in Houston, he met with Oilers owner Bud Adams and general manager Don Klosterman and got an astounding offer for the time—three years at $250,000 per year.

Adams wrote the offer on a napkin and signed it, as did Klosterman and Brodie. Brodie called 49ers executive Lou Spadia with the news. Spadia almost fainted; his offer to Brodie was $55,000 per year, plus incentives.

Brodie's adviser, Sonny Marx, told him to take the napkin. Marx feared that the war between the leagues might end before Brodie got his money, and he wanted a record of the offer. Marx's intuition was dead center. The next day, when Brodie and Marx met again with Adams and Klosterman, the conversation was much different. Adams, trying to change his proposal, offered to set up Brodie with a car dealership and some cattle. "I let Adams know that I didn't want any cattle or cars," Brodie said. "I was a football player."

Behind the scenes, NFL Commissioner Pete Rozelle was meeting with Lamar Hunt, owner of the Kansas City Chiefs of the AFL, and Tex Schramm, general manager of the Dallas Cowboys, to work out a merger agreement.

Meanwhile, Brodie lost the napkin. From that point, he and Marx were running a bluff. Fortunately for them, nobody ever asked to see their hole card.

The two leagues reached an agreement on June 8, 1966. It took another six weeks for the contract to be approved because the understanding had been that all the AFL clubs would share in paying it, not just the Oilers. In the end, however, Brodie remained with the 49ers at the terms he'd arranged in Houston. The 49ers received the difference between their offer and the Oilers' offer from the other AFL clubs and paid it to Brodie.

another important source of talent: the black colleges. "The AFL teams such as Kansas City and the Raiders went out to the black colleges," Washington said. "They got guys like Buck Buchanan and Willie Brown. The good AFL teams had so much speed. When they brought the leagues together and we started to play with them, we couldn't keep up with them."

THIRD TIME A CHARM?

In 1972, though, the full effects of what was going wrong with their drafts had not yet hit the 49ers. Even though Brodie missed eight weeks during the season with a badly sprained ankle, the 49ers won their third consecutive division title. Spurrier played surprisingly well as Brodie's replacement, completing almost 55 percent of his passes and throwing for 18 touchdowns, including 5 in a 34-21 victory over the Chicago Bears.

Spurrier's effectiveness, however, ended in the final game of the season. Against the Minnesota Vikings at Candlestick Park, a game the 49ers needed to win for the division title, he completed only 7 of 14 passes for 64 yards as the Vikings took a 17-6 lead into the fourth quarter.

Nolan brought in Brodie to start the fourth quarter, and the veteran quarterback sparked a memorable comeback, though his first two possessions ended in interceptions. With eight minutes remaining and the 49ers on their own 1-yard line, Brodie marched his team 99 yards for a touchdown. The key play was a 53-yard pass to Washington, and the touchdown also came on a pass to Washington—a 24-yard strike.

With only 1:39 left, the 49ers still trailed 17-13, but had the ball on their 35-yard line. Quickly, they moved downfield to Minnesota's 20-yard line, and Vic Washington's 18-yard run got them down to the 2-yard line. With 25 seconds to go, Brodie rolled to his right, motioned to Witcher in the end zone and, when the receiver broke free, threw to him for the winning touchdown. In just one quarter of play, Brodie completed 10 of 15 passes for 165 yards, and the 49ers won 20-17.

In the first round of the playoffs, the 49ers again faced the Dallas Cowboys. Their mood was

HOLD THAT THOUGHT

Before the 49ers' divisional playoff game with Dallas in San Francisco in 1972, promotions director Dick Berg prepared "Super Fever" buttons to hand out to the fans if the 49ers won.

With five minutes to go and the 49ers leading 28-13, Berg wanted to start handing out the buttons. Club president Lou Spadia, remembering the 49ers' collapse against Detroit in a 1957 playoff game, told him to wait. With two minutes to go, the 49ers still had a 28-16 lead. Again, Berg wanted to hand out the buttons. Again, Spadia told him to wait.

Spadia was right to be cautious. Two Roger Staubach touchdown passes later, the Cowboys won 30-28, and the "Super Fever" buttons still are locked in a 49ers' safe.

I'VE GOT SUPER FEVER

optimistic, despite losses in each of the previous two seasons. "The Cowboys weren't a really good team that year," Washington remembers. "They were trying to work some young players in, and they weren't settled."

They also had a different quarterback than they did in 1971. Roger Staubach, who led the team to victories in its last ten games and was the most valuable player in the Cowboys' win in Super Bowl VI, separated his shoulder in training camp and had hardly played in 1972; Craig Morton replaced him. Morton was an excellent passer, but Staubach was one of the best quarterbacks in NFL history. He was a gifted passer, a good runner who could scramble out of trouble, and an exceptional leader who could rally his team to win when defeat seemed inevitable—a quality that would be important for the Cowboys, especially in this game.

Staubach was on the bench as the 49ers—playing at home—dominated for more than three quarters. Vic Washington returned the game's opening kickoff 97 yards for a touchdown, and Larry Schreiber scored 3 touchdowns as the 49ers took a 28-13 lead into the fourth quarter.

Dallas coach Tom Landry brought in Staubach in the final minute of the third quarter, but the Cowboys could not score again until six minutes had elapsed in the fourth quarter, and then it was just a Toni Fritsch field goal that cut the 49ers' lead to 28-16. There was no hint of the horror to come.

A short punt by the 49ers went out of bounds at Dallas's 45-yard line, and the Cowboys had the ball with 2:02 left. Staubach completed three consecutive passes to get to San Francisco's 20-yard line. Though Landry normally called plays from the sideline, there was no time for that in the two-minute offense, so Staubach was calling everything. In the huddle, Billy Parks said he could get open on a post pattern. He did, and Staubach hit him for the touchdown.

That cut Dallas's deficit to 28-23, but the Cowboys' chances still seemed slim. Their only hope was to recover an onside kick. Otherwise, the 49ers would be able to run out the clock. Nolan put his most sure-handed players into the front row of the receiving team, but the ball

took a crazy bounce. Wide receiver Preston Riley fumbled it, and Mel Renfro recovered for the Cowboys at midfield.

On the next play, Staubach dropped back to pass but saw an opening and ran for 21 yards. He followed that with a pass to Parks for 19 yards. From the 49ers' 10-yard line, Staubach then called for a sideline pattern to Parks, but when the 49ers blitzed, he unloaded quickly to Ron Sellers, open in the middle of the end zone, for a touchdown.

All 49ers' fans remember the Staubach touchdown passes and the onside kick. Few remember that the 49ers still had a chance to win the game. There were 52

John Brodie (12, above) was not known as a scrambler. He preferred to throw to wide receivers such as Gene Washington (below), a four-time Pro Bowl selection.

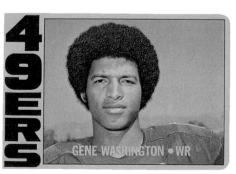

GENE WASHINGTON • WR

seconds left, and they needed only to move into position for Bruce Gossett to kick a field goal. Brodie completed three consecutive passes, the last to Riley at Dallas's 22, which would probably have been enough—but on that final pass, Banaszek was called for holding and the ball came back. That was the 49ers' last shot.

As with the 1957 playoff loss to Detroit, this game was much more than just one defeat. A pall settled over the entire organization, and many individuals were affected. Riley's career was ruined because he was always identified as the culprit who had not been able to hold on to the onside kick. "That was very unfair," Brodie said. "He was a fine young receiver who was on his way to being a very good player, and he had played well in that game."

The loss precipitated a downhill slide for the 49ers, and that caused Brodie to retire after the 1973 season. "I probably could have played at least two more years," he said, "and I would have if I'd thought we had a chance to win again. But I could see the [downward] direction the franchise was heading, and I didn't want to be a part of that."

Most of all, the loss affected Nolan. "I remember some times later when we'd come back from a loss on the road and would be in meetings the next day," Rohde said, "and he just looked terrible — like he hadn't slept in forty-eight hours. I knew he'd been replaying the [most recent] game, over and over."

"After that Dallas loss, he took the defensive play-calling responsibility away from me," Nunley said. "I thought it was wrong, but I never blamed him for it. He was under tremendous pressure."

At the same time, Nolan was losing assistants he couldn't afford to lose. He had always been on the defensive side of the ball, first as a player (he played defensive back for nine NFL seasons), then as a coach, so he needed help offensively. He got it from Ed Hughes in 1970 and, when Hughes left after that season, from Jim Shofner for the next three years. When Shofner left, Dick Stanfel became the offensive coordinator. Stanfel had been a very good offensive line coach, but he lacked the imagination to be a coordinator.

The 49ers dropped as quickly as they had risen, and after three consecutive seasons below

Monte Clark's 49ers were the surprise of the NFL the first half of the 1976 season, winning six of seven games. But they stumbled down the stretch and finished 8-6.

SELECT GROUP

Quarterback John Brodie's number was retired after he played his last game in 1973. The 49ers whose numbers have been retired by the club:

Uniform	Player	Position	Years
12	John Brodie	QB	1957–1973
34	Joe Perry	RB	1948–1960, 1963
37	Jimmy Johnson	CB	1961–1976
39	Hugh McElhenny	RB	1952–1960
70	Charlie Krueger	DT	1959–1973
73	Leo Nomellini	T	1950–1963
87	Dwight Clark	WR	1979–1987

SHORT-LIVED REVOLUTION

For a time in the early 1960s, it seemed as if the 49ers' Shotgun formation would be as revolutionary as the T-formation of the 1940s.

The Shotgun was similar to the old Double Wing that had been one of the two major formations (with the Single Wing) in the days before the T. It called for the quarterback to take a direct snap from center and either pass the ball, run, or hand off to the other deep back. Coach Red Hickey shuttled in three quarterbacks: John Brodie, an outstanding passer and a fair runner; Billy Kilmer, who had been a Single-Wing tailback at UCLA and was an excellent runner; and Bobby Waters, who passed and ran with equal skill.

The running part didn't thrill Brodie. On one play, he was supposed to spin and fake a hand-off, then turn and run into the line. One time, he ran straight into a big defensive lineman, who said, "What are you trying to do?" Brodie replied, "I think I'm trying to get myself killed."

So after a time, it came down to Brodie passing, Kilmer running, and Waters either running or passing. Hickey first tried the Shotgun in 1960, beating a much better Baltimore Colts team with it.

After splitting the first two games the next season, the 49ers unveiled the Shotgun in the third game. It was a sensation. First the 49ers blitzed the Detroit Lions 49-0. Then they dismantled the Los Angeles Rams 35-0. In their third game with the formation, they had a less spectacular but still convincing 38-24 victory over the Minnesota Vikings. "The 49ers were the talk of football," announcer Bob Fouts said.

But one thing is certain in the NFL: When a team comes up with something new, other teams will soon devise a way to stop it. In this case, the 49ers' nemesis was Clark Shaughnessy, a Bears' assistant coach who put together a five-man line, with middle linebacker Bill George directly over center.

"With the Shotgun, we split our offensive linemen wider than normal," tackle Bob St. Clair said. "That required everybody to move quickly to fill the gap if a defensive lineman came through. Our center, Frank Morze, wasn't very quick. George just went around him on one side or the other. He was in the backfield before the quarterback could even make a handoff. They just killed us."

The final score was 31-0, Chicago. That was the end of the Shotgun.

.500 (1973–75), Nolan was fired. His successor would have a memorable beginning and a tempestuous end.

A DREAM COME TRUE

Monte Clark was the right man at the right time. The 49ers' talent level was on the upswing because bad teams had given them an improved draft position. Cleveland Elam and Jimmy Webb had joined Cedrick Hardman and Tommy Hart on what was one of the best defensive front fours in the league. Two top running backs, Wilbur Jackson and Delvin Williams, had been drafted in 1974. Tackle Keith Fahnhorst (1974) and center Randy Cross (1976) were beginning careers that later would make them mainstays in the offensive line of Super Bowl champions. Fahnhorst, like Cas Banaszek before him, had been a Big Ten tight end (Minnesota) who had to find another position in the pros.

"I could block, but I wasn't fast and I wasn't a good pass catcher," he said. "I reported with the rookies in 1974 and, after about three days, Dick Nolan told me that when the veterans reported, we were going to be short of offensive linemen for awhile, so he was just going to put me there for a few days. I could see what was happening. I remember calling my wife and she started crying and saying, 'You're going to have to get fat and tape up your hands.' Well, I did that, all right, but I had a good career, so it worked out."

In addition to their drafts, the 49ers made judicious trades for outside linebacker Dave Washington, who would be a Pro Bowl player in 1976, and wide receiver Willie McGee, to take the double-teaming pressure off Gene Washington.

They also needed the right coach, and Clark was the man. A physically imposing man at 6-feet, 6-inches and perhaps 260 pounds, Clark had a manner to match his stature. "Everybody liked Monte and wanted to play for him," Williams said. "He created an atmosphere that was congenial and allowed us to win." The thirty-nine-year-old Clark, who had been the offensive line coach at Miami, was the league's youngest head coach. Dolphins coach Don Shula gave Clark a good share of the credit for teaching the blocking schemes that had enabled Miami to put together a running game that was the key to its offense in the 1970s.

It was a homecoming for Clark, who played with the 49ers the first three years (1959–61) of his eleven-year career, mostly as a defensive tackle. "It was like a dream come true," he said. "I remember when I came to the 49ers and looked around and saw Tittle, Nomellini, Perry, McElhenny. To think that a few years later I could come back as the coach was pretty special. I remember the night I signed the contract, I was looking out at the lights of the city from the hotel and feeling so good."

Though he had coached in the other conference, Clark actually knew the 49ers quite well because he lived in the Bay Area in the offseason and visited often with players and coaches. Ironically, he was close to the coach he followed, Dick Nolan, who recommended Clark for his job in Miami. With the 49ers, Clark was given more authority than Nolan ever had. He was named director of football operations and given authority over all player moves.

The 49ers needed a quarterback, and negotiations to get Jim Plunkett from the New England Patriots were basically completed before Clark signed his contract.

Plunkett was a local hero. He had grown up in San Jose, won the Heisman Trophy at Stanford in 1970, and was the player of the game in Stanford's upset of Ohio State in the 1971 Rose Bowl. The Patriots made him the first pick in the 1971 draft. Unfortunately for Plunkett, the Patriots didn't draft an offensive line to play in front of him. He took a tremendous pounding and suffered several injuries, the most serious being injuries to his right shoulder and ribs.

Clark agreed with the decision to trade for Plunkett, but he wasn't happy about the stiff price the 49ers had to pay: two first-round draft picks in 1976 (one had been acquired from Houston in a previous trade), first- and second-round picks in 1977, and quarterback Tom Owen, who had been the starter for part of the previous season.

Clark's fears were justified. The trade turned out to be very costly to the 49ers' future, and even during

FROM DALLAS GUARD BLAINE NYE, AFTER THE COWBOYS RALLIED FROM A 15-POINT, FOURTH-QUARTER DEFICIT TO BEAT THE 49ERS IN A 1972 DIVISIONAL PLAYOFF GAME:

"I FELT SO SORRY FOR THOSE GUYS THAT WHEN IT WAS OVER, I COULDN'T EVEN LOOK AT THEM."

the one good year the team had while Plunkett was quarterbacking, 1976, he was only a minor figure in their success for reasons beyond his control.

Plunkett's health still was a problem. "I'd had surgery on my shoulder and knee when I was at New England," he said, "but the biggest problem I had with San Francisco was rib injuries. I had to have ten or fifteen pain-killing shots before every game because they had to deaden each rib." Plunkett ranked only eighth in 1976 in passing efficiency among the conference's fourteen starting quarterbacks, which bothered him. "That was the worst period of my pro career. I had been so excited about coming home, and then I couldn't do what I wanted to do."

Though he did use it as an excuse, others thought Plunkett's physical problems undercut his confidence. "I think for psychological reasons as much as anything, he wasn't able to play as well as he did later," Clark said. "I ended up having to bench him for the last game. It was very disappointing to me."

Plunkett's play also suffered because of an injury to another player, Willie McGee, who was sidelined with a broken leg in the sixth game of the season. "With McGee in the lineup, the defense had to set up deeper because Willie had great speed," Williams said. "When he was out of there, the defense could double cover Gene [Washington]."

Injuries also devastated the offensive line. "Somebody named it the 'Soup Line,'" Clark said. "We had so many injuries, we were picking up guys off the waiver wire who nobody had ever heard of." Despite those problems, Clark put together a very effective running game in 1976. "That was really the only year I played in the NFL that was really fun for me," Williams said. "Monte changed a lot of things. Wilbur and I had been running at the same position, but he put us both in the backfield at the same time. He gave us a scheme that enabled us to run the ball well, using a lot of misdirection. He brought surprise back into our running game." Williams set a club record with 1,203 rushing yards that year while Jackson added 792.

The 49ers started the season strong, winning six of their first seven games. The most notable was a 16-0 shutout of the Rams in Los Angeles in the fifth game of the season, a Monday-night game.

"Before the game, I was talking with [defensive line coach] Floyd Peters," Clark remembers, "and I said, 'Damn it, Floyd, we're jumping offsides all the time. Can't we stay onsides?' He told me, 'Sure we can, if you don't want a pass rush.' I threw up my hands. 'All right, you've made your point.'"

A fearsome defensive line was the scourge of the NFC in 1976. Cleveland Elam (72) wraps up the Redskins' Mike Thomas on this play.

Nobody remembers how many offsides penalties the 49ers got in the game, but everybody remembers that the defense got 10 quarterback sacks with Hart alone accounting for 6 of them. The defense continued to pressure opposing quarterbacks in the next two games, 33-3 and 15-0 victories over New Orleans and Atlanta. The 49ers had 25 sacks in the three-game stretch. "We really had a solid defense that year," Clark said, "with a great pass rush. Tommy Hart was the best competitor I ever saw. Frank

GROUND FORCES

On October 31, 1976, Delvin Williams rushed for a club-record 194 yards on 34 carries against the St. Louis Cardinals. One week later, he gained 180 yards — the fourth-best single-game mark in club history — against the Redskins. The top ten rushing days in 49ers' history:

Yards	Player	Opponent, Date
194	Delvin Williams	at St. Louis, October 31, 1976
190	Roger Craig	at L.A. Rams, October 16, 1988
190	Wilbur Jackson	vs. New Orleans, November 27, 1977
180	Delvin Williams	vs. Washington, November 7, 1976
174	Joe Perry	vs. Detroit, November 2, 1958
170	Hugh McElhenny	at Dallas Texans, October 5, 1952
168	J. D. Smith	vs. Minnesota, November 26, 1961
163	Ricky Watters	at L.A. Rams, November 22, 1992
162	Roger Craig	at Phoenix, November 6, 1988
162	Ken Willard	at Atlanta, December 15, 1968

Nunley, playing middle linebacker, was the only player I've ever known who knew everything that happened on the football field. He'd come out of the game after a series and tell me what happened on every play."

After completing the first half of the season 6-1, the 49ers lost four games in a row. The only bad loss was the fourth in that streak, 23-3 to the Rams at Candlestick. It was the only game the 49ers lost by more than a touchdown that year. A breakdown

of the 49ers' six losses that season is amazing. Two losses, to St. Louis and San Diego, came in overtime. Another was by three points to Washington, a fourth loss by only five points to Atlanta.

The 49ers were at a great disadvantage in close games because of Steve Mike-Mayer, their kicker. Mike-Mayer started the season with a streak of 10 consecutive field goals but was successful on only 6 of 18 from that point, and he missed 4 of 30 extra-point attempts. The players called him "Miss-a-Mile," which soon was picked up by the media. A soccer-style kicker, Mike-Mayer had problems getting the ball airborne. "We used to cringe when he came into the game," Fahnhorst said, "because he was known for not getting the ball high enough and hitting one of the linemen. We'd come out of the game with bruises."

"I remember that in the St. Louis game, our two return men [Paul Hofer and Tony Leonard] each thought the other was going to catch a kick, and St. Louis recovered on the ten-yard line," Clark said. "I remember that we had Washington beat until they faked a field goal and went on to score a touchdown. But mostly, I remember 'Miss-a-Mile.' That's one change I should have made but didn't."

The 49ers usually had to be much better than the other team to win. Except for a four-point victory

The 49ers had high hopes when they acquired local hero Jim Plunkett from the Patriots in 1976. But after releasing him prior to the 1978 season, they had nothing to show for the trade. Plunkett, meanwhile, went on to lead the Raiders to two Super Bowl victories.

over Minnesota in a Monday night game, they won all their games by at least twelve points. When the games were close, they lost them. Still, though the team's 8-6 record wasn't good enough for the play-offs, it generally was an upbeat year.

"I definitely felt that we had the nucleus to go on and be a contending team," Williams said. "We had the veterans, and if we'd just filled in here and there with some young players, we could have done it. The important thing in football is continuity. That's why the 49ers are so successful now. They've basically been using the system Bill Walsh brought

Tommy Hart had 6 of the 49ers' 10 quarterback sacks in a 16-0 shutout of the Rams on a Monday night in 1976. That was the beginning of a three-game stretch in which the 49ers recorded 25 sacks and allowed only 3 points.

with him in 1979. We were just starting to learn Monte's system. We could have done much more once we learned it."

Fahnhorst echoes that. "I think we could have had a lot of success with Monte. He was tough but fair, and I think he could have produced a champi-onship team."

But Clark never got the chance.

UNDER NEW MANAGEMENT

The 49ers had always been owned by the Morabito family and friends — Tony's wife, Jo, and Vic's wife, Jane, inherited majority ownership of the team when their husbands died — but times were changing in profes-sional sports. Family ownership was dying out. Corporations and very rich men were buying into professional sports. The 49ers' owners could see what was coming.

"We felt that, to be an owner of a professional football team, you had to be very wealthy," Al Ruffo said. "We anticipated that salaries would take off. I felt that pay-TV had to come in before teams would make much money. The owners were very apprehensive."

So the club was being shopped.

The first potential buyer was Wayne Valley, who had been one of the general partners in the Oakland Raiders. After a long, complicated feud with Al Davis, Valley had sold his interest to Davis. The 49ers' negotiations with Valley progressed enough that Valley was given a chance to look over the team's books, and he also had a long talk with Clark about the team's future. All of the minority partners had a clause in their partnership agreement that gave them the option of matching an offer from the outside. After Valley presented his offer, Franklin Mieuli said he would exercise his option, so the negotiations with Valley were put on hold while Mieuli tried to come up with the money to buy the team.

Nobody thought that would be Mieuli's own money because Mieuli was already highly leveraged with his basketball team, the Golden State Warriors. Finally, Mieuli had to tell his fellow 49ers' owners that he could not put together a group that would be able to buy the team.

So it was back to Valley's proposal. "We couldn't come to terms with Wayne," Ruffo said. "We had a certain amount in mind, but Wayne wouldn't come up. He was tough. He might have thought that we didn't have any choice because nobody else was interested, and because it was hard to negotiate since our partners were so eager to sell."

At Super Bowl XI in January 1977, Ruffo was approached by Oakland Raiders owner Al Davis, who asked if the club was still for sale. "I told Davis that we were clear," Ruffo said. "He said he had two or three people, and he wanted to pick out the best one financially."

Davis is a man who hates to travel in a straight line, and his talk about "two or three people" is an

Larry Schreiber was a determined runner, a bruising blocker, and a gifted pass catcher out of the 49ers' backfield from 1971 to 1975.

example. There was never another mention of more than one group, but there was no quarreling with the candidate he eventually picked: the DeBartolo Corporation.

The DeBartolo family had been involved in sports for some time, owning horse-racing tracks and an NHL team in Pittsburgh. Before the NFL expanded into Tampa for the 1976 season, Ed DeBartolo, Sr., had been approached. "My father was interested," Ed DeBartolo, Jr., said, "but Hugh Culverhouse had the inside on that franchise."

Sometime after the Ruffo-Davis meeting, Davis called Joe Thomas, who had been born and raised in Cortland, Ohio, only a few miles from the DeBartolos in Youngstown. "Al Davis and Joe Thomas were

always kind of buddies," said Ed, Jr. "Even during the period when Joe worked for us, I remember him bouncing a lot of ideas off Davis. He used him as an adviser."

Thomas called Ed DeBartolo, Sr. Meanwhile, Davis called Ruffo, and a meeting was set up at the Edgewater Hyatt in Oakland, across the street from the Coliseum. That meeting gave the 49ers' partners a chance to meet the DeBartolos. At a second meeting, the two groups began to negotiate seriously, and Ruffo asked Ed DeBartolo, Sr., for a letter of credit.

"There was a silence, which seemed like five minutes," Ruffo remembers. "DeBartolo finally said, 'This is the first time I've ever been asked for a letter of credit.' I explained that we asked for it because we wanted to close off Mieuli, who couldn't come up with a letter of credit."

The deal came together quickly after that. Ed DeBartolo, Jr., remembers that it was for a little over $17 million, though the liabilities that the new owners had to assume probably pushed it to around $20–22 million.

Al Davis, who orchestrated everything, got $100,000 as a finder's fee. It was a perfect deal for him. He thwarted his rival, Valley, and he brought in Thomas, whose actions would guarantee that the 49ers would be no threat to Davis's Raiders for at least the immediate future. Davis should have been the one paying a fee.

A ROCKY START

The DeBartolos held a press conference with Joe Thomas present. Thomas pointed to running back Delvin Williams, standing in the back of the room—and called him Wilbur Jackson. Ed, Jr., the team owner and president, was only thirty, and this was the first time he had been in charge of a separate entity within the corporation, as well as his first press conference. Addressing a hostile media audience, he talked of running the team like a business, which was not what anybody wanted to hear. "They almost tarred and feathered me," he remembers.

The reaction to the DeBartolos' purchase would have been different in another city but this was San Francisco and the 49ers. The 49ers always had close

BLANKET COVERAGE

Jimmy Johnson made the Pro Football Hall of Fame as a cornerback, but he started his 49ers career in 1961 as a wide receiver. "I had played some defense at UCLA, and the 49ers kept shifting me back to defense every time a defensive back got hurt. When [Jack Christiansen] became head coach, he asked me which I preferred. I thought I'd have a longer career as a defensive back, so I said defense."

That was a wise choice, for Johnson and for his team. Johnson has a vivid memory of the first game he played as a full-time defensive back, against Baltimore. The Colts featured John Unitas at quarterback and Raymond Berry, Lenny Moore, and Jimmy Orr as wide receivers.

"Berry was a great moves man," Johnson says. "Moore was really fast, a great deep threat. Orr had great moves, and he was very verbal, abusing you all the time.

"At the end of that game, each one of the receivers came up and told me what a great job I'd done. That was a great lift for me."

It wasn't the Colts' receivers, though, who were the most memorable for Johnson. "I had tremendous respect for Tommy McDonald [a flanker who played for five teams between 1957 and 1968]," he said, "because he was such a great technician and he put out such a great effort.

"The first time I played against Tommy was after he'd been traded to the Rams [1965]. They tried a long pass to him and I batted it away at the last second. When you make a play like that, you usually lounge around on the ground for a time, enjoying the moment, but Tommy jumped up and started sprinting back to the huddle. Well, I wasn't going to let him do that with me just laying there, so I got up and ran after him, almost like we were still in pass coverage.

"He always hustled like that, so when we played against him, I made a point of jumping up after a play as fast as he did."

Johnson's 47 career interceptions stood as a 49ers' record until the mark was broken by Ronnie Lott, but Johnson was best known for his blanket coverage of receivers.

"It takes skill for backs to read a quarterback when they're playing zone and figure out where he's going," Johnson said, "but for me, I loved the challenge of just taking a receiver on man-to-man." The way he responded to that challenge landed Johnson in the Pro Football Hall of Fame.

Paul Hofer (36) was a hard-working running back and a fan favorite during the lean years in the late seventies. The eleventh-round draft choice rushed for 1,746 yards in six seasons for the 49ers, but his career was hampered by knee injuries.

ties to the community. The owners were local people. Now, outsiders had bought the club and refused to pay the usual tributes. The DeBartolos did not say over and over how wonderful San Francisco was, and Ed DeBartolo, Jr., didn't bother to pretend that he would move to San Francisco. The outsiders would remain outsiders. It was unforgivable.

Soon, the 49ers lost their coach. Clark accompanied the DeBartolos to the NFL meetings in Arizona, where the sale was approved by league owners, but he resigned shortly after that. Before the public announcement, Clark told the DeBartolos he

was through. "When I first heard about the deal," Clark said, "I heard that Joe Thomas would be the general manager and that he'd have authority on all trades and player decisions — the same things that were very clearly in my contract. Those were the things I'd fought for. It was a matter of principle and a matter of integrity. The DeBartolos offered to extend my contract, to give me more money, but I felt that if I agreed to what I really didn't believe in, I'd have a 'Sold' sign on my forehead."

Thomas had been player personnel chief at Miami, and Clark remembers one humorous incident when the Dolphins were working on the draft. "Before Joe came into the room, we [the coaches] put up a phony name on the draft board. When Joe was going down the list of players and came to this name, he just faked his way through it, saying the guy could do this or that, just making up things."

Thomas was not a popular figure in the NFL. Why, then, did the DeBartolos hire him to run their franchise?

"Joe Thomas had a fairly good reputation as a football man," Ed, Jr., said. "At that time, I didn't know whether a football was pumped up or stuffed. Thomas knew talent. He didn't always go about it the right way, but he'd put some good players on some good teams."

DeBartolo, Jr., was right: Thomas did have a good reputation throughout the NFL for player evaluation, first with the Dolphins and then as general manager of the Baltimore Colts. In San Francisco, though, he lost his touch.

DeBartolo, Jr., gave Thomas complete responsibility. "I was sitting three thousand miles away in Youngstown," he said. "I couldn't tell him to do this or do that. He was empowered to run the football team."

THE SCULPTOR by MURRAY OLDERMAN

Management was all smiles after acquiring O. J. Simpson in 1978, but the price turned out to be too high for the running back—he never approached his past glory. Flanking Simpson are general manager Joe Thomas (left and above), owner Edward DeBartolo, Jr., and coach Pete McCulley (far right). The signing was one of a series of poor moves by Thomas that nearly left the franchise in ruins.

Given that authority, Thomas ruined himself, the team, and very nearly, the franchise. Thomas seemed determined to eliminate the 49ers' past. As club president, Lou Spadia had worked hard to mend fences, to end Tony Morabito's feuds with the newspapers, and to cultivate a close relationship with the community, but Thomas nearly destroyed all that in less than two years.

When he met with members of the Recreation and Parks Commission, Thomas insulted them. He eliminated perks for season-ticket holders and broke up clubs formed for them. He threw away pictures and memorabilia — a friend of Gene Washington's brought Gene a picture that he had found in a trash can.

"Now I'm detached from it," Washington said, "but when you're in it, you're numb. Monte had a lot of stability. We had a sense we were going to make progress, but with these changes, it was like the team just fell off the cliff. There was no light at the end of the tunnel. It was all darkness."

Thomas hired only coaches who would do his bidding, going through Ken Meyer, Pete McCulley, and Fred O'Connor in two years, the last two splitting the 1978 season between them.

"We all knew Thomas was pulling the strings," Williams later recalled. "The coach is your leader. He's the guy you look to for inspiration. When you know he's not making the decisions—even if it's not in your area—he loses credibility and you lose your motivation. You try to tell yourself you have to keep going, but it's really hard to play under those circumstances."

"After playing on teams like we had in nineteen seventy, seventy-one, and seventy-two," Washington said, "to play with these coaches, it was disbelief, a state of shock. We were in disarray."

The unrest among the players probably was the main reason the 49ers, who had looked like a team on the rise the season before, slipped to 5-9 in 1977.

The silver lining to the Joe Thomas years was that they paved the way for Bill Walsh to become head coach. Steve DeBerg (17) was Walsh's first quarterback with the 49ers. Joe Montana and Sam Wyche (who would go on to coach the Bengals and Buccaneers) confer in the background.

Players were going in and out of the starting line-up, seemingly on a whim—and everybody knew whose whim it was. Former tackle Len Rohde had opened a Burger King restaurant in Mountain View, California, and mounted pictures of the 49ers' starting lineups, offense and defense, on two walls. "There were so many changes, I was putting up ten new pictures every week," Rohde said. "That got to be too expensive, so I said, the hell with it, and put up pictures of former players. I knew Thomas couldn't get rid of them."

Thomas made a series of blunders in 1978. He released Plunkett before the season began so the 49ers had nothing to show for the 1976 trade. "That was devastating to me," Plunkett said, "but to be out

from under Joe Thomas, well, there was a tremendous sense of relief." Picked up off the waiver wire by Al Davis, Plunkett eventually came back to lead the Raiders to Super Bowl victories following the 1980 and 1983 seasons.

Thomas also cut or traded Washington, Williams, cornerback Bruce Taylor, linebacker Skip Vanderbundt, defensive end Tommy Hart, and guard Woody Peoples. He traded for O. J. Simpson, once the premier running back in football but now near the end of his career because of a serious knee injury, giving up second- and third-round picks in the 1978 draft, first- and fourth-round picks in 1979, and a second-round choice in 1980. The 49ers plunged to 2-14 in 1978, which would have given them the first pick in the 1979 draft as a consolation prize. Instead, Buffalo got it.

The draft was supposed to be Thomas's strong point, but it wasn't while he was with the 49ers. The Plunkett trade wiped out the first two picks in 1977, and none of Thomas's subsequent nine picks helped the team. In 1978, the 49ers were picking high (seventh) in the first round, but Thomas selected Notre Dame tight end Ken MacAfee, who ranks with the all-time 49er draft busts. Later picks included Dan Bunz, Archie Reese, and Fred Quillan, all good players for Super Bowl teams, but by the time they started producing, Thomas was long gone.

It was ugly. On game days at Candlestick Park, fans would put up signs reading, "Blame Joe Thomas." Thomas would send security men around to confiscate the signs. While the team was deteriorating, Thomas was making more bad news off the field, including fighting with a beat reporter on a hotel dance floor during a 49ers' road trip.

Even more than the team's bad record, Thomas's relationship with the fans, media, and community bothered DeBartolo when he learned of it. "I didn't realize for a time the underlying animosity that was being created," he said. "It was terrible the way Joe Thomas pushed, the way he represented himself."

For DeBartolo, the culmination came on

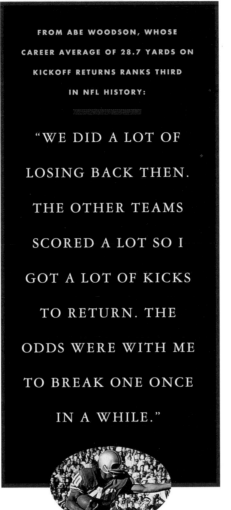

FROM ABE WOODSON, WHOSE CAREER AVERAGE OF 28.7 YARDS ON KICKOFF RETURNS RANKS THIRD IN NFL HISTORY:

"WE DID A LOT OF LOSING BACK THEN. THE OTHER TEAMS SCORED A LOT SO I GOT A LOT OF KICKS TO RETURN. THE ODDS WERE WITH ME TO BREAK ONE ONCE IN A WHILE."

November 27, 1978, the day San Francisco Mayor George Moscone was assassinated. The 49ers were scheduled to play the Pittsburgh Steelers in a Monday-night game at Candlestick, and Thomas didn't want to play the game. "Joe thought it was a conspiracy, that somebody would try to kill him," DeBartolo said. "I talked to Dan Rooney [son of Art Rooney, then the Steelers' owner] and he convinced me we should play the game. That Monday-night fiasco was the straw that broke the camel's back."

It wasn't until after the season that DeBartolo fired Thomas, but the decision had been made in his mind that night. "Eddie told me that he'd told his dad, 'I've been taking all the heat, and if that's going to happen, I'm going to make the decisions,'" said Carmen Policy, then an attorney for DeBartolo and later the club president.

"I think he was the first guy I'd ever fired," DeBartolo said. "He was really startled. I told him, 'We can't have this. Our company has been in business for years. Our company has been a people company. We've always treated our employees like members of the family. You're not running my franchise right. You're creating a lot of animosity. It's filtering back to me, to my family.' He gave me a lot of reasons why he should stay, but he had to go."

The worst period in 49ers' history had ended.

A SILVER LINING

Like the lotus flower growing out of the mud, though, Washington thinks the 49ers ultimately benefited from the Thomas years, because DeBartolo then made the decision to hire Bill Walsh, who ushered in the greatest period in 49ers' history — by far.

"If Thomas hadn't done what he did, Walsh may not have come here, and who knows what would have happened," Washington said. "Bill is clearly the reason for the 49ers' success. If you were to ask me if I would go through what I went through to get to where this team is now, I'd say yes."

ddie DeBartolo needed a new coach. Fortunately, he didn't have far to look. The man he needed, Bill Walsh, was coaching at Stanford University, just a few miles from the 49ers' headquarters. ⁋ Walsh's success at Stanford, where his teams won bowl games in two consecutive years, got the attention of NFL executives. Walsh, in fact, remembers being approached in 1978 by Joe Thomas, though he quickly said he wasn't interested. There was also a feeler from the Chicago Bears and serious talks with the Los Angeles Rams before Walsh's second season at Stanford. ⁋ Walsh was anxious to prove he could succeed in the NFL. When he and DeBartolo met in 1979, it took very little time for the 49ers' owner to offer the coaching job to Walsh, and no longer for Walsh to accept.

(Above) Coach Bill Walsh and quarterback Joe Montana confer during a time out; (pages 104–5) Montana prepares his troops in warmups prior to Super Bowl XXIV; (page 106) wide receiver Dwight Clark; (page 107) 49ers quarterback Steve DeBerg (17) and Raiders quarterback Ken Stabler (12) exchange pleasantries; (pages 108–9) Montana readies for kickoff against the Saints; (page 110) wide receiver Jerry Rice; (page 111) Montana passes in his final game as a 49er; (page 112) running back Ricky Watters; (page 113) quarterback Steve Young exults in the aftermath of victory in Super Bowl XXIX; (opposite) linebacker Todd Shell celebrates.

"We met at the Fairmont Hotel [in San Francisco] and talked for about forty minutes," DeBartolo said. "I just liked him. I liked his temperament, his disposition, his intelligence. We hit it off very well."

DeBartolo was accompanied by Carmen Policy (now the club president), who was meeting Walsh for the first time. "He was very impressive," Policy said. "He had a presence. You got the feeling that this guy could be teaching at Stanford, not just coaching. He just impressed the hell out of me."

It is customary in the NFL to first hire a general manager, who then hires a coach, but these were desperate times and DeBartolo first wanted a man in place that he could trust. "I knew I was going to be an absentee owner, with the way our operation was

set up in Youngstown," he said. "I wasn't going to live in San Francisco."

Because the 49ers were in such disarray, it proved difficult to attract a reputable football man to be general manager, so DeBartolo suggested to Walsh that he act as his own general manager. Walsh agreed. He hired two former NFL head coaches, John McVay (as player personnel director) and John Ralston (as vice president for administration), but the main drafting and trading decisions would be made by Walsh.

The first two seasons, when the 49ers went 2-14 and 6-10, were very hard for both coach and owner. Walsh thought the 49ers had enough talent to win perhaps a half dozen games in his first season, but he

THE GENIUS

When Bill Walsh was hired as head coach in 1979, he brought with him a reputation as an offensive genius.

Walsh had spent almost all of his coaching career as an NFL assistant, including eight years with the Cincinnati Bengals. When Paul Brown retired in 1975, Walsh expected to be named his successor, but Brown picked Bill (Tiger) Johnson, who had started his coaching career as an assistant with the 49ers in the 1950s. A disappointed Walsh moved to the San Diego Chargers and, after one season as the offensive coordinator there, was named head coach at Stanford University.

Nobody ever questioned Walsh's ability to put together an offense or coach quarterbacks, but many NFL coaches and executives thought Walsh was too professorial—and not tough enough to be an NFL head coach. Players would later wonder about that reputation because nobody ever had tighter control of his team than Walsh. They did not question him on the practice field or in a game. Walsh could wither a player or assistant coach with a well-chosen phrase.

"Players were afraid of Bill," said Guy Benjamin, a reserve quarterback for the 49ers from 1981 to 1983. "They knew better than to talk back to Bill. They'd be gone the next day if they did."

Billy Wilson, an assistant in Walsh's early years, remembered the time in training camp when starting tackle Ron Singleton got into a fight with another player

and then argued with Walsh. Walsh called Wilson over and said he wanted Singleton out of camp a half hour after practice. "R. C. Owens and I got his plane ticket, packed his clothes, and had him in a car to the airport twenty minutes after practice," Wilson said. "That got everybody's attention."

"Bill was always challenging you," former wide receiver Dwight Clark said. "You never felt you had it made." Toward the end of Clark's first training camp in

1979, when he was feeling good about himself, Walsh passed him in the dormitory hall and said, "You're fading a little on me out there." Clark was crushed—but he worked extra hard in the next few practices.

Benjamin played for Walsh at Stanford and then, after an interlude with Don Shula in Miami and one year in New Orleans, came to the 49ers as a reserve quarterback behind Walsh.

"I was just amazed at how he developed the team in San Francisco," Benjamin said. "One of the things that really impressed me was the way he'd bring in veteran players like Jack Reynolds and Charle Young, who had been leaders on other teams, for their last hurrah. They'd dig down a little more, maybe work harder to get in shape, and they'd be leaders for him."

Benjamin considered Walsh less a coach than a corporate manager who made decisions solely on the basis of what was best for the team. When Benjamin was at Miami, Shula had three quarterbacks—Bob Griese and Don Strock were the others. Shula traded Benjamin to New Orleans but told him, "I really should have traded Griese [then thirty-five], but you know I can't do that."

"Bill would never have hesitated," Benjamin said, "if he thought that would be the best thing for the team."

Walsh's offensive system brought the 49ers their initial success, but it was his great organizational ability that enabled the 49ers to sustain their success even after he left.

realized very quickly how Thomas had stripped the roster of good veteran players without bringing in good young talent to replace them.

Perhaps the biggest disappointment for Walsh was running back O. J. Simpson. Though Simpson was past his prime, Walsh thought he could be productive for the 49ers, but a knee injury Simpson had suffered while with the Buffalo Bills often prevented the once-great running back from even practicing. When he could play, he couldn't cut sharply, and in 1979, his final season, he ran for only 460 yards and averaged just 3.8 yards per carry. Simpson was a shadow of the player who had been the first NFL back to rush for more than 2,000 yards in a season.

A SENSE OF OPTIMISM

Even in that first season, though, there were signs that Walsh would succeed with the 49ers. The most obvious indication was the offense, which was not only productive but exciting. Walsh's organization, on and off the field, was equally important.

(Above) Quarterback Steve DeBerg had to be equipped with a voice amplifier prior to a game in 1980; (right) John McVay spent sixteen years in the 49ers' front office, the last six as vice president for football operations. He remains a consultant.

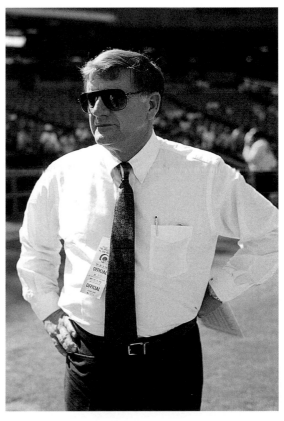

Randy Cross, who joined the 49ers as a rookie in 1976, noted that the players who survived the Thomas years were skeptical when Walsh arrived, but their skepticism soon turned to belief. "Basically, we'd had coaches who were going to do anything Joe Thomas said," Cross said. "Bill was different. We knew we had a great offense and we knew we had a plan.

"Bill put together an organization that made it more comfortable. He encouraged a relationship with former players. He encouraged the civic things, the charities, which were time-consuming for the players but really helped establish us with the community."

Walsh knew he would have to make many changes before he'd have a competitive team. The quickest way to get help was by picking up players

Joe Montana arrived in 1979 replete with Fu Manchu mustache; by 1981, "next year" had arrived for long-time equipment manager Chico Norton (below) and 49ers fans.

waived by stronger clubs during training-camp cutdowns, as he did in getting defensive end Dwaine Board and free safety Dwight Hicks. Players were coming and going, but those who stayed saw brighter days ahead. "When you were around Bill," wide receiver Dwight Clark said, "you knew that sooner or later, we were going to win. He was so smart."

Walsh selected quarterback Joe Montana in the draft that year, envisioning Montana as the 49ers' quarterback of the future, even though Steve DeBerg would set an NFL record in 1979 with 347 completions. DeBerg, who threw 17 touchdown passes and ranked fifth in the NFC in passing, was also a strong leader.

"Steve might have been the best quarterback for Bill's system," said Cross, whose analytical ability has enabled him to succeed as a commentator on NFL telecasts, "except for two things. He lacked Joe's mobility and, with his strong personality and great football knowledge, he challenged Bill. He asked why. Not all coaches like challenges, and certainly Bill didn't, but Steve never hesitated."

DeBerg's lack of mobility often forced him into hurried throws which resulted in incompletions or interceptions, of which he threw 21 in 1979. The interceptions were not always DeBerg's fault. As Walsh admitted, he sometimes called "one pass too many" on a drive. The 49ers had to throw because they were usually playing catch-up; DeBerg averaged 36 passes a game.

The interceptions were intolerable to Walsh, who referred to them as "gross errors," but DeBerg performed a valuable service for the 49ers. "If we hadn't had Steve, we might have had to throw Joe in there immediately, with catastrophic results," Walsh said. "We didn't have very good pass protection and we had to throw on virtually every down because it seemed we were always trailing. With Steve available, we were able to slowly but surely move Joe into the system. He didn't have the pressure of having to win because we were such a poor team.

"Joe had his problems. He wasn't consistent, he made mistakes, and he showed his lack of experience, but he really made it very quickly. Some quarterbacks have made it a little faster, but they played on teams with a strong supporting cast where they were the final piece."

Safety Dwight Hicks was in only his third season in 1981, but he was the senior member of a defensive backfield that included three rookies.

Walsh picked his spots to play Montana, usually near the other team's goal line, and he would give him a play that was likely to have an open receiver so Montana could do well and thereby build his confidence.

At least as important was when Walsh didn't play Montana, as in the 59-14 shellacking by the Cowboys in Dallas in the sixth game of the 1980 season. "One of my most enduring memories," Cross said, "is Steve getting beat to death and Joe trying to hide from Bill because he didn't want to go in there."

The game that sealed DeBerg's fate with the 49ers came against Detroit during the 1980 season. Montana started the game, but DeBerg was in at the end, with the 49ers trailing 17-13. Tight end Charle Young broke free in the end zone but, with a Detroit defender in his face, DeBerg threw incomplete. "How many times had we seen that," Walsh

Dwight Clark earned a reputation as a valuable possession receiver, but he also was capable of outrunning supposedly faster defensive backs.

said, "with Steve just throwing blindly because he didn't have the mobility to get away? We just knew, watching that play, that Joe could have stepped to the side to complete the touchdown, and we'd have won the game."

Meanwhile, in 1980 the 49ers were making progress. They won their first three games but lost Board, their best defensive lineman, in the third week, starting a string of injuries which also deprived them later of their best running back, Paul Hofer. They lost eight consecutive games in what Walsh would call the most devastating period of his coaching career. "I can't take this," Cross remembers Walsh telling the team, "I didn't get into coaching for this."

"We weren't too thrilled about it, either," Cross said.

The season ended on an upbeat note, however, as the 49ers won three consecutive games before dropping decisions to Atlanta and Buffalo, division winners that year. At 6-10, the 49ers were approaching mediocrity, a big step up from back-to-back 2-14 seasons. Offensively, they already ranked among the league's top teams, and with Montana and Clark as their mainstays, they figured to have a top-notch offense for years to come. Defense, however, was another story, so Walsh made a firm commitment to go for help in the draft. Specifically, he wanted to strengthen his defensive backfield, which had only one player of true NFL caliber, free safety Dwight Hicks.

DRAFTING FOR SUCCESS

While Walsh was with the 49ers he made all the important decisions regarding players, but he did not make those decisions without help. He sought information both inside and outside the organization. Nothing was left to chance. Prospective draftees were interviewed and given personality and intelligence tests. Scouts and coaches were asked specific questions about each player's ability to help the 49ers and fit into their offensive or defensive systems. Walsh had tapes made that showed the ten best and the ten worst plays a player had made, so he had a good idea of the span of a player's performance.

Walsh's first great draft came in 1981, when

A SIGN OF THINGS TO COME

Late in the 1980 season, the 49ers trailed the winless New Orleans Saints 35-7 at halftime at Candlestick Park.

On the first play of the second half, Joe Montana hit Dwight Clark for a 48-yard gain, and the 49ers drove 88 yards for a touchdown on Montana's 1-yard run. The next time the 49ers had the ball, Montana teamed with Clark on a 71-yard touchdown. Clark caught a short pass, cut across the field, and outran supposedly faster defensive backs.

The stunned Saints fumbled on two of their next three possessions, and the 49ers drove 83 yards and 78 yards to touchdowns, tying the score at 35-35 on Lenvil Elliott's 7-yard run with 1:50 left in the fourth quarter.

Ray Wersching's 36-yard field goal 7:40 into overtime won the game.

It was the greatest regular-season comeback in NFL history but, more than that, it was the unofficial beginning of the championship years. For the first time, Montana asserted himself as the team's leader, and the 49ers showed how explosive their offense could be. Though they lost their last two games that season, the 49ers were on their way.

he picked Ronnie Lott, Eric Wright, and Carlton Williamson, who became starters in the defensive backfield; Lynn Thomas, a solid backup in the secondary; and Pete Kugler, who became a good nose guard.

Walsh was not through. Before the start of the season, he traded for Dan Audick, who became the starting left tackle; Johnny Davis, who became the starting fullback, and Guy Benjamin, who had been his first quarterback at Stanford and would be the backup for Montana. Then he signed middle linebacker Jack (Hacksaw) Reynolds, who became the heart and soul of the defense. For the first time in years, the 49ers had good overall talent.

Walsh and defensive backfield coach George Seifert didn't waste any time with the rookies, starting them immediately in the secondary with the closest thing they had to a veteran, Hicks at free safety. "I had all of a year-and-a-half's experience," Hicks said.

"We knew they were going to be starters, come hell or high water, so we just had to get it done," Seifert said. "I coached Eric at the Senior Bowl so I knew a little about him. There was a question at first whether he could play corner [Wright had been a safety in college], but after the first couple of days in camp, we knew he could. Ronnie's strong personality came out right away. There was a question whether Carlton had the athletic ability to cover receivers one-on-one, but we decided that in our system he didn't have to do that very often, so that wasn't a problem. Dwight, of course, was our glue."

Hicks was thrilled when the 49ers drafted three defensive backs because he knew he'd finally have some help. "I thought, 'Wow, they're making a big move,'" he said, "because I knew they'd be starters right away. I was delighted to play with Ronnie, Eric, and Carlton. They were unbelievable athletes and even greater people. We worked well together from the start. There was a chemistry among us."

That chemistry wasn't obvious at the start, though, mostly because the 49ers played a cautious defense. The rookie corners, Lott and Wright, played so far off receivers to prevent deep passes that opponents were catching 10-yard passes with ease.

Hicks noted that it was the same coverage the Philadelphia Eagles had used successfully. "The

corners would play ten yards off the line of scrimmage and then watch the first three steps of the quarterback," he said. "They were supposed to read the play and either move up if the play looked like a run, or backpedal, but being so inexperienced, they just instinctively started to backpedal as soon as the ball was snapped."

Lott remembers that "we weren't playing with the confidence and reckless abandon you need to win in the NFL," but he thought that changed in the second half of an exhibition game against the Seattle Seahawks. "We just looked terrible in the first half," he said. "We were missing tackles, we were running into each other. I missed the quarterback when he was running with the ball. George Seifert came in at halftime and told us, 'I don't want you guys to think any more. I want you to go out and have fun.' And in the second half, Eric Wright made a really big play, an interception, and it gave everybody confidence that we could make plays."

Seifert looks back at that time with fondness and says, "I wouldn't trade that for any other experience in my coaching career," but he also remembers how tough it was at the time. "There was a lot of pressure on both coaches and players," he said. "It was very intense. I remember we lost an exhibition game to San Diego when Eric tried to make a tackle with one arm and missed, and the receiver scored a touchdown. Well, you would have thought we'd lost the championship game or something. Bill really got on us about that."

Despite the uncertain beginning, the defensive backfield developed an amazing confidence. "Because our chemistry was so good, we made a pledge to each other," Hicks said. "We felt that if we played well, the team could win. If we played poorly, the team would lose. So we vowed to play our best the whole season and, week after week, the defensive backfield was making plays to help win games."

There was no hint of a Super Bowl season as the 49ers split their first four games, losing two on the road and winning two at home, but Cross remembers that the players were confident. "We

The 49ers struck gold in the 1981 draft with defensive backs Ronnie Lott (24), Eric Wright (21), and Carlton Williamson (27).

almost beat Buffalo, the AFC East champions, in our final game in 1980," he said. "We knew that with any luck, we could have won ten games that year, so we thought we had a pretty good chance, going into the 1981 season, of having a good year, especially after getting defensive help in the draft.

"Plus, we were very close. The losing had a lot to do with how good we became. When you'd lose, you could only go out with players on the team because they were the only ones who wouldn't ask you why you were so bad. And when we won, we wanted to share it with each other."

TURNING POINTS

There were several games in 1981 that can be regarded as turning points, and Lott thought the third game, a humiliating 34-17 loss to the Falcons in Atlanta, was the first one. "They just demolished us," he said. "Bill came in at the end of that game and said, 'We've got to make a commitment that we won't get out hit again.' I can't think of a game the rest of the season that we got out hit."

Three Atlanta touchdowns came on passes from Falcons' quarterback Steve Bartkowski, and Walsh was losing patience with his rookie defensive backs. He called Seifert into his office and said, "When are we going to get this done? We've invested a lot in these defensive backs, making them practically our whole draft. When are we going to see the benefit?"

The sign Walsh was looking for came in practice one week after his outburst.

"Everything seemed to come together," Seifert said. "We were working on our Nickel defense in practice against the first-team offense and it was like a game, not a practice. We were shutting them down, and they were really getting frustrated. They weren't used to anybody stopping them, whether it was a game or practice. At that point, I felt we could do the job."

The new-found cohesiveness would show in the next game in Washington, but it appeared for a time the 49ers might not even be able to get to the game against the Redskins.

"We were standing around at the gate and there

HACKSAW

Jack (Hacksaw) Reynolds, the middle linebacker on the 49ers' Super Bowl championship team in 1981, was a genuine character. He earned his moniker when he sawed an old car in half as an angry gesture after his college team, the University of Tennessee, lost an important game.

Reynolds was a fiery competitor who head coach Bill Walsh called "our Pete Rose," and a student of the game who took home game films to study on his own.

Hacksaw put on his game-face early. Hours before home games, he would don his uniform and drive to the game. Those passing him on the freeway assumed he was just another fan dressed up in a 49ers' uniform.

"They thought I was nuts," Reynolds said. "Little did they know, they were right."

was no plane," Cross said. "After awhile, the guy from United told us they had a stretch-eight that they could use for us. [Business manager] Keith Simon told him, 'That won't do. We want the best plane you have or we won't charter with you any more.' So, we went back in the terminal and we were just sitting there when we saw a DC-10 taxiing up for us. We all let out a big cheer."

Psychology is very important in football, and this seemingly small incident gave the 49ers the feeling that they were special. In Washington, they played one of their most impressive games of the season.

The 49ers, ahead 30-3 at one point, coasted to a 30-17 victory over the Redskins. Hicks intercepted 2 passes and recovered a fumble, returning them for 184 yards and 2 touchdowns. Not surprisingly, he calls it the best game of his pro career and also regards it as a turning point for the 49ers. He wasn't alone. Though the Redskins were struggling — 0-4 on the way to an 8-8 season — Walsh later called the win the most significant of the year because it came on the road, where the 49ers had lost 26 of their previous 28 games. "That started the stretch where we won about ninety percent of the time on the road," Cross said.

One week later defensive end Fred Dean joined the 49ers after being acquired from the San Diego Chargers. Dean was embroiled in a contract dispute with the Chargers, and the 49ers were able to get him on the cheap: a second-round pick in the 1983 draft.

When Dean first came to the club, defensive coordinator Chuck Studley was using the 3-4 (three defensive linemen, four linebackers) as his basic defense. Dean was used only in obvious passing situations and was so effective that Studley quickly changed to a 4-3 defense (four defensive linemen, three linebackers), enabling Dean to play virtually every down.

"Dean was really incredible," Cross said. "The first time he came to practice, he just ran around [49ers' left tackle] Dan Audick. It wasn't good for Dan, but we were laughing.

"Dean was like [pro football Hall of Fame defensive end] Leroy Selmon—guys who weren't very big but could pick up 290-pound tackles and throw them. He was the lineman's equivalent of

Ronnie Lott. If you hit Ronnie hard, you'd always hurt more than he would. Some guys have an extremely dense muscle mass, so if you hit them, it hurts. Fred Dean was like that.

"He had a unique personality, too. He smoked these big menthol cigarettes, and his eyes were always red. You'd go into the weight room and there would be Fred, sitting in the corner, smoking a cigarette. If you asked him if he lifted weights, he'd say, 'Sometimes I think about it, but then I lie down until I get over it.'"

Much of the time, Dean was unstoppable. He was so quick off the ball that often he appeared to be offsides, and though he weighed just 230 pounds, he had enormous upper body strength and could

A 17-14 victory over the Steelers at Three Rivers Stadium midway through the 1901 season served notice to the rest of the league that the 49ers were for real.

push aside much heavier offensive linemen. Dean usually was double-teamed, and he was virtually tackled at times — but nothing worked.

Perhaps the best example of Dean's value came in a game against the Rams at Candlestick Park. The 49ers secured a 20-17 victory by stopping the Rams on four fourth-quarter drives into San Francisco territory. Dean sacked quarterback Pat Haden four times and ran him into defensive end Lawrence Pillers for another sack.

The milestones kept piling up that year. "With every win, we just got more and more confidence," Clark said.

"Sports is so much momentum," Benjamin said. "You start playing better and you believe in yourself,

Not Your Average Joe

Before the 1979 draft, Bill Walsh worked out a skinny quarterback from Notre Dame—Joe Montana. History was about to be made. "As soon as I saw Joe drop back from a supposed center position ... oh, he was beautiful," Walsh said. "As he began to throw, I knew there wasn't anything he didn't have for our system."

Montana was not rated highly by other NFL teams. Though he engineered some sensational comebacks for the Irish, he was inconsistent and did not have the strong arm most coaches look for in a pro quarterback. Neither of those factors bothered Walsh. His system depended more on accuracy than on arm strength, and he felt that, with work, Montana could develop into a consistent quarterback. So he drafted him.

Walsh worked Montana into the lineup gradually, playing him only in specially selected situations his first year—usually when the 49ers were inside the other team's 20-yard line.

"We'd put in plays where we were certain there would be an open receiver," Walsh said, "to allow him to succeed and build up confidence." Montana improved swiftly, and by the end of the 1981 season he was the best quarterback in the league.

Walsh traded Steve DeBerg, the starting quarterback in 1979 and much of 1980, after the 1980 season. DeBerg was much more outgoing than Montana, and Walsh feared that the quiet quarterback would not assert himself as long as DeBerg was around.

Montana's competitive nature sometimes has been masked because he is reserved in public. With his teammates, though, he's always been more relaxed, quick to play pranks and practical jokes.

"He always messed with the bicycles in camp," former wide receiver Dwight Clark said. "There was a rental agency for bikes, and guys would rent them to get around the campus. [Then assistant coach] George Seifert had his name in big block letters on his, but if he parked it outside the cafeteria, Joe would just take it wherever he was going. And he was always taking bikes of other players and putting them up in the trees.

"One time, he got the sunglasses of [kicker] Ray Wersching and [guard] Guy McIntyre and put sunblack on the inside, so when Ray and Guy took off their glasses that day, they had big rings around their eyes. They looked like raccoons."

In the 49ers' locker room at their practice facility, there is a big bulletin board where players put up stories in which teammates say or do something ridiculous. Montana, Clark remembers, put up more articles and pictures than anybody else."

"Joe never wanted to be bothered," said defensive back Ronnie Lott, who became as close to Montana later in their careers as Clark had been early on. "He wanted to be like a Joe DiMaggio. He wanted to fit in, to be one of the boys. I admired him because he stuck to the way he was. He could easily have gone into the fast lane, to become another 'Broadway Joe,' but he didn't. He didn't compromise who he was."

On the field, of course, Montana was extraordinary, and his coach gave him the help and support he needed. Walsh eased Montana into the system by restricting his choices. On pass plays, for instance, Montana would use only half the field, with perhaps three receivers on that side. It was 1984 when Walsh finally opened the whole field, by which time Montana had become as adept as any other quarterback in NFL history at seeing all the possibilities on the field.

"I don't think there was any defining moment for Joe in 1981," said Guy Benjamin, who played behind Montana at quarterback and roomed with him in training camp and on the road. "He just manipulated the offense the way it's designed. Joe's ability to run the offense allowed other people to take advantage of it, and they started to believe in themselves.

"He wasn't a natural leader. But he commanded a tremendous amount of respect from other players, and I really think that, intuitively, other players respected his 'athletic intelligence.' They could look at him and say this was a different kind of player, that he was operating at a different level.

"He was tremendously motivated, tremendously competitive. I've never seen an athlete as competitive as he was. He just had something in him that was not going to let him fail. In 1981, he bought this big ranch in the Bay Area but he couldn't sell his house in Manhattan Beach. The guy had nothing in his bank account. I told him, 'You're going to lose everything if you're cut or get injured.' He looked at me like, 'What are you talking about? I'm going to make a lot of money.' It was not even in his thought process that he wouldn't."

There was another big factor in Montana's success: his courage. He never was a physically robust player, and he sustained a series of injuries over the years—the last time he played a full 16-game schedule was 1983. He had back surgery in 1986, and elbow injuries that sidelined him for all but one game in his last two seasons as a 49er (1991 and 1992).

Yet Montana always rebounded, even from the back surgery that convinced many, including his coach, that his career was over. Indeed, he led the 49ers to two more Super Bowl titles after that surgery, tying him with Terry Bradshaw as the only quarterbacks in NFL history with four Super Bowl rings.

"When you think about how fragile he's always seemed, and all those times that people were convinced that he was through," said Cross, his teammate for the first three of those Super Bowls, "it's truly remarkable what he's accomplished."

and then your buddy starts playing better and you've got to play even better to keep up with him—and then the breaks start coming."

A LANDMARK VICTORY

Another big victory came in Pittsburgh. "It was our defining moment," Benjamin said.

The Steelers, who won four Super Bowls in the 1970s, were especially tough at home where their vocal fans pack Three Rivers Stadium. They were also tough against NFC teams — they had not lost to an NFC team in Pittsburgh in ten years.

It's often gone unnoticed by the media, but consistency from the offensive line has played a big role in the 49ers' success. Tackle Keith Fahnhorst (71) and center Randy Cross (51) take a breather.

Walsh was pulling out all the emotional stops. "Bill was very, very good at getting people to work together," Cross said, "and he would get people psychologically ready to play better than anybody."

Walsh wasn't a typical football coach. "Don Shula was like a general," Benjamin said. "Bill was more like a captain in Army Intelligence. He had to convince you. He'd sometimes get angry and when he was spontaneous like that, it was effective, but that wasn't usually his personality. So instead of giving a traditional pep talk, he'd tell stories."

For this game, Walsh talked to his team about British troops in Burma during World War II

when they retreated until they had their backs to a mountain and had no choice but to fight. The 49ers, he said, also had their backs to the wall. "It's forty-five [players] against fifty thousand [fans]," Walsh said, sounding what would become a familiar "us-against-the-world" theme on road trips.

On a more practical note, Walsh also emphasized that the 49ers would have to out hit the Steelers. "This is the toughest team in the league," he told his team. "You've got to beat them physically or nobody will take you seriously."

His team took his message to heart. The game was very emotional and very physical—Carlton Williamson knocked two receivers out of the game, Calvin Sweeney and John Stallworth, breaking Stallworth's ribs. It was also another defensive triumph. Williamson set the tone for the game and he, Hicks, and Wright all had interceptions.

"To come into the locker room and see Bill Walsh jumping up and down like a kid—well, you knew it was something special," Clark said.

The victory over the Steelers raised the 49ers' record to 7-2, and there was an inevitability to the division championship because no other team in the NFC West won even half its games that season. Yet, it seemed incredible that this team, after all the bad years, could be doing what it was doing.

It wasn't until the 49ers beat the Cincinnati Bengals 21-3 to improve to 11-3 that their fans began to realize that, yes, it truly was happening. The Bengals were on their way to a division title too, but the 49ers beat them with ease. Two games later, San Francisco was 13-3, holding the best record in the NFL that season.

THE SECOND SEASON

Everybody was overwhelmed by the 49ers' presence in the playoffs, except the players. "We didn't think anything about it because we didn't know what we were doing," tackle Keith Fahnhorst said. "If we'd known what

FROM 6-FOOT, 6-INCH, 266-POUND TACKLE KEITH FAHNHORST, ON DEFENSIVE END FRED DEAN, WHOM THE 49ERS ACQUIRED IN 1981:

"I REMEMBER PLAYING AGAINST HIM IN A PRESEASON GAME IN 1975 WHEN HE WAS A ROOKIE. I LOOKED IN THE PROGRAM AND SAW SIX-TWO, 230 POUNDS, AND I LICKED MY CHOPS. ON THE FIRST PLAY HE FLEW BY ME SO FAST I NEVER EVEN SAW HIM."

we were doing, we probably wouldn't have done it."

"Bill made a huge deal about the playoffs," Cross said. "[Linebacker] Jack Reynolds talked about how different playoff games were. [Tight end] Charle Young did, too. We just felt, hell, we're happy to be playing another game. You guys have done this a lot—Hacksaw and Young had come from playoff teams in L.A.—but we'd never done it. If we win this one, they'll let us play another game."

Reynolds, the ultimate competitor, felt frustrated at first because he thought his teammates had a bad attitude. He told them, "You don't understand how this works." They told him, "No, you're the one who doesn't understand. You've never been two and fourteen."

"Our young guys got so good so fast," Cross said. "Those three defensive backs, specifically. They didn't have any time to get any perspective."

The offensive line was also coming together, developing the cohesiveness that made it an outstanding group for much of the 1980s. Fahnhorst came to the 49ers in 1974, Cross and guard John Ayers in 1976, and center Fred Quillan in 1978. Cross began his career at center, his college position, but Walsh moved him to guard in 1979 so Quillan could play center.

The one weak link was at left tackle where Walsh had to play the undersized (245 pounds) Audick, who had been playing guard. (The left tackle spot was a problem throughout the Walsh years. "It always seemed it was four of us and a tackle to be named later," Cross said.)

Of course, in 1981 the 49ers also had Joe Montana, who justified Walsh's confidence by having the first "great year" in a brilliant career that has led many football observers to call him the best quarterback of all time.

By his standards, Montana's statistics were good but not overwhelming that season: 311 completions in 488 attempts for 3,565 yards, 19 touchdowns, 12 interceptions, and a quarterback rating of 88.4. He later would have four seasons in which he threw for more yards, six in which he threw for more touchdowns, and six in which he had a higher quarterback rating.

Montana's better statistical years, though, came when he was playing for teams that had weapons such as the receiving duo of Jerry Rice and John Taylor, and runners such as Wendell Tyler and Roger Craig. In 1981, the 49ers' offense was Montana throwing to Dwight Clark (who led the NFC with 85 receptions) and Freddie Solomon. The running attack, which averaged only 3.5 yards per attempt, was almost nonexistent. The 49ers had to pass to win.

Montana was a dynamic, exciting player that year. He danced around in the backfield, eluding and frustrating pass rushers, while spotting an open receiver when it seemed the play was doomed to failure. His mobility was an integral part of Walsh's game plan that often called for Montana to roll out and throw on the run, which he did with incredible accuracy.

Most important, Montana had a special aura, exuding a confidence that — no matter what the circumstances — he could pull out the game. Walsh's design helped because Montana and the rest of the offense repeatedly practiced the plays that were used in the final two minutes of a half or game, so they were in a "comfort zone" when that time came during the game. But it took Montana's special competitive personality to make the most of Walsh's preparations.

"He's a person who likes to be against the odds, like Indiana Jones," said Lott, who became Montana's teammate that year and has remained a close friend. "It's not that he doesn't get nervous. He gets scared just like everybody else before the games. He's sitting there with his palms sweating. But then he goes out and does his thing."

The 49ers' first playoff game was against the New York Giants, an average team with one extraordinary player: rookie linebacker Lawrence Taylor, whose blitzes terrorized opposing quarterbacks.

As a result, teams ran more against the Giants than they normally did, but that actually made Taylor more of a factor because they would often get into obvious passing situations on third down, when Taylor would go full-bore for the quarterback.

BREAKING OLD HABITS

The 49ers won three of their first five games in 1981, but their next opponent was Dallas. The Cowboys had made a habit of beating the 49ers, and they'd smashed them 59-14 in Dallas the previous season. This game was different from the start, though, as the 49ers drove 61 yards to score after the opening kickoff, with Joe Montana throwing to Freddie Solomon for the touchdown.

The next time the 49ers got the ball, they marched 68 yards and scored on Paul Hofer's 4-yard touchdown run. Still in the first quarter, they scored again. After Ronnie Lott recovered a fumble at Dallas's 4-yard line, Johnny Davis ran 1 yard for the touchdown that made it 21-0.

The final score was 45-14. Montana completed 19 of 29 passes for 279 yards and 2 touchdowns. Overall, the 49ers had a 23-10 edge in first downs, ran 80 plays to Dallas's 53, and outgained the Cowboys 440 to 192.

Yes, the Cowboys had a bad day, but the 49ers obviously had arrived, as Landry noted after the game. "Most games that start out that way end up as lopsided games, if you're playing a good team. The 49ers are a good team."

Landry would discover just how good three months later in the NFC Championship Game.

Walsh knew the 49ers would first have to slow Taylor down, and he devised a two-pronged scheme to do it: first, instead of having a back try to block the 237-pound Taylor, he had guard John Ayers pull back from the line of scrimmage to block him; and, second, instead of running more, he passed more. He called 17 passes on the 49ers' first 23 plays, throwing in situations where the Giants expected a run and thus giving Montana the advantage of surprise.

The Giants were off balance for most of the game and the 49ers won 38-24. They were headed to the NFC Championship Game for the first time in a decade.

Bring on the Cowboys.

DETHRONING AMERICA'S TEAM

Growing up in New Jersey," safety Dwight Hicks said, "I hardly ever saw the 49ers. So the 49ers and Cowboys didn't mean anything to me until the week before that championship game. All I heard was Dallas, Dallas, Dallas — how the Cowboys had beaten the 49ers in the playoffs, how much everybody hated the Cowboys. So it became a very big game to us. We were ready for the challenge."

The Cowboys were an arrogant bunch, the self-proclaimed "America's Team." They crushed Tampa Bay 38-0 in the divisional playoffs and they were confident they'd beat the 49ers. All week long they made public comments to the effect that "the real Cowboys" hadn't shown up when they'd been routed 45-14 by the 49ers during the regular season.

"That's all we heard about — big, bad, Dallas, with the big physical Doomsday Defense," Cross said. "Poor little 49ers. First time was a fluke. We were insulted by all the talk."

Walsh was circumspect with his public comments, but he let loose in a tirade to his players about Dallas's arrogance. Walsh often used dramatic techniques to inspire his players, but this was from the heart. He hated the Cowboys. Beyond the rhetoric, though, Walsh felt his team matched up well against the Cowboys. Dallas was big and tough but the 49ers were quicker. "Bill always talked about beating people to the punch," Cross said. "He used a boxing analogy. If you beat your opponent by three-quarters of an inch, maybe it didn't mean

much in the first round or the fourth round, but by the seventh and eighth rounds, it would start to make a difference. He thought we could beat Dallas to the punch."

Walsh also knew he could dictate how the Cowboys would play defensively, just by the way the 49ers' lined up. Dallas was very predictable, using specific defenses against specific offensive formations. That was part of the Cowboys' arrogance because they were saying, in effect, "It doesn't make any difference that you know what we're going to do because we're going to do it anyway."

Walsh would make them regret that philosophy

Dwight Clark (87) and Freddie Solomon (88) gave Joe Montana a solid one-two punch at wide receiver in the early 1980s.

in this game because he would run plays that were not what they seemed. One example: He'd have a guard pull out to simulate a running play and when the Dallas defense "read" the "run," Montana would pass. That kind of play calling caused observers around the league to label the 49ers as a "finesse" team, which was a not-so-subtle way of saying that the 49ers weren't very physical. That was nonsense because Walsh emphasized hard-hitting to his team. It was true, though, that he put a premium on both mental and physical agility.

"That offense requires you to think more than any other offense," Cross said. "If you can't think,

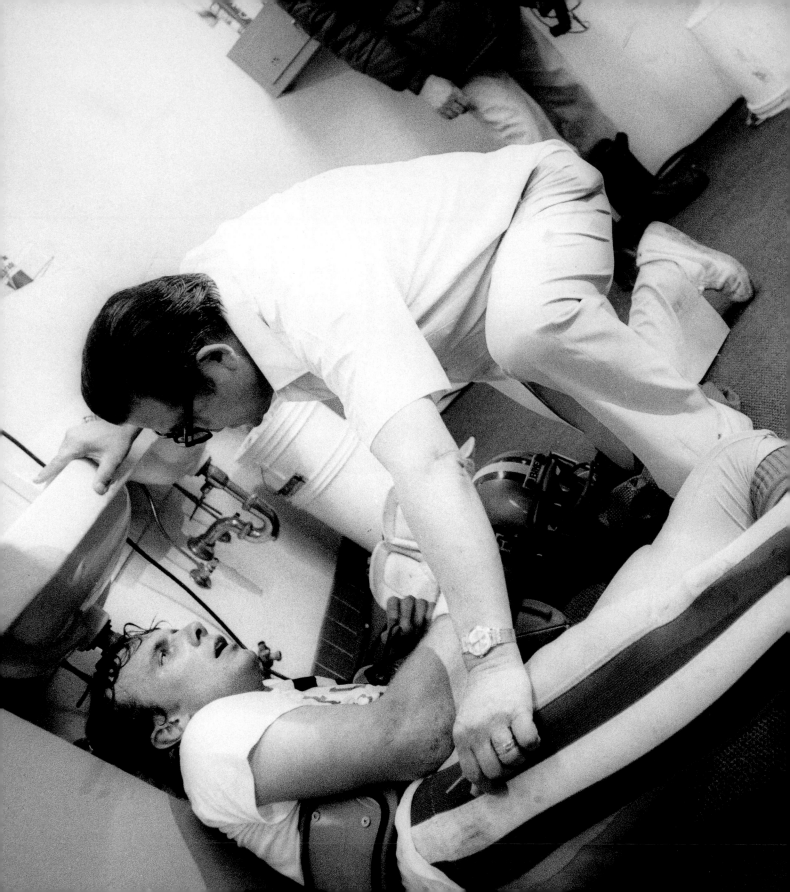

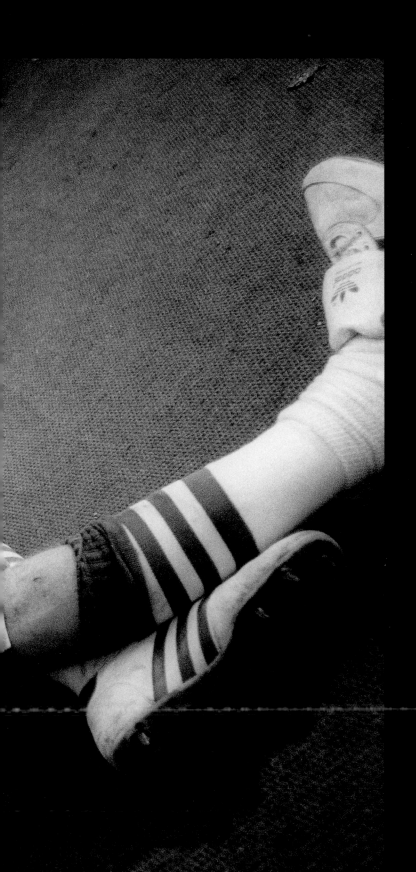

Scenes from the 49ers'
dramatic 28-27 victory over
the Cowboys in the 1981
NFC Championship Game.
Joe Montana (left) collapses
from exhaustion in the locker
room afterwards and is
attended to by equipment
manager Chico Norton; defensive back Ronnie Lott (above)
celebrates after Jim Stuckey
recovered Danny White's fumble in the closing seconds.

I WILL NOT BE OUT HIT ANY TIME THIS SEASON

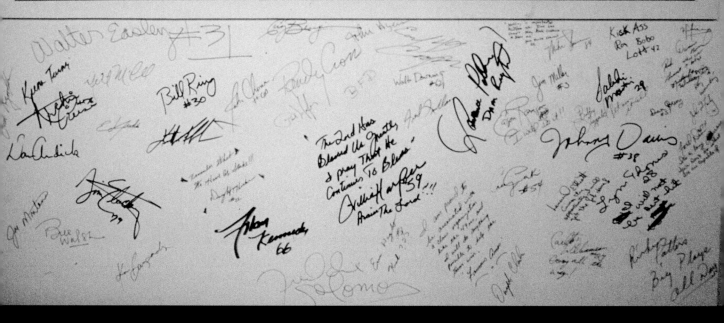

(Above) Bill Walsh vowed early in the 1981 season the 49ers would not be out hit by their opponents, and the players concurred; (left) Joe Montana's heroics gave him celebrity status; (opposite) guard John Ayers.

you can't play. Bill never liked really big linemen, either. He wanted guys who could move."

The Cowboys' bragging didn't shake the 49ers' confidence. "The closer the game got," Clark said, "Bill and [quarterbacks coach] Sam Wyche and all the rest of the coaches seemed to get more confident and looser about the game, like they knew we were better and they knew we should win. The day of the game, there was so much excitement and so much tension, but Bill was joking around in the dressing room. He had a way of getting people to just the right kind of tension. If he saw guys getting too tight, he'd come up with some kind of prank. We were at just the right level."

The game lived up to the pregame hype. It was almost nonstop excitement for three hours, give and take, up and down the field by both teams. The lead changed hands six times. There were spectacular plays on both sides of the line of scrimmage, controversial calls, an incredible drive by the 49ers at the end and, of course, the most memorable play in San Francisco sports history, "The Catch." The 49ers had a 28-27 victory and their first conference championship.

THE FIRST SUPER BOWL

The Dallas win, Dwight Clark said, made Super Bowl XVI seem "almost anticlimactic," which was one reason the 49ers were so much more relaxed about the game than their opponent, the Cincinnati Bengals.

Another reason was the coaches. Cincinnati's Forrest Gregg was grim. Walsh was determined to keep his players loose. When the 49ers arrived at their hotel in Detroit, a white-haired bellman came out to help with their bags, saying, "Let me help you with that." It took a few moments for the players to realize it was their coach. Walsh had arrived early because he had been in Washington, D.C., the night before to receive an award as coach of the year, and he conceived this gag to get his players laughing.

It went that way all week. The 49ers lost the coin flip for practice—both teams were practicing

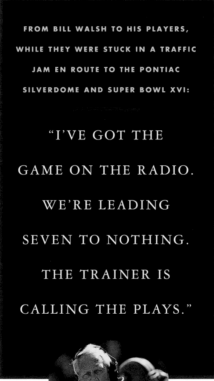

FROM BILL WALSH TO HIS PLAYERS, WHILE THEY WERE STUCK IN A TRAFFIC JAM EN ROUTE TO THE PONTIAC SILVERDOME AND SUPER BOWL XVI:

"I'VE GOT THE GAME ON THE RADIO. WE'RE LEADING SEVEN TO NOTHING. THE TRAINER IS CALLING THE PLAYS."

(Opposite) Joe Montana is introduced prior to Super Bowl XVI. He was named the most valuable player in the 49ers' 26-21 victory over the Bengals. This was the first of his record three Super Bowl MVP awards.

at the Silverdome—which meant they had to work out in the morning. Ostensibly, that was a disadvantage (the 49ers already were three time zones removed from San Francisco), and Walsh made much of it during press conferences during the week, but there was a flip side.

"We were done by two o'clock in the afternoon [after media interviews]," Cross said. "We had a really good time in Detroit. We partied like crazy. We went out every night. We had guys who didn't get a bunch of sleep. Friday night, we had a team meeting. Fahrnie [Fahnhorst] was up there saying, 'We've all been having a lot of fun here, and we really think it would be a good idea to impose a curfew on ourselves. Everybody in bed by eleven.'

"Some guys were saying, 'Yeah, that's a good idea,' and other guys were saying, 'No way.' Ronnie Lott got up and said, 'Look, I think we should just keep on doing what we've been doing because it's working. If you've been getting to bed at four in the morning and getting three hours sleep, do it. If you've been in bed at eleven, do it.' Well, that was just carte blanche, so everybody loved it."

The day of the game, one of the 49ers' buses, the one with Walsh on it, got caught in a traffic jam caused by the motorcade for then Vice President George Bush. Walsh kept everybody on the bus loose by carrying on a running gag about the trainer playing quarterback in the game and throwing touchdown passes to the equipment manager.

Walking down the tunnel into the dressing room, Dwight Hicks saw Cincinnati kicker Jimmy Breech. "We had played together briefly at Detroit, before both of us got cut," Hicks said. "Jimmy looked at me and said, 'Take it easy on us, Dwight.' You might think he was being sarcastic, but I was there. I could see his eyes. He meant it."

The 49ers were in an almost trance-like state, and none more than their star wide receiver. "I was walking down the sideline, just taking it all in, all the excitement and the noise," Clark said, "and then I realized I was on the wrong sideline. I had to get over to the right side in a hurry."

The 49ers weren't even shaken when Amos Lawrence fumbled the opening kickoff, with the Bengals recovering on San Francisco's 26-yard line. Six plays later, Cincinnati was on the 49ers' 11-yard line, and quarterback Ken Anderson dropped back to pass.

"I knew they were going to line up with three wide receivers and run a pick play on one of our DBs because we were in a man-to-man defense," Hicks said. "Sure enough, they ran a play and picked Eric, to try to free Isaac Curtis. I left my man and went over to defend Curtis."

When Anderson tried to hit Curtis, Hicks stepped in front of the receiver to intercept the ball and return it to the 49ers' 32-yard line.

"Two weeks later," Hicks said, "I was watching game films with George Seifert and he told me to look at that play. When we were in a man defense, I never took my eyes off my man because if you do that, you're lost. But this time I did. I never would leave my man, either, but again, I did this time. George said, 'Great play, but if your man had scored, I'd have jumped all over you.'

"Then he told me to look at what Eric was doing, and I saw that Eric, as soon as he'd seen me leave my man, had picked him up. George asked me if we'd talked about doing that before the game and I said we hadn't. It was incredible because it looked as if we'd planned it, but that was just the kind of chemistry we had that year."

After the interception the 49ers drove sixty-eight yards to score the game's first touchdown on a 1-yard sneak by Montana. Once again, Walsh's strategy paid off. The day before the game he added an un-balanced line to his game plan, and the Bengals were unprepared for it.

The first half was all 49ers. They recovered a Cincinnati fumble on their own 8-yard line and drove 92 yards, with Earl Cooper catching an 11-yard pass from Montana for the touchdown.

They got a 22-yard field goal from Ray

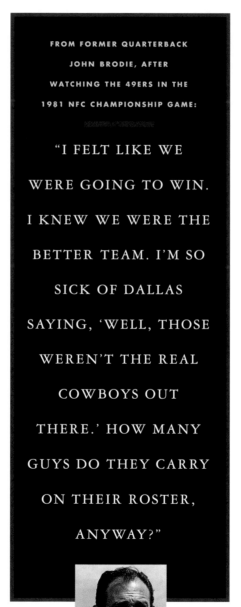

FROM FORMER QUARTERBACK JOHN BRODIE, AFTER WATCHING THE 49ERS IN THE 1981 NFC CHAMPIONSHIP GAME:

"I FELT LIKE WE WERE GOING TO WIN. I KNEW WE WERE THE BETTER TEAM. I'M SO SICK OF DALLAS SAYING, 'WELL, THOSE WEREN'T THE REAL COWBOYS OUT THERE.' HOW MANY GUYS DO THEY CARRY ON THEIR ROSTER, ANYWAY?"

Wersching just fifteen seconds before the half, and then a gift on the ensuing kickoff. Wersching had been practicing squib kicks all week, and this one was fumbled by the Bengals' Archie Griffin. Milt McColl recovered on the Bengals' 4-yard line, and Wersching kicked another field goal with only two seconds left on the clock.

The 20-0 lead was the biggest yet at half-time of a Super Bowl, but quarterbacks coach Sam Wyche wrote on the dressing room blackboard, "This game is not over yet." Wyche knew how quickly momentum can swing in a football game, which it did in the second half.

When the 49ers' offense suddenly stalled, Cincinnati dominated the third quarter. The Bengals drove 83 yards for a touchdown following the second-half kick-off, got into 49ers' territory on their second drive before being forced to punt, and drove to a first down on San Francisco's 3-yard line on their next possession. The game's most dramatic sequence would follow.

On first down, 249-pound fullback Pete Johnson punched the ball to the 1 yard line. On second down, linebacker Dan Bunz stopped Johnson for no gain. On third down, Bunz again made a great save, stopping running back Charles Alexander, who caught a pass from Anderson, perhaps six-inches short of the goal line.

In the regular-season game between the 49ers and Bengals, Johnson averaged more than 7 yards per carry. Defensive line coach Bill McPherson told Jack Reynolds that Johnson tipped off when he was going to carry the ball: if he wasn't going to get the ball, he draped his left arm loosely over his knee, but when he was going to get it, he had that arm held tightly against his body. McPherson waited until after the game to tell Reynolds because the 49ers were winning easily and the coach felt the teams might meet again in the Super Bowl, when that knowledge would be important.

Reynolds didn't tell his teammates—"I didn't want to confuse them," he said—but he used that

Bill Walsh rode the shoulders of his team after the 49ers' first Super Bowl victory (XVI). He would experience the euphoria of NFL titles twice more (Super Bowls XIX and XXIII).

Ray Wersching gave the 49ers consistency in the kicking game for eleven seasons (1977–87).

Johnson, and Reynolds shot the gap between the linemen, standing up the fullback short of the goal line. The entire 49ers' defensive line collapsed around Johnson with Archie Reese on the top of the pile squirming with joy.

There were still many anxious moments ahead, though. After forcing the 49ers to punt, the Bengals drove 53 yards for a touchdown, with Anderson passing 4 yards to Dan Ross for the score. Now it was 20-14 with more than ten minutes left—plenty of time for Cincinnati to win the game, especially since the 49ers' offense was moribund: no first downs in the second half.

Finally, the 49ers put together a drive. With the key play a 22-yard pass to Mike Wilson on the second play of the drive, they moved to Cincinnati's 23-yard line. Wersching's 40-yard field goal increased the advantage to 23-14 with 5:25 remaining.

Wersching was renowned for refusing to look at his target before kicking. He would walk onto the field with his head down, put his hand on holder Montana's shoulder to line himself up with the goal post, and then kick. The 49ers didn't care what kind of routine he followed, only that he was very accurate. Wersching got another chance minutes later after Eric Wright intercepted Anderson's pass and returned it 25 yards to the Bengals' 22-yard line.

Playing conservatively to use up the clock, the 49ers settled for a 23-yard field goal, Wersching's Super Bowl-record-tying fourth, to make it 26-14 with 1:57 to go. Cincinnati came back to score a touchdown, but only 0:16 remained. Clark smothered the subsequent onside kick to clinch the 26-21 victory.

The players were in a trance. "That was the weirdest feeling," Cross said. "We were getting in the bus afterward, and somebody had 'We are the Champions' playing. We're just having a good time and suddenly it was like, 'Who do we play next?' We realized our season was over."

At a party that night, Walsh was savoring the experience. "You know, if you told me I'd have to wait twenty years for this, I'd have done it because this is such a great feeling," he said.

"Bill, we need another of these," Eddie DeBartolo, Jr., told him. "And in less than twenty years."

information early in the Super Bowl, in less critical situations. Now it was vital. He noticed that Alexander had cheated a little toward the line of scrimmage on the right side, so he probably would be the blocker. Johnson, a human bowling ball, had his left arm tight against his side.

When the ball was snapped, Bunz hit Alexander so hard he lost his chin strap and broke the clamp on his helmet. Alexander was knocked back into

THE NIGHTMARE SEASON

The 1981 season was a dream; 1982 a nightmare. Everything went right in '81; everything went wrong in '82.

The 49ers avoided injuries to key players in 1981, but in 1982, there were dozens of injuries. The miserable year included a players' strike that limited the season to nine games, of which the 49ers could win only three.

"I was more embarrassed going three and six that season than two and fourteen in 1978 and 1979," Cross said. "We had too much ability for that."

Joe Montana had a different problem: coming to grips with his new-found celebrity. In the aftermath of the victory in Super Bowl XVI, he noted, "People come up at seven in the morning and knock on my door. They'll sit in their cars in the driveway and just stare at the house. They're driving me crazy."

In 1981, Montana married Cathleen Castillo, an airline stewardess. By 1982, that marriage was dissolving, though the divorce wouldn't be final until 1984, and he moved in with Dwight and Ashley Clark. "People would come up to the house just to see Joe coming and going," Ashley said. "One couple sat out in front and painted my picture while I was sitting at the breakfast table in my robe. One girl used to come by and leave beer for Joe. She didn't try to see him. She'd just leave it and say, 'This is for Joe.'"

Some athletes love that kind of attention, but Montana was acutely uncomfortable with it. Still, even though the team was disintegrating around him, Montana continued to play at a very high level. He completed more than 60 percent of his passes in 1982, threw more touchdown passes (17) than interceptions (11), and had a quarterback rating of 87.9, almost as good as his 88.2 the season before. He was the only bright spot in an otherwise dismal season.

Walsh was so upset that he did not even talk to the team in the traditional postseason meeting the day after the final game, leaving that to administrative vice president John McVay. "I seriously thought at that point that I was going to leave coaching," Walsh said. "I told Eddie DeBartolo, and he said he understood what I was feeling and that he would support whatever decision I made."

For those who knew Walsh, his emotional turmoil came as no surprise. On the sidelines, he

MONTANA'S SIDEKICK

Dwight Clark is the best example of how Bill Walsh made independent decisions. Walsh was looking for a quarterback in the 1979 draft, and he had gone to Clemson to scout Steve Fuller, who threw to Clark in workouts staged for the 49ers' coach. Walsh quickly dismissed Fuller as a draft possibility, but he was intrigued by Clark, who hadn't even been Clemson's number-one receiver that season and was not listed among the top fifty prospects in scouting reports.

Walsh liked a big wide receiver who could catch passes over the middle and take punishment, and Clark was exactly that kind of receiver. The 49ers took him in the tenth round, surprising Clark as much as anybody.

"I was just real excited about the opportunity," Clark said, "and I thought that was all it was — an opportunity to come out here and have a tryout, and then be cut. [In fact, Clark brought his golf clubs to camp, figuring that he would play some of California's top courses before he returned home.] I remember thinking at the time that it would be a great story to tell my kids, that I was actually drafted by a pro team.

"That first year, they'd bring in receivers every week. I never really knew for sure that I was going to make it. I didn't catch a pass until the tenth or eleventh game. I didn't feel I was part of the team until then."

That first year was also memorable because in training camp Clark met quarterback Joe Montana, and the two became fast friends.

Clark remembers sitting at the lunch counter of a restaurant. "The guy opposite me was kind of frail looking, with a Fu Manchu moustache. I'm trying to figure out if this guy is a player. I thought he was a kicker. I introduced myself. When he said, 'Joe Montana,' my jaw dropped. We played Notre Dame when I was at Clemson. We were beating them seventeen to seven, and he brought them back and beat us twenty-one to seventeen, so I thought he was a great quarterback even then."

Within three years, Montana had become the 49ers' star quarterback and Clark the team's most dependable wide receiver. They combined on many important pass plays, including The Catch that won the first championship ever for the 49ers.

Clark and Montana were inseparable. Between marriages, Montana stayed with Clark and his wife, Ashley.

Just after the 49ers' first championship, Ashley, Dwight, and Montana were sitting in a restaurant. A stream of people came by to say hello, ask for autographs, and say, "That Dallas game was fantastic. You guys were something else! What a great play that was against Dallas!"

"I didn't watch the Dallas game," Ashley said. "I didn't even watch the Super Bowl because I wasn't a football fan before I met Dwight. So finally I had to say, 'Just what the hell is it that you guys did in the Dallas game that was so good?'"

appeared almost professorial, in complete control, but that masked an emotional cauldron within. Walsh has always internalized problems. He could not separate his emotions from the team, and the problems players were having were his as well.

"The stress of the first two years showed up in 1982," he said. "I'd been personally managing the whole operation and didn't even realize how big a job that was. Most other teams had four people doing what I was doing."

As he went away to sort out his emotions, Walsh considered three college coaches who might replace him: Mike White, who had been a member of his first staff and was the head coach at Illinois; John Robinson, head coach at USC; and Terry Donahue, head coach at UCLA. He was confident that any of the three would work as the 49ers' coach.

Each of the three, though, told him he was comfortable with his job and didn't want to leave to come to the 49ers. Walsh later realized that White, Robinson, and Donahue all knew that the best move would be for Walsh to remain as coach and that he would eventually understand that himself.

The final nudge, if it can be characterized so gently, came from football friends Jim Finks and Jim Hanifan, when they joined Walsh at the Senior Bowl in Mobile, Alabama. Both Finks and Hanifan told him, in effect, to quit feeling sorry for himself and get back to work.

Walsh came back from the Senior Bowl recharged—but also came back to a significantly depleted coaching staff. Sam Wyche left, with Walsh's blessing, to become head coach at the University of Indiana, and special teams coach Milt Jackson, running backs coach Billie Matthews, and defensive coordinator Chuck Studley all left for jobs with other NFL teams. Walsh may have delayed his decision to return to allow time for assistants to leave. He undoubtedly would have made some changes, as he did throughout his time with the 49ers, because he believed that bringing in new assistants with different ideas kept his approach fresh.

It was especially important that Studley leave on

Bill Walsh was an introspective coach, and the disastrous season of 1982 had him contemplating retirement. But by 1984, the 49ers were again the best team in football.

A LOTT OF HEART

Bill Walsh knew he needed to strengthen his defensive backfield in the 1981 NFL draft. He coveted USC All-America Ronnie Lott, but thought he'd be gone before the 49ers' turn came in the first round. His backup choice was Ken Easley. The UCLA safety wanted to come to San Francisco so much that he had his attorney, Leigh Steinberg, send out a letter to clubs drafting ahead of the 49ers, saying he wouldn't play for them.

Easley's bluff didn't work: Seattle drafted him. Then came one of those draft-day surprises: the St. Louis Cardinals selected linebacker E. J. Junior instead of Hugh Green, another line-backer who was rated much higher. Tampa Bay, which probably would have taken Lott, grabbed Green. The grateful Walsh picked Lott.

The 49ers had caught a break, and a big one. Easley played well for the Seahawks before a kidney ailment prematurely ended his career, but Lott was a great player for the 49ers, first as a cornerback and then as a safety. He is all-but-certain to be elected to the Pro Football Hall of Fame.

In 1981, the 49ers also drafted cornerback Eric Wright and safety Carlton Williamson. All three rookies were immediate starters and became very good very fast. They were an important part of the 1981 Super Bowl champions.

"We all pushed ourselves," Lott said, "and we were fortunate to have George Seifert as our backfield coach. George was a no-nonsense kind

of coach. He really got the most out of us. He might have pushed us when we didn't want to be pushed, but I have to attribute a lot of our success that year to him.

"He kept us out at practice every day after everybody else was finished. It became a joke with the rest of the team. They'd say, 'God, are you ever going to give those guys a break?' George would go on his runs and he'd take us with him. That's how close we were as a group."

Lott was a ferocious competitor, known for his bone-jarring tackles. "There would be games where we'd be playing at one level," Seifert noted, "and then Ronnie would really stick somebody, and all of a sudden, our level of play would go up a notch."

It is no coincidence that the rest of the defensive backfield was very physical when Lott was with the 49ers. "If you play in a backfield with Ronnie Lott," wide receiver Dwight Clark said, "you either hit or you don't play."

Lott was the heart and soul of the 49ers. On the field, he was constantly screaming at his teammates to play better and do more. Off the field, he was just as vocal, a leader in the club-house and a man willing to counsel younger players who were struggling.

Away from football, there is another side of Ronnie Lott that is quite different from the foot-ball competitor. He is a soft-spoken, thoughtful man who has generously given time and money to charities, especially youth groups.

A very special player, a very special man.

his own because Walsh would have found it difficult to fire him. Walsh and Studley had been close when they were assistants in Cincinnati, driving to prac-tice together and bouncing ideas off one another, and Walsh had brought Studley to the 49ers. Studley's approach worked well in 1981, but the 49ers slipped defensively in 1982, and Walsh thought that an important part of the problem was that Studley had not adjusted to changes in the game.

Studley's defenses were designed to stop the run, but Walsh felt he needed a defensive coordinator who could devise more sophisticated defenses against the pass, and he thought defensive backfield coach George Seifert was his man. When Studley left voluntarily, Walsh was free to elevate Seifert to defensive coordinator.

Seifert had an innovative defensive mind. More than anybody else, he popularized the use of "sit-uation substitution," using defensive specialists at a time when teams generally were making few sub-stitutions. When the 49ers' drafted Jeff Fuller in 1984, he used Fuller as a combination linebacker/ defensive back, making use of Fuller's rare combina-tion of strength and speed. Seifert was as imagina-tive with his defensive approach as Walsh was on offense, and the two worked together brilliantly until Walsh retired and recommended Seifert as his successor.

In 1981, the 49ers had been dismissed as "doing it with mirrors." Dallas coach Tom Landry, bitter in defeat after the NFC Championship Game, said, "They've got Joe Montana and nothing else." Walsh was called a genius for taking unknown players and making them champions, but the feeling was that 1981 was a fluke. When the 49ers fell to earth with a resounding thud in 1982, that opinion was reinforced.

ON THE MEND

Nineteen eighty-three, then, was special. Though it was not a Super Bowl year (San Francisco went 10-6 but lost in the NFC Championship Game), it proved that the 49ers' belonged among the NFL's elite teams. In fact, it was the first of twelve consecutive ten-victory seasons (through 1994)—an NFL record.

There was also a significant attitude change:

from that point, the 49ers would play with special determination. Walsh made some important changes. First, he traded second- and fourth-round draft picks to the Rams for running back Wendell Tyler and two others.

Tyler was superfluous for the Rams, who had drafted Eric Dickerson, but he turned out to be the 49ers' best running back since Delvin Williams. When Walsh drafted Nebraska's Roger Craig that spring, the 49ers suddenly had two quality backs.

The difference Tyler and Craig made was apparent from the beginning. The 49ers demolished Minnesota 48-17 in week 2, and trounced St. Louis 42-27 in week 3. Montana threw 4 touchdown passes against the Vikings and 3 against the Cardinals. In each game, Tyler balanced Montana's passing with more than 100 yards rushing.

The 49ers would go on to score 432 points in 1983, 75 more than the 1981 Super Bowl champi-

Veteran Wendell Tyler (far left) and rookie Roger Craig (33) teamed in 1983 to give the 49ers their best rushing attack in years.

ons and more than any other 49ers team since the club joined the NFL in 1950. The 49ers had to win their final game to win the division, and they walloped Dallas 42-17 on Monday Night. Perhaps the "real Cowboys" didn't show up for that game, either.

The 49ers got lucky in their first playoff game, beating Detroit 24-23 when the Lions' Eddie Murray missed a 43-yard field-goal attempt on the final play. Their luck, though, ran out the following week against the Washington Redskins in the NFC Championship Game.

The Redskins were building a reputation — which would be deflated rudely by the Raiders in Super Bowl XVIII — as a dynasty. The defending Super Bowl champions went 14-2 during the regular season in 1983, then crushed the Rams 51-7 in a divisional playoff game. Their offensive line was known as "The Hogs" because of its immense size,

WOULD ONLY ROO for DALLAS PLAYED

MAMA'S DON'T LET YOUR BABIES GROW UP TO BE COWBOYS

MERRY XMAS RANDY, BETTY, CHAD, AND NAY!!!

and many of their fans wore pig-snout masks to the games. Their fullback, John Riggins, was regarded as unstoppable, and few experts gave the 49ers much of a chance in the championship game, especially since wide receiver Dwight Clark was out with a torn tendon suffered in the season's final game.

The scouting reports seemed accurate when the Redskins breezed to a 21-0 lead after three quarters. Everybody was convinced of the outcome — except the 49ers. "We were embarrassed, because they weren't better than us," Cross said. "We'd just played badly."

In the fourth quarter, Joe Montana mounted a comeback that ranks among his best. First, he took his team 79 yards in nine plays, hitting Mike Wilson for the touchdown that made it 21-7. Then, one play after Mark Moseley missed a 41-yard

Passion for the 49ers (and disdain for the Cowboys) is more than skin-deep among San Francisco citizens.

field-goal attempt, Montana teamed with Freddie Solomon on a 76-yard touchdown pass. The 49ers trailed by just a touchdown, and nearly ten minutes remained.

The 49ers scored quickly again the next time they got the ball, moving 53 yards in four plays. Montana's 12-yard touchdown pass to Wilson tied the game 21-21. "That was the weirdest feeling," backup quarterback Guy Benjamin said. "When we tied the game, there was dead silence. People were in total shock."

Then came controversy. On the Redskins' next possession, they faced second-and-10 from San Francisco's 45-yard line when quarterback Joe Theismann threw long to Art Monk. The ball sailed far behind Monk's reach but Eric Wright was called for pass interference on the 18-yard line. An irate

Walsh later said, "A Boston Celtics player couldn't have caught that pass." Three plays later, on third-and-5 from the 13-yard line, Theismann threw an incomplete pass, but Ronnie Lott was called for holding a receiver on the other side of the field.

Given an automatic first down, the Redskins were able to run three more plays, taking the clock down to 40 seconds left. Moseley, who had missed 4 field-goal attempts, made this one from 25 yards away. The 49ers had little time left to come back, and Montana was intercepted.

So the Redskins won the game, but the 49ers came away thinking they were the better team.

"We could have sneaked into the Super Bowl that year," Walsh said, "but that game launched us into a great 1984 season."

THE PERFECTIONISTS

Before that season, though, there was a public exchange of words between coach and quarterback. "There are too many times when Joe runs out of the pocket and can't get the ball to his receivers," Walsh said after the championship game. "The worst is when he runs to the right and the pattern is set up to the left. Then he really has no chance to complete the pass.

"This is a common problem for teams with mobile quarterbacks. The Vikings had it with Fran Tarkenton early in his career. There's a 'fine line.' We don't want Joe to never leave the pocket because his ability to scramble when the protection breaks down is a real asset, but we do want him to develop more discipline."

"It works both ways," Montana said. "Sometimes I should stay in the pocket, but sometimes there's nothing there so I try to make something happen. I admit, sometimes I get carried away, but what difference does it make if I throw the ball away from the pocket or throw it away after I've been running around for awhile?"

Both public and private comments reflected a tension in the Walsh-Montana relationship that existed until Walsh retired as the 49ers' coach, at which point the two became close in a way they never could be while they were collecting Super Bowl rings.

On one level, each recognized the debt he owed to the other: Montana would not have been as effective a quarterback in another system; Walsh would not have been so successful with another quarterback. They worked together as well as any other coach and quarterback in NFL history, ever, with Montana the physical extension of Walsh's intellect. But both wanted their full measure of credit, too. There were times Walsh thought people idolized Montana without fully realizing how important the system was, and there were times Montana thought that people talked of Walsh as a "genius" without fully understanding that the system wouldn't be so successful if he hadn't been there.

Joe Montana and Bill Walsh worked together as well as any other coach and quarterback in NFL history.

Each man was a perfectionist, too. When Walsh criticized Montana (he praised Montana far more than he ever criticized), it was only because his quarterback fell short of perfection—though not by much.

A STEAMROLLER

In 1984, though, both Montana and the 49ers would come as close to perfection as anybody ever could in the football world, and it started with a great draft that showed how far Walsh had taken the team.

In his early years, Walsh had to draft players who could help immediately, even if there was little chance they would improve. Now he could draft players who had some question marks but good potential.

After the 49ers' first pick, linebacker Todd Shell (whose career ended prematurely due to injury), the next four picks all came with questions attached: Tight end John Frank was a pre-med student who would retire early to become a doctor, but not until he'd given the 49ers five good years; guard Guy McIntyre was undersized at 271 pounds but had great agility and soon became a fixture in the offensive line; Michael Carter was an Olympic shot-putter for whom football appeared to be a sideline, but he became the dominant nose tackle in the NFL; and Jeff Fuller seemed a man without a position, not quick enough to play cornerback and not big enough to play linebacker. But defensive coordinator Seifert created a position for Fuller, who sometimes played zone pass coverage and sometimes defended against the run.

The 1984 season established Walsh's credentials as a special kind of football man, one who had combined coaching ability with executive talent to assemble a great franchise.

In 1981, Walsh was hailed as a genius because he won the Super Bowl with a team that did not seem to be supremely talented. By 1984, he put together a team that was far better than the 1981 champions, one that would rank with the NFL's all-time best.

Of his three Super Bowl teams, Walsh regards the 1984 champions as the best, and players who were members of all three of those teams agree. "That's the Super Bowl ring I wear," Cross said.

The acquisition of defensive end Fred Dean was the last piece of the defensive puzzle for the 49ers in 1981.

"It's the best team I ever played on," Lott said. "That was a great team, a dominating team. We had a lot of great players. I don't know if you could ever put anybody in a category with [defensive end] Fred Dean. We had [nose tackle] Gary [Big Hands] Johnson. [Defensive end] Dwaine Board had one of his best years. [Nose tackle] Michael Carter was a young, aggressive guy. The front seven was more dominant than the front seven we had in later years."

The loss in the NFC Championship Game the year before was the great motivator. "Everybody was on such a mission," Cross said, "because we knew the Redskins weren't better than us. We were obsessed in training camp with the idea that we were going to the Super Bowl. We really got on a

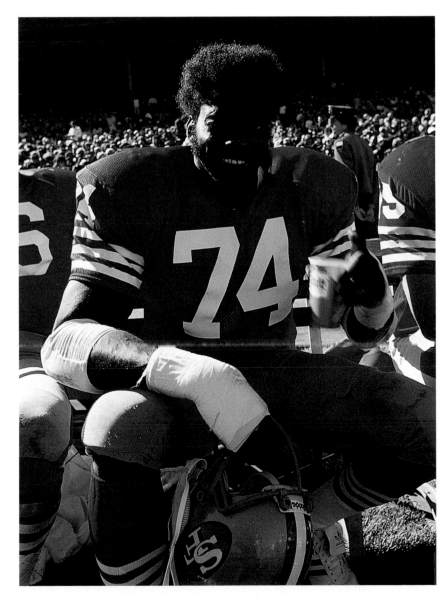

THE WEST COAST OFFENSE

Bill Walsh's offensive system has been the key to the 49ers' success.

Walsh's system was flexible enough to improve every quarterback he coached, whatever their skill level. He coached Guy Benjamin and Steve Dils to NCAA passing championships at Stanford—yet neither quarterback was more than a backup in the NFL. He coached Virgil Carter, a good athlete with an average arm who led the NFL in completion percentage in 1971. He won games for the 49ers with journeymen quarterbacks Jeff Kemp, Mike Moroski, and Matt Cavanaugh.

When he had quarterbacks with outstanding skills—Ken Anderson, Dan Fouts, Joe Montana, Steve Young—he made them great.

Options are the key to Walsh's system. "At Tampa Bay, I'd be told just to look for an open man and hit him," Young said. "With the 49ers, there's a definite progression. You look for your first receiver. If he's covered, you look to your second, then to your third. There's always an open man."

In Walsh's offense, quarterbacks and receivers both read the defense. Receivers take a couple of steps to see how the defense reacts. If defenders drop back in a zone, the receiver runs one type of pattern; if they take a receiver man-to-man, the receiver runs a different route. The quarterback is reading the defense at the same time, so he knows where the receiver will be.

There are endless variations—literally hundreds of pass plays in the 49ers' playbook—because the same patterns can be run from different formations, making it impossible for the defense to predict where the ball will be thrown.

The innovative Walsh made it even more difficult by "scripting" the offense's first twenty to twenty-five plays of the game.

By the 1980s, NFL coaches were using computers to detect patterns, or tendencies, in their opponents' play-calling. Should circumstances so dictate, the 49ers could change their planned plays, but for the most part they stuck to what Walsh had written before the game. That made it impossible for coaches to plan on what the 49ers might call on third-and-6, for instance, because the call had been made before Walsh knew what the down and distance would be.

Walsh was certainly conscious of that. Knowing that coaches got films of the previous three 49ers' games, he often would go four games back to repeat unusual plays.

His system was a low-risk, high-percentage one, designed to give quarterbacks wide-open receivers. "Any quarterback should be able to complete sixty percent of his passes in this system," Young said. In fact, both Young and Montana have been well over 60 percent in their 49ers' careers, and each quarterback had a season in which he completed more than 70 percent of his passes.

Walsh's system was also designed to keep the chains moving with first downs. That helped San Francisco's defense because, by controlling the ball on offense, it gave them additional rest.

roll after awhile. It was an amazing feeling, like Mike Tyson fighting middleweights. It didn't matter who we played. We stomped everyone."

Cross called it "justifiable arrogance."

"We knew the season wouldn't be over until the Super Bowl," he said. "That's one of the things that makes this organization special. They regard the dates of postseason games as important as the regular season because they expect to get there."

Walsh finally achieved the team attitude that he had been striving for, an attitude that would carry the 49ers through traumatic moments in years to come. "As each year passed," he said, "we had more and more of a really committed football player. The selection of players, the peer pressure. People molded right into it."

The 49ers' 1984 edition had an excellent defense that exerted unrelenting pressure on other teams. It had a great one-two running punch in Wendell Tyler and Roger Craig, plus balance among its receiving corps, with Craig the top pass catcher (71 receptions), Dwight Clark the leader in yardage (880), and Freddie Solomon tops in touchdowns (10).

Most of all, that team had Joe Montana at his best. "He might have thrown better later," Cross said, "but as far as the complete package, with his ability to throw the ball and his ability to run with it, that was the peak of Joe's abilities." Like the question of which came first, the chicken or the egg, the question for those who have looked closely at the 49ers is whether the system made Montana or vice versa. The right answer is: both of the above.

Montana was the ideal quarterback for Walsh's system because he had the ability to use all of it. His mind could process what his eyes were seeing on the field within seconds of the snap from center, and his arm would then deliver soft passes to his receivers with such accuracy that the receivers could catch the balls in stride and often turn short passes into long gains.

Walsh could have done well with another quarterback, but he realized that to get the absolute most out of his system, he needed Montana. "Joe is as coachable an athlete as any I've ever worked with," Walsh said. "He will listen and learn and adapt. He has great intuition and instinct. He became measurably better each year."

With Montana at the controls, the 49ers

The 49ers of 1984 achieved the team cohesiveness and unity that Bill Walsh longed for.

bulldozed the field that year, losing only one game (to Pittsburgh 20-17) and outscoring their opponents by more than two-to-one (475 points scored, only 227 allowed).

The tipoff came in the second game of the season, when the 49ers jumped to a 27-0 lead over the Redskins at Candlestick Park. Though Washington came back in the second half to make the game respectable, eventually falling 37-31, the 49ers were never in danger of losing. "We just outplayed them completely, just overwhelmed them," Walsh said, "so you could see we were a much better club."

The season's lone loss was marred by a disputed pass-interference call on Eric Wright at the goal line that set up a Pittsburgh touchdown, a penalty that still rankles Walsh. "If it hadn't been for that call, we could have had a perfect season," he said. "On the other hand, maybe it sobered us up and made us play better the rest of the year."

The loss came in the seventh game of the season, and the 49er steamroller picked up speed after that. The 49ers had a couple of letdowns against weak opponents—they trailed Cincinnati 17-7 at halftime before pulling out a 23-17 victory and beat Tampa Bay by only a touchdown—but they won most games easily. There were a number of routs in the second half of the season: 33-0 over the Rams, 41-7 over Cleveland, 35-3 over New Orleans, and 51-7 over Minnesota.

DEMANDING RESPECT

Even after such an overwhelming season and a 21-10 victory over the New York Giants in the divisional playoffs, some observers thought the 49ers would lose to the Chicago Bears in the NFC Championship Game. "Our battle cry all year," Lott said, "was that nobody gave us the respect we earned."

The Bears, who played defensive coordinator Buddy Ryan's "46 Defense," were an intriguing team. They would put as many as eight men on or close to the line of scrimmage with the intent of both pressuring and confusing the quarterback, who never knew how many of the eight would be rushing him. Nor could the offensive linemen be sure who they should be blocking, which meant the running lanes often were blocked, too.

Any defense is only as good as the players, of course, and Chicago had some great ones, including defensive linemen Richard Dent and Dan Hampton and middle linebacker Mike Singletary. The Bears also had a great tradition dating to founder George Halas, one of the most important figures in the early development of the NFL. In another year,

Jack Reynolds (64) brought leadership and experience to the 49ers' defense. Below, rookies Michael Carter (95) and Mike Walter (99) get a sideline lesson in 1984.

they would be the league's dominant team.

Not this year, though. It was the 49ers' defense that was overwhelming in the title game, sacking Chicago quarterback Steve Fuller nine times en route to a 23-0 victory. Fuller passed for just 87 yards and gave back 50 of them on sacks.

There was a sidelight to the game. To get stronger blocking on the goal line, Walsh put guard Guy McIntyre into the backfield on what he called the "Angus" play. Bears coach Mike Ditka, who never liked Walsh and tended to take everything personally, saw that as an insult, so the next year, he put defensive tackle William "The Refrigerator" Perry in the backfield and even used him as a ball carrier on similar plays.

The Angus play was significant only as a trivia

Defensive ends Dwaine Board (left) and Lawrence Pillers stretch in the locker room prior to Opening Day, 1984.

item. More important, Walsh learned from a 13-3 loss to the Bears the previous season when Singletary destroyed the 49ers' offensive continuity with blitzes up the middle. In that game, the 49ers used a back to block Singletary, but that didn't work. This time, Walsh had guards Randy Cross and John Ayers check to see if Singletary was coming and then to check for a blitz from an outside linebacker. The Bears never sent the middle and outside linebackers on the same play.

Walsh also instructed Montana to throw quickly, before the Bears' outside pass rushers could get to him, and he was sacked only once in the game. The 49ers' offense wasn't overwhelming at first, scoring only on 2 field goals by Ray Wersching in the first half, but Tyler's 9-yard touchdown run in the third quarter helped break the game open.

THE SECOND RING

The 49ers were back in the Super Bowl.

Unlike baseball's World Series, which alternates between the two teams' home parks, the Super Bowl almost always has been played at a neutral site. Only in January,

1980, when the Los Angeles Rams played in Super Bowl XIV at the Rose Bowl in Pasadena, California, had a team played in its home area.

Stanford Stadium, site of Super Bowl XIX, wasn't the home field for the 49ers, but it's only a short drive down the peninsula from Candlestick Park.

The pregame buildup centered on Dan Marino, the Miami Dolphins' quarterback who set NFL records with 362 completions, 5,084 yards, and an astounding 48 touchdowns in 1984.

Montana had an outstanding year, too, statistically his best yet (3,630 yards, 28 touchdowns, a quarterback rating of 102.9), but he had been operating in a balanced offense. The Dolphins seldom ran the ball, but they scored more points than the 49ers in the regular season (513 to 475). They had beaten Pittsburgh 45-28 in the AFC Championship Game.

Though the 49ers had nothing but compliments for the Dolphins —Walsh continually cautioned against saying anything that would wind up on an opponent's bulletin board — some players were stewing inside.

"You could tell that Joe [Montana] was really

bothered because all the talk was Marino, Marino, Marino," Cross said. "He didn't say anything, but he was tight all week."

Montana did caution writers that they were underestimating the 49ers' defense, and the defenders felt the same way. "Sure, we knew [Mark] Duper and [Mark] Clayton were great receivers," Lott said, "but we'd played against good receivers before. We felt we just had to go out and play our game."

Walsh was confident. "Miami had been throwing the ball with Marino about as well as anybody ever had," he said, "but we had a great defense. And we felt they couldn't play defense against us. Overall we were much stronger, much better balanced. We didn't feel they'd be able to score with us."

Arguably, nobody is better at preparing a team for a big game than Walsh. In this one, he thought his offense could take advantage of the physical weakness of the Dolphins' linebackers, who often covered running backs man-to-man in pass defense. Walsh devised plays that forced one of those linebackers to cover Roger Craig, knowing they couldn't do it. Craig caught 7 passes and scored a record 3 touchdowns in the 49ers' 38-16 victory.

The Dolphins' defense was vulnerable in another way: the linebackers had to turn their backs to the line of scrimmage to chase a running back or receiver down the field.

Walsh told Montana to seize any opportunity to run because the linebackers wouldn't be in position to tackle him until he'd made a sizable gain. Montana ran 5 times for 59 yards and 1 touchdown, and his scrambles set up two other touchdowns. The most memorable was a 19-yard run down the sideline in which three players were running in tandem: Craig, a Dolphins' linebacker chasing Craig, and Montana.

Walsh's confidence increased when he watched the teams before the start of the game. "I stood with our group as they were going out, and I looked out and saw the Miami players. What a revelation. They weren't nearly as physical as we were. Marino was a

great quarterback, but I knew they weren't as good as we were. I thought at that point that Don Shula had done a great job to get this team as far as he had."

The game was close for a time. Miami scored first on a field goal, and the 49ers countered with Montana's 33-yard touchdown pass to Carl Monroe. Marino answered by marching the Dolphins right down the field. He completed five consecutive passes, including a 2-yard touchdown to tight end Dan Johnson, and the Dolphins led 10-7.

The game turned right after that. The 49ers had anticipated that the Dolphins would run the ball at least some of the time, so they started the game with their base defense of three defensive linemen and four linebackers. But the Dolphins were throwing the ball on virtually every down and they went to a "No-Huddle" offense to keep the 49ers from changing defenses. That forced San Francisco to stick to one defense, the one most effective against a passing team.

"We really got our best athletes on the field," defensive coordinator Seifert said. "We took out [linebackers] Dan Bunz and Jack Reynolds and put in Jeff Fuller and Keena Turner, who were better against the pass. That made us a much stronger defense." Seifert also went to a four-man defensive line that put more pressure on Marino, and the 49ers shut down the Dolphins' offense the rest of the way, yielding just 2 field goals.

Meanwhile, the 49ers' offense was in high gear, scoring 3 touchdowns in the second quarter. Craig got 2 of them on an 8-yard pass from Montana and a 2-yard run. Montana scored the other on a 6-yard run.

The game was all but over at halftime, although McIntyre gave the Dolphins a glimmer of hope by mishandling a kickoff just before the intermission. The Dolphins kicked a field goal to close the gap to 28-13 with just 12 seconds remaining in the second quarter. Miami tried a squib kickoff. Members of the receiving team had been told to fall on the ball. McIntyre did that, but rookie running back Derrick Harmon told him to get up and run. When

FROM LINEBACKER DAN BUNZ, ON THE DRAWBACKS OF PLAYING SUPER BOWL XIX SO CLOSE TO HOME:

"I WAS GETTING CALLS FROM PEOPLE AT TWO IN THE MORNING SAYING, 'REMEMBER ME? I SAT BEHIND YOU IN FOURTH GRADE. CAN YOU GET ME TWO TICKETS TO THE GAME?'"

Super Bowl XIX provided cause for celebration for the 49ers, who defeated the Dolphins 38-16 at nearby Stanford Stadium. Guard Guy McIntyre (62) and others exulted as the clock wound down.

McIntyre did, he fumbled the ball and the Dolphins recovered. "Talk about a botched, stupid play," said Walsh, the perfectionist in him still enraged ten years later. Miami scored to make it 28-16 at half-time, but that would be Miami's last points.

ANOTHER WEAPON

Because he'd put together such a complete team, Walsh had the luxury in 1985 of going after just one star player in the draft. The player he wanted was Jerry Rice, a wide re-ceiver playing for NCAA Division I-AA Mississippi Valley State.

Walsh feared that Rice would be gone long before the 49ers' pick, the last in the first round. Walsh talked to other teams about packaging his first two picks to move up in the first round, but he assumed that Rice would go early—probably in the first half-dozen picks and certainly in the first ten—and he doubted that he could move up that far.

Walsh had gotten an unusual look at Rice. The night before the 49ers played in Houston during the 1984 season, he was watching the television news before going to bed. The sports segment featured shots of Rice catching touchdown passes in a game that day, and Walsh was intrigued by the thought of putting Rice in the 49ers' offense.

Fortunately for Walsh, other clubs doubted Rice's ability. He had set eighteen NCAA records but at a low level of competition. Scouts questioned his speed because he usually ran 40 yards in 4.6 sec-onds—marginal speed for his position. But Walsh talked of football speed. "Scouts always regarded [49ers wide receiver] Dwight Clark as slow," he pointed out, "but I never saw a defensive back catch Dwight from behind."

There were at least two other excellent wide receivers in the draft: Wisconsin's Al Toon and Miami's Eddie Brown. The New York Jets took Toon with the tenth selection, and Cincinnati picked Brown thirteenth. Walsh realized that he still had a chance to get Rice.

John McVay had talked before the draft to Dick Steinberg, director of player development for the Patriots, who had expressed some interest in trading New England's first-round pick, the sixteenth, for the 49ers' first- and second-round picks. Walsh told

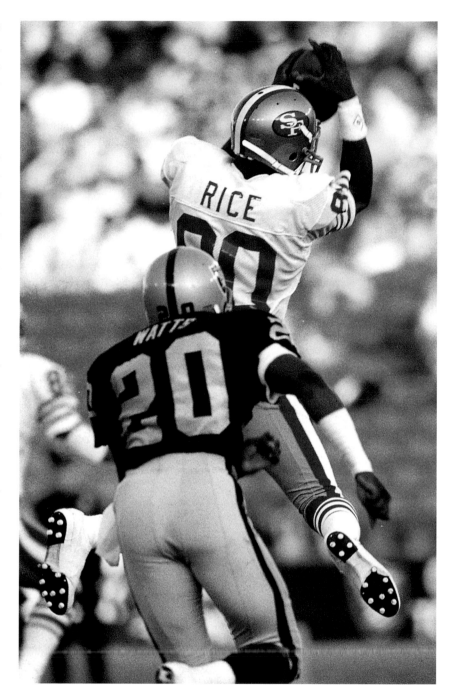

(Above) Wide receiver Jerry Rice joined the 49ers as a rookie out of Mississippi Valley State in 1985; (opposite) defensive back Ronnie Lott (42) and linebacker Riki Ellison pun-ished opponents with bruising hits.

McVay to call Steinberg again, and the trade was made (the teams also swapped third-round picks in the deal). The 49ers grabbed Rice.

Adding Rice to a 49ers' team that dominated the league the previous year seemed almost unfair. Yet, the 49ers fell behind early in 1985, barely made the playoffs as a wild-card team, and were eliminated easily by the New York Giants in the first round.

The problems started in the season opener at Minnesota, a loss that still causes Walsh great anguish. "God, we were a beautiful team," he said. "We went up there and played so well, and then Wendell Tyler fumbled and Derrick Harmon fumbled and we lost the game. That was a killer."

The 49ers were leading the Vikings 21-14 when Tyler's fumble set up Minnesota's tying touchdown in the fourth quarter. Walsh cautioned Harmon about protecting the ball on the ensuing kickoff, but Harmon fumbled, the Vikings recovered, scored, and won the game 28-21. The 49ers gained 489 total yards, nearly 200 more than the Vikings, but lost the game.

The 49ers won their next two games but then fell into a pattern of sloppy play and lost three of their next four to fall to 3-4.

Walsh was playing Rice more than popular veteran Freddie Solomon, but the rookie wide receiver couldn't hang on to the ball. Newspapers were running weekly charts on how many passes he dropped. When he couldn't hold on to two against Kansas City, he had 11 dropped balls in 11 games, and the Candlestick crowd booed him. "He was weeping at halftime," Walsh said. "I remember [linebacker] Keena Turner comforting him. We won the game, but he learned the hard, cold facts of NFL life."

"I had a seventy-yarder right in my hands," Rice said. "I had never been booed in my life. I felt like just taking off my stuff and going to the locker room." In college, everything revolved around Rice. Wherever he ran, it was up to the quarterback to find him. But with the 49ers he had to run precise routes. When he broke off a pattern, assistant coach Paul Hackett would remind him that he wasn't at Mississippi Valley State anymore.

"I came into the league wanting to be an impact player from the start, but it didn't work out," Rice said. "I was totally confused. They handed me this big playbook that was very complex. I had to learn to pick up so much in different situations. The thing I forgot was to catch the football."

That finally ended in a late-season game against the Rams when Rice caught ten passes for a club-record 241 yards. "I felt totally relaxed in that game," he said. "I knew exactly what to do. I knew my reads and everything fell into place for me."

Rice finished the season with 49 receptions for 927 yards. He was UPI's choice as the NFC rookie of the year.

The 49ers rallied late in the season, too, winning five of their last six games, but they had so many injuries when the playoffs came around that their 17-3 loss to the Giants in the first round was almost a relief. Walsh said several players, including Montana, wouldn't have been able to play another game.

The most difficult accomplishment in sports is not winning a championship, but repeating, as the 49ers learned in 1982. But the 1984 champions had been so good it was surprising when they failed to make a serious run at another championship. One problem was that the competition was improving. "There were some really good teams coming along," Walsh said. "You could see the Giants making progress, and the Chicago Bears were a great team. Those were some golden years in pro football."

DIFFICULT DECISIONS

The 49ers were growing older, too, and about that time, Cross noted, "Bill started calling in players privately, informing them that their careers were over or when their careers would be over. He brought me in and told me he thought I had three or four strong years left."

"He called me in before training camp in 1987," Clark said, "and told me he thought I should retire. I had arthroscopic surgery on my knee in the offseason. I didn't think I was ready to retire, but he was right. I played that season, but I didn't have much left."

"He didn't call me in, but I remember reading in the papers that he thought 1987 would be my last year," tackle Keith Fahnhorst said. "Before that, I remember listening to the radio on draft day in 1987, and when I heard the 49ers had drafted Harris Barton, I thought, 'Uh-oh.'"

Walsh was always trying to improve the 49ers, and that often meant bringing in younger players. He had seen too many teams decline because coaches hung on to players past their prime. "Who knows? It might have been one of the reasons we won," Fahnhorst said. "Nobody ever felt secure, not even Joe Montana, and maybe that made us play harder. I know that when I look

Player's Owner

As owner of the 49ers, Eddie DeBartolo, Jr., has set the tone for the team, creating a family-like atmosphere within the organization that has enabled it to thrive even during rare periods of adversity.

In the 1980s, before the NFL's salary cap was instituted, DeBartolo spent freely to keep the 49ers on a championship level. The 49ers traveled first class wherever they went, and DeBartolo not only paid high salaries to stars, he also paid to have high-salaried back-ups. At one point, the 49ers employed about $8 million worth of quarterbacks, with Joe Montana backed up by Steve Young and Steve Bono.

"The big difference in my former team, the Patriots, and the 49ers when I first came was Eddie DeBartolo's willingness to spend money," tight end Russ Francis said. "Eddie did more than anybody. We always had incentive bonuses, for instance.

"Eddie was committed to winning, and he expressed his appreciation and even his affection with money. That was very important to us because, as a player, you always wonder how committed the coach and the owner are to winning. We had the attitude that we were all in this together, we were all committed to winning. We had the best organization and the best coaching staff. It was just terrific."

DeBartolo has always been close to his players.

That attitude carried over even when the free-spending era ended. Other teams in the league hoped that the salary cap would bring down the 49ers, but top-quality free agents came to the club for the 1994 season because the 49ers had the reputation of being winners and of being a good organization.

For the most part, DeBartolo has had a hands-off attitude toward the club, allowing his coach and front office free reign in making decisions. With Bill Walsh, he admits, "there were times I would storm into the dressing room after losses or confront Walsh on the team plane coming home."

The emotions quickly blew over, though. "You had two people who were emotional," DeBartolo said. "I was rambunctious, spirited—a lot more than now. Bill was the perfectionist. But considering the length of our relationship, on a scale of one to ten, we were maybe nine-and-a-half.

"He had a remarkable career. He set a standard for the organization. He wasn't just a great coach. He saw the big picture. He was always one step ahead."

Through the years, DeBartolo has been close to the players, especially Joe Montana, Dwight Clark, and Roger

DeBartolo gets a lift from the five players who participated in each of the 49ers' first four Super Bowl victories: (left to right) Eric Wright, Mike Wilson, Joe Montana, Keena Turner, and Ronnie Lott.

Craig. "I became very close to Montana and Clark in that period when they were young kids doing great things on the football field."

There is a downside, though: when his favorite players leave. When Craig signed with the Raiders as a free agent in 1991, DeBartolo saw him off at the airport. "Boy, it was tough to talk to him," the 49ers' owner said.

Three years later, when Craig decided to end his career, DeBartolo and club president Carmen Policy arranged to have Craig put on the roster for one day so he could retire "officially" as a 49er.

It was even more painful when Montana told DeBartolo he wanted to be traded to Kansas City. The two met at DeBartolo's home in Youngstown and flew out to San Francisco for the press conference. "That was a rotten day," DeBartolo said. "We tried to talk about kids, about the state of Montana—everything but the 49ers and Kansas City."

down at my two Super Bowl rings, I wouldn't have won them if it hadn't been for Bill Walsh."

There is no disputing the effectiveness of Walsh's policy. The problem was that while Walsh tried to make it easier for the players, he was, in fact, making it more difficult. "Bill felt that getting guys to retire was the dignified way," Benjamin said. "He'd tell players, 'You don't want to be hanging on, to be bouncing from team to team. Go out in style.' He felt he was doing it in their best interests, but that's the last thing an athlete wants to hear. He doesn't want to quit thinking he might have been able to play another year."

Walsh didn't realize the bitterness that resulted from his approach. When he retired, he expected that he would get together with his former players, play a little golf, maybe go to lunch. "But the players were still scared of him," Benjamin said. "He was the last guy they wanted to have lunch with."

Walsh finally realized that he was the one who would have to make the phone calls, and he did. He is now close to a number of his former players, who have a better understanding of why he did what he did. A happy ending—but it took time.

RELOADING THROUGH THE DRAFT

The 1985 and 1986 drafts are the best examples of how Walsh built a dynasty. In 1985 he went after a superstar, Jerry Rice. In 1986, he employed a much different approach.

The 49ers were drafting low (eighteenth), and had only eight picks in the twelve-round draft. Moreover, the draft seemed weak at the top with no more than a handful of players who were certain to be stars. None of those players would be available by the eighteenth pick, and the 49ers saw very little difference between players who would be selected in the bottom of the first round and those who would go in the second and third rounds. So Walsh made the decision to trade down and get more picks, even though it meant giving up his first-round selection.

The strategy worked beautifully, yielding not only quantity (six trades yielded fourteen picks in

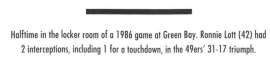
Halftime in the locker room of a 1986 game at Green Bay. Ronnie Lott (42) had 2 interceptions, including 1 for a touchdown, in the 49ers' 31-17 triumph.

the draft) but quality. Walsh considers this his best draft because he got eight players who eventually became starters: defensive end Larry Roberts (second round); fullback Tom Rathman, cornerback Tim McKyer, and wide receiver John Taylor (third round); defensive end Charles Haley, tackle Steve Wallace, and defensive end Kevin Fagan (fourth round); and cornerback Don Griffin (sixth round).

Walsh also sent reserve quarterback Matt Cavanaugh to the Philadelphia Eagles for a second-round pick in 1987 and acquired quarterback Jeff Kemp from the Los Angeles Rams for a third-round pick that same year. Acquiring Kemp, the son of politician Jack Kemp, himself a former pro quarterback, became very important when Montana was sidelined by a back injury that required surgery after the first game of the 1986 season, a victory over Tampa Bay.

It appeared Montana would be out for the rest of the season and that his career might very well be over. As he did so often, Walsh used a military analogy, the Battle of Midway, to tell his players that when one player went down, another one had to step up.

The players may or may not have believed that, but Walsh had built a team with great character. The 49ers, who could have folded at that point, played surprisingly well with Kemp, going 3-2-1 in his six starts. Then Kemp got hurt, and Walsh was down to his third-string quarterback, Mike Moroski. The 49ers beat the Packers 31-17 in Moroski's first game, but then lost 23-10 at New Orleans.

THE MONTANA WATCH

Meanwhile, the Joe Montana story was playing out in three-inch headlines in San Francisco newspapers. It was news when Montana had surgery. It was news when he ate his first solid food. It was news when, incredibly, it seemed his season might not be over.

Dr. Arthur White, who operated on Montana, cleared him to practice the week before the New Orleans game, but Walsh held the veteran quarterback out of that game to give him an extra week to recuperate.

Montana was eager to play. He felt better than he had in some time because the pain he'd been playing with for at least two years was gone. Montana started

Montana was remarkably resilient and bounced back from numerous injuries in his 49ers career, including a devastating concussion suffered in a playoff loss to the Giants in 1986 (opposite).

against St. Louis a week later. He played as if he'd never left, completing 13 of 19 passes for 270 yards and 3 touchdowns in a 43-17 victory.

Montana's return sparked the 49ers to five victories in their last seven games, but after winning the NFC West for the fourth time in six years, the 49ers ended their season on a crushing note. The New York Giants humiliated the 49ers 49-3 in the divisional playoffs, the most lopsided defeat in Walsh's NFL career. Even worse, Montana was knocked out of the game with a concussion in the second quarter, once again raising the question of whether his career was just one big hit from being finished.

"With Joe, you never really knew," Walsh said.

Ronnie Lott (middle) and 49ers players discuss the players' strike before a workout in 1987.

"Every injury was career-threatening because he's not a big, strong, indestructible guy."

Tampa Bay was willing to trade Steve Young, and Walsh thought Young could replace an injured Montana, so he made the trade. He also thought that 1987 would be a rebuilding year—the playoff loss to the Giants showed him how far his team had to go to reach the Super Bowl again—and Young would be part of that.

A SEASON INTERRUPTED

Walsh's pessimism seemed deserved when the 49ers lost their season opener in 1987 to Pittsburgh, and they would have gone 0-2 but for an incredible ending against Cincinnati a week later. The Bengals led 26-20 and faced fourth down from their 30-yard line with only six seconds left. Instead of risking a blocked punt, Cincinnati coach Sam Wyche decided to try to run out the clock. He called for running back James Brooks to run wide, but 49ers defensive tackle Kevin Fagan blew into the backfield unblocked and dropped Brooks for a 5-yard loss. The clock showed two seconds left.

Given one last chance, Montana threw a 25-yard touchdown pass to Jerry Rice as time ran out. Ray Wersching's extra point gave the 49ers' a 27-26 victory, and the giddy Walsh actually skipped off the field into the dressing room.

Before the 49ers could spend time savoring that win, however, NFL players went on strike. When the Players Association announced the work stoppage, the NFL countered with a plan to continue the season with replacement teams, though regular players who did not want to go out on strike were also welcome. After one week without games, the season resumed with replacement squads.

"That was a very, very difficult time," said Fahnhorst, the 49ers' player representative. "I was trying to keep the team together, to keep it from disintegrating. We certainly weren't striking against Eddie DeBartolo, because he'd taken very good care of us. I felt we had to support the union, but I knew there were many players who didn't agree with that."

Walsh, too, was trying to keep the team together. He met with a group of players, including Fahnhorst, to urge them to stay together—to all stay out or all go back. It was impossible to reach agreement, though, because there were some who strongly believed in the union's cause and others, including stars such as Montana, Clark, Roger Craig, Jeff Fuller, and Russ Francis, who believed they should be playing.

Walsh was able to persuade all his players to stay out for the next game, against the Giants in New York, because it wasn't necessary for them to play. Expecting that there would be a strike, Walsh had prepared a replacement team of players who had been in training camp with the 49ers. The Giants, who had thought that replacement games wouldn't count in the standings (they did), had a very poor replacement team. The 49ers beat the Giants 41-21, and Walsh

The 49ers' replacement team in 1987. San Francisco won all three games during the players' strike and finished the regular season 13-2.

even used the Wishbone formation in the game.

Walsh was also feeling pressure from others in the league. "Tex Schramm had somehow convinced himself that the 49ers should come back to break the strike, but not the Cowboys," he said. "He heard that we were about to do it, but the players had loyalty to me and Eddie, so they stayed out that week.

"That was the relationship 49ers players had with coaches and management. Some other teams were totally separated and had confrontations. We didn't have that. People envied that in the 49ers. We had such great *esprit de corps*."

The next week, many of the 49ers players came back, but against a Falcons team that had virtually none of its regular players, they weren't needed, so Walsh used them sparingly. Montana threw only 8 passes in the 49ers' 25-17 victory.

In the strike's third and final week, the 49ers were playing the St. Louis Cardinals, who had twenty of their regular players in uniform. Montana passed for 334 yards and 4 touchdowns as the 49ers won an exciting game, 34-28.

After that, the season resumed with regular

teams, but it wasn't easy for those players who had been on opposite sides of the issue to forgive and forget. Walsh scheduled a team meeting in the middle of the practice field to give players a chance to vent their opinions.

"There was a lot of tension during that meeting," said Ronnie Lott, the 49ers' fiery leader. "We always felt the strong suit of our team was unity, and we thought that had dissipated because some players had crossed the picket line. We decided that we needed to move forward.

"There were guys who said they wanted to go after certain players in practice. What good would that have done? We had to win all our games to win the division, and we couldn't have done that if we hadn't gotten together. We had games to win. That was our objective."

As a team, the 49ers stayed together. "We had a stretch where we played as well as a team as we ever did," Randy Cross said. On a personal level, though, it was difficult. "That strike broke up a lot of friendships," Fahnhorst said. "There were some guys who just couldn't fight their way through that disagreement."

A STUNNING UPSET

Still, the 49ers finished 13-2 in the regular season, tops in the NFL. They had the league's top-ranked offense and top-ranked defense. They were regarded as the best team in football and were heavily favored to beat Minnesota in a divisional playoff game at Candlestick Park.

The underdog Vikings not only won but dominated the game from the start. Minnesota's defensive line, led by Chris Doleman and Keith Millard, put unrelenting pressure on Montana while Vikings wide receiver Anthony Carter was having the best day a receiver ever had against a Walsh-coached team, catching 10 passes for 227 yards.

"We were just totally overconfident," Cross said. "Plus, we didn't adjust. They were obviously prepared to just get after Joe. We had always been a team that made adjustments, but we didn't change a thing."

Owner Edward DeBartolo, Jr., joins the team in prayer after a thrilling one-point victory over the Bengals in 1987. The 49ers scored the winning touchdown with no time left on the clock.

The 49ers were so flat that day that defeat probably was inevitable, but one play in the second quarter was pivotal. Under pressure, Montana threw to Dwight Clark, but Vikings defensive back Reggie Rutland stepped in front of Clark, intercepted the pass, and raced 45 yards down the sideline for the touchdown that gave the Vikings a 20-3 halftime lead.

In the first two offensive series of the second half, Montana was sacked twice and could not get a first down. Walsh thought that Young's running might force the Vikings' pass rushers to back off, so he replaced Montana — the first time since Montana had become the starter that he had been replaced when he was not injured.

Young played well, completing 12 of 17 passes for 158 yards and a touchdown and rushing for 72 yards and another touchdown, but he could not get the 49ers closer than nine points. The Vikings won the game 36-24.

It was a crushing loss and a seminal game for the 49ers, setting the stage for the quarterback

The 49ers have become international favorites, too. They opened the 1988 preseason with a game against the Dolphins in London's historic Wembley Stadium.

controversy of 1988 and hastening Walsh's retirement. DeBartolo, enraged by the loss because he had been certain the 49ers would be back in the Super Bowl, stripped Walsh of the title of team president. Though purely a symbolic move because Walsh still had complete control of team operations, it wounded the sensitive coach.

"We tore ourselves apart because of that game, as though it was the only one that would ever be played," Walsh said. The breach between DeBartolo and Walsh did not heal until Walsh retired.

The relationship between Walsh and DeBartolo, idyllic in the beginning, had changed dramatically over the years. The first two Super Bowls only whetted DeBartolo's appetite for more, and his frustrations and outbursts were duly chronicled in the press. Even in its most stormy moments, though, the DeBartolo-Walsh relationship did not set any standards in pro sports. More important, DeBartolo always gave Walsh autonomy to run the team. Many owners cannot resist meddling, either personally or

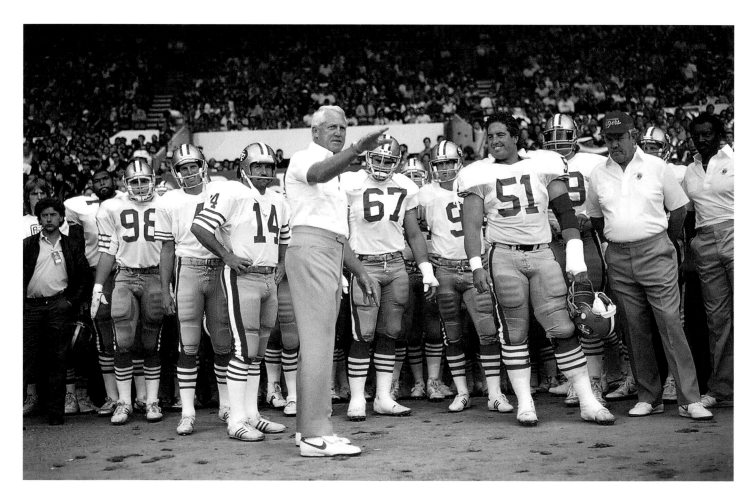

through the team's general manager. Walsh never had to worry about that, and he has said many times how important it was to the 49ers' success.

Walsh and DeBartolo now look back at those years with a clearer perspective. Both savor the good times and have become close again.

A ROLLER-COASTER SEASON

The next season was the wildest roller-coaster ride in Walsh's ten years with the 49ers.

Before a preseason game in London in the summer of 1988, Walsh and Miami coach Don Shula were talking about their teams to reporters when Walsh was asked if anything worried him. "We may have a quarterback controversy," he said.

Walsh later said that it was a slip of the tongue, that he meant to say only that Steve Young was a legitimate NFL quarterback and would provide competition for Joe Montana. But Walsh usually was adroit at his press conferences, and he was not above using newspapers and telecasts to get his message to the public — or to his players. A suspicion lingers that he wanted to plant the unthinkable thought: Joe Montana would not go on forever.

That did not mean he was phasing out Montana early. There was never any doubt that Montana would start the season opener, and when he did not play at times, there was always a good reason for Walsh's decision. But because Walsh himself mentioned a quarterback controversy, all those decisions were viewed by outsiders — and sometimes by Montana — within that framework.

Walsh had legitimate concerns about Montana's health, and, in fact, Montana injured his elbow on the artificial turf of the Superdome as the 49ers edged the Saints 34-33 in the season opener. Young started the next game, against the Giants in New York, but Montana relieved him and teamed with Jerry Rice on a 78-yard touchdown pass with only 42 seconds left, giving the 49ers a dramatic 20-17 victory.

Montana returned as the starter for the next six games, but Walsh replaced him with Young late in games against the Denver Broncos and Chicago Bears. Both were special situations.

The Denver game was played on the windiest

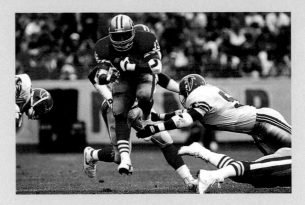

HIGH STEPPER

Running back Roger Craig was a classic leader-by-example for the 49ers, both with his great running and pass catching and with his incredible work ethic.

In practice, Craig would run thirty or more yards beyond where a play was supposed to end. In a game, he was always squirming and fighting for extra yards.

His trademark, though, was his rigorous offseason workout regimen, which was so strenuous that wide receiver Jerry Rice was the only teammate who could stay with him. Craig would get up at 5:30 A.M. to run distances up hills, sprint on flat land, and then go into the gym to continue with workouts on the weights and exercise machines.

"I first got the idea of working so hard by watching my older brother at practice in high school," Craig said. "He was always the head of the pack when they ran, always the one working hardest.

"When I got into pro ball, I emulated Walter Payton. His work ethic was what kept him so good for so long. I really admired him. It helps if you get into competition on your own team. Jerry and I used to compete to see who could run the farthest on plays in practice."

Craig, a second-round draft choice out of Nebraska in 1983, had an unusual high-stepping running style, a carryover from running high hurdles in high school. He had the speed to turn the corner on the sweep and a slashing, powerful style that made him an effective inside runner.

Though not particularly elusive, Craig could break tackles because he always kept his legs churning, which enabled him to turn short gains into big plays (he holds the NFL postseason record with an 80-yard touchdown run against the Minnesota Vikings in a 1988 playoff game).

Craig was an unselfish player who always did what his coach asked. At Nebraska, he moved to fullback so Mike Rozier could play tailback; Rozier won the Heisman Trophy, but Craig had a much more productive pro career.

Wendell Tyler was the main running back when Craig came to the 49ers, so he played fullback, where he was used as a runner, receiver, and blocker. In 1985, Craig became the only player in NFL history to gain 1,000 yards both rushing and receiving, rushing for 1,050 yards and catching 92 passes for 1,016 yards.

When Tyler retired, Craig became the 49ers' main running threat, and he set a club record by rushing for 1,502 yards in 1988.

Craig's dedication probably shortened his career as a top running back. In 1990, he tore a knee ligament against Houston, but he refused to give the injury time to heal.

"I should have stayed out six or eight weeks," he said, looking back. "But I couldn't wait to get back in the lineup. I was running sprints before the Atlanta game the next week to prove I could play. I missed a couple of games, but then I got back in there. That killed me. A knee injury to a running back is critical. I couldn't cut."

Joe Montana (left) and his eventual successor, Steve Young.

day anybody could remember for football at Candlestick Park. The wind got worse and worse, and it became almost impossible to pass the ball. When the game went into overtime, Walsh put in Young, thinking he could run the ball if he could not pass. But Young forced a pass that was intercepted deep in 49ers' territory, and the Broncos kicked a field goal to win 16-13.

The Bears game, played in Chicago, presented an entirely different weather problem: subfreezing temperatures. In addition, Walsh overcompensated for the Bears' blitzing defense, using running backs Roger Craig and Tom Rathman and tight end John Frank as blockers instead of sending them out on pass routes. The Bears shut down the 49ers, and Walsh put in Young in the fourth quarter, again hoping the elusive quarterback could keep Chicago's defense off balance. The strategy failed as the 49ers lost 10-9.

Montana had been weakened by dysentery before the Bears game, and with the 49ers at 5-3, Walsh decided it would be best to rest him for the next game so he would be strong for the stretch run. Shortly after Walsh made that decision, Montana started having back spasms, and team doctor Michael Dillingham told Montana not to practice. Two days later, Dillingham advised Walsh not to play him.

Dr. Dillingham's role was largely ignored by sports writers, who speculated on Walsh's reasons for starting Young. Ironically, the start came against the Minnesota Vikings, who had initiated all the turmoil when they beat the 49ers in the playoffs the previous season.

Young's performance against Minnesota was typical of his early play with the 49ers, alternating between miserable and brilliant with no stops in between. Walsh's game plan called for the 49ers to block Vikings defensive end Chris Doleman to the outside, giving Young the opportunity to step up in the pocket and throw to the right side. Instead, Young often tried to circle to his left to evade Doleman, which meant he was out of position to throw to the right side. At halftime, the 49ers trailed 7-3.

In the second half, Young led the 49ers on a 97-yard touchdown drive (Roger Craig ran 1 yard for the score) and teamed with John Taylor on a

PARIS WEIGHT PROGRAM

The one player Bill Walsh could never control was tackle William (Bubba) Paris, whose weight problems kept him from being the dominant player he could have been.

Paris is a very intelligent man. With the 49ers, he applied his intelligence to circumventing Walsh's attempts to control his weight. One time when the scales were placed next to a soft drink machine, Bubba draped an arm on the machine, just enough to bring his weight down to an allowed level.

Conditioning coach Jerry Attaway put Paris on a restricted diet at training camp, but the player's weight just kept going up. "Metabolism," Paris said.

Then Walsh got a call from the maid who cleaned Paris's room. "What do I do with the chicken bones?" she asked. Paris had been calling out at night for fried chicken and storing the bones in boxes in his closet.

So much for metabolism.

73-yard touchdown pass. But the Vikings countered with touchdowns each time and led 21-17 with just over two minutes to play. Then, seemingly trapped behind the line of scrimmage, Young broke loose and burst downfield, breaking tackles and collapsing in the end zone after a spectacular 49-yard run that was replayed coast-to-coast by many stations airing that night's NFL highlights. Young's touchdown gave the 49ers a 24-21 victory.

Young started the next game, too, against the Cardinals in Phoenix, a game that had an effect beyond the win-loss column. The 49ers led 23-0 in the third quarter, and Young had played well, more consistently than before. "I remember it was so hot that day," Young said, "but I felt very confident with that lead. I thought it was just a matter of playing it out."

But the 49ers' defense fell apart, and Walsh became too conservative in his play calling. The Cardinals came back to win 24-23, scoring the winning points on Neil Lomax's 9-yard touchdown pass to Roy Green with three seconds left.

Would Young have remained the starter if the 49ers had won that game? "Steve should have remained the starter," Walsh said. "He wasn't to blame for that loss. But there was tremendous pressure to start Joe. He played the next week and he played terribly. He wasn't ready."

The 49ers lost 9-3 to the Raiders at Candlestick Park in as bad an offensive game as they ever had under Walsh. Montana completed 16 of 31 passes for only 160 yards, and the 49ers managed just 219 total yards. Their record now stood at a paltry 6-5, with a Monday night game coming up against the defending Super Bowl–champion Washington Redskins.

For the 49ers, there were two significant meetings that week. The first was between Walsh and DeBartolo. For Walsh, the pressures of coaching in the NFL had become too much. It didn't help his frame of mind when, on his way out of the stadium after the loss to the Raiders, he was confronted by two rowdy fans who berated him before they were taken away by security guards. It no longer was a question whether Walsh would resign, but when.

The 49ers survived an inconsistent midseason stretch in 1988, and Bill Walsh stepped down as coach after winning his third Super Bowl.

Owner Edward J. DeBartolo, Jr. (above, left), with his father. The senior DeBartolo died at age eighty-five in December 1994; (right) assistant coach Bobb McKittrick and the offensive line.

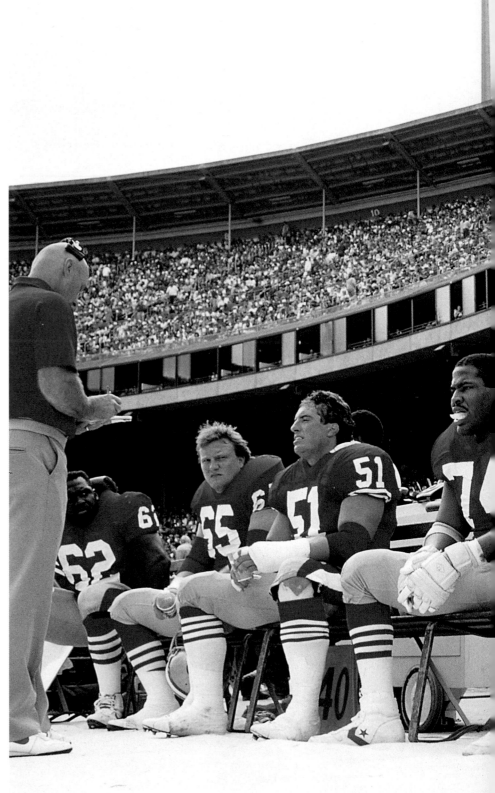

"I was emotionally exhausted," Walsh said. "I felt like I was being shipped home from the front. I don't think it affected my work, though there were times when I was short-tempered. I had the feeling I had run the course with the 49ers."

Walsh didn't say that directly when he met with DeBartolo. "He never said he had decided to quit," DeBartolo said. "We did discuss a lot of different things. It was a very emotional meeting, and I don't mean that we were screaming at each other. We just expressed our emotions on a lot of different things. It was a good meeting. We hadn't had a chance to do that in a long time."

Neither Walsh nor DeBartolo is quite certain whether it was then or later, but at some point, they discussed different scenarios for the future, including the possibility of Walsh moving to a front-office position and defensive coordinator George Seifert taking over as coach, which ultimately is what happened.

No decisions were made at the time, though. The important thing was that the two men cleared the air. "We reminded ourselves of the good times we'd had," DeBartolo said. For the rest of the season, Walsh was a much more focused coach.

The other meeting was held by the players, without coaches present. "That made a big difference," Cross said. "It was the first time in a couple of years that we'd sat down and had a conversation

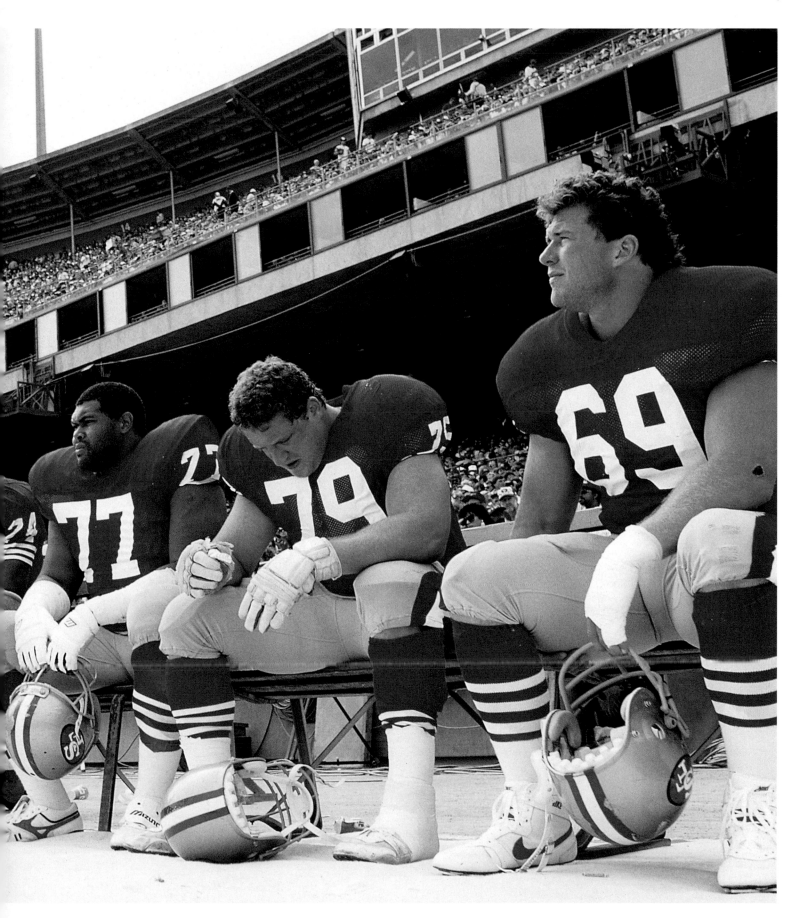

about a lot of things. Ronnie Lott got up and talked, Jerry Rice talked, which was unusual for him, Joe Montana talked. It was a pretty lengthy session. We decided we were going to find a way to win."

The 49ers routed the Redskins 37-21, starting a four-game winning streak that lifted them to another division title. Montana played brilliantly during the streak. "I've always given him a lot of credit for the way he came back," said Young, who knew how close he'd been to replacing Montana.

The competition from Young may have been a spur to Montana. "Joe was notorious for being motivated when people thought he was on his way out," said Dwight Clark, who remained close to Montana though he no longer played for the 49ers. "He was determined to prove they were wrong. I think that had a lot to do with the way he played for the next two years."

Montana's play down the stretch in 1988 through the 1990 season solidified his Pro Football Hall of Fame credentials. Before then, he was a superb quarterback with a relatively short career, but when Montana added two more Super Bowl rings to bring his total to four, football people started talking of him as the best quarterback of all time.

Their late-season success in 1988 put the 49ers in the playoffs again and set up two of their best back-to-back games ever, considering the quality of the competition.

Minnesota came first. The Vikings were convinced they lost to the 49ers during the regular season on a fluke (Young's incredible run), and they remembered how they took the 49ers apart in the 1987 playoffs. But familiarity always worked in Walsh's favor. He knew how to dissect a defense, while his offense and George Seifert's defense were much less predictable.

The Vikings' pass rushers, particularly Doleman and Millard, were quick and strong, so Walsh devised plays that would lure them in one direction while the play was going another. That worked on running plays as well as passes. Roger Craig started to the right on one play and the Vikings moved swiftly in that direction, but then Craig cut back across the flow and went 80 yards for a touchdown —the final score in the 49ers' 34-9 victory.

That lopsided win didn't convince anybody in

(Above) Wide receiver Jerry Rice was named MVP of the 49ers' 20-16 victory over the Bengals in Super Bowl XXIII after catching 11 passes for a record 215 yards; (opposite) Joe Montana, who threw the winning touchdown pass to John Taylor in the final minute, exchanges a high-five with tight end John Frank.

Chicago, where the Bears were regarded as a cinch to make it to the Super Bowl. "The Bears were the so-called team of destiny," Walsh said. "They had to have an opponent [in the NFC Championship Game], and there we were. Nobody gave us a chance to win."

Walsh learned from his mistakes in the 10-9 loss to the Bears in the regular season. This time, he made the Bears react to his team, not the other way around. Instead of just two receivers, he would have five flood the Chicago zone, and he felt confident that Montana's short, timed passes would beat the Bears' pass rush.

The Chicago media assumed that the 49ers would not be able to function in the cold weather—it being an article of faith in the East and Midwest that players on California teams turn blue if the temperature drops below 60 degrees—but even the icy conditions worked to the 49ers' advantage. Late in the first quarter, Montana threw a short pass to Rice. He zipped past two Bears' defenders who could not keep their footing on the slippery field and went 61 yards for a touchdown. That was the most spectacular play of the day as the 49ers moved the ball consistently, rolling up 406 yards against the supposedly impregnable Bears' defense. They dominated from beginning to end and won 28-3.

A DRAMATIC SUPER BOWL

The 49ers were solid favorites over the Cincinnati Bengals in Super Bowl XXIII, a rematch of the game seven years earlier that started the 49ers' great run. En route to Miami, Randy Cross slipped into the seat next to Bill Walsh. "I've got something to tell you," he said. Walsh motioned to the stewardess to bring a bottle of wine, then poured two glasses. "Okay, what is it?" Walsh asked.

Cross told him he'd decided to retire. Walsh asked him why, saying he thought Cross could play two more years if he wanted. "I don't think I'm playing well, and it isn't fun anymore," Cross said.

"I know what you mean," Walsh said. "If we win this game, I might not be around much longer, either."

Walsh and Cross had each made their decisions much earlier, of course. Cross waited until the Wednesday before the game to make his announcement.

Walsh waited even longer. Speculation mounted about his decision. Eddie DeBartolo told reporters that he hoped Walsh would come back. Walsh deliberately withheld comment, not saying anything even to his players. "I felt proud of myself that I didn't

COACHING TREE

Bill Walsh was one of a generation of coaches who learned their trade under the watchful eye of the legendary Paul Brown. Walsh also tutored a number of assistants who went on to become NFL head coaches, including the 49ers' George Seifert. In turn, Seifert's staffs have continued the tradition. In fact, nearly one-third of the league's head coaches in 1995 were 49ers assistants at one time:

Coach	Team	Years 49ers' Assistant
Rich Brooks	St. Louis	1975
Jeff Fisher	Houston	1992–93
Dennis Green	Minnesota	1979, 1986–88
Mike Holmgren	Green Bay	1986–91
Ray Rhodes	Philadelphia	1981–91, 1994
George Seifert	San Francisco	1980–88
Mike Shanahan	Denver	1992–94
Sam Wyche	Tampa Bay	1979–82
Mike White	L.A. Raiders	1978–79

(Opposite) Former defensive coordinator George Seifert succeeded Bill Walsh as head coach in 1989, and the 49ers didn't miss a beat, winning Super Bowl XXIV. Seifert's winning percentage of .778 through the 1994 season is the best in NFL history.

bring that to the team," he said. "The players had enough pressure as it was. It wouldn't have been fair to add to that."

The 49ers were confident, probably too confident. "We were so relaxed during the week," Rice said, "we were laughing in practice." No doubt, that overconfidence hurt the 49ers, who struggled throughout the game.

"We were so much better than Cincinnati, it was ridiculous," Cross said. "They had a good offense but only an okay defense. We just didn't play very well. We kept fumbling and getting penalties at the wrong time."

For almost three quarters, field goals accounted for all the scoring. But after Mike Cofer's 32-yard field goal tied the score at 6-6 with 50 seconds remaining in the third quarter, Cincinnati's Stanford Jennings breezed 93 yards with the ensuing kickoff to give his team a 13-6 lead.

The 49ers countered with a four-play, 85-yard drive capped by Montana's 14-yard touchdown pass to Rice to tie the game, but Jim Breech's 40-yard field goal gave the Bengals a 16-13 lead with just 3:20 remaining. Cincinnati was on the brink of an upset, especially when a penalty on the kickoff pushed the 49ers back to their own 8-yard line.

San Francisco fans thought back to the 1981 NFC Championship Game when the 49ers marched 89 yards to the winning touchdown against the Cowboys in the game's final minute. There was a key difference in the two drives, however. The 49ers trailed by six points against Dallas and needed a touchdown. In this game, trailing by three, they could settle for a field goal and try to win the game in overtime. Walsh cautioned Montana not to take unnecessary chances.

From Cincinnati's 45-yard line, Montana hit Rice over the middle. "When I caught the ball, I turned up field, and I really thought I was going to score," Rice remembers. Cincinnati cornerback Lewis Billups got around John Taylor's block to tackle Rice at the 18-yard line, but the 49ers were close enough that Montana started thinking touchdown. He teamed

with Craig on an 8-yard pass and called time out with thirty-nine seconds left.

Walsh again cautioned Montana not to force a pass because they had time to run more plays if necessary. He then called virtually the same play that just worked, the difference being that this time Montana would look first to Taylor, who would fake to the outside and turn inside to the end zone, with Craig drawing the attention of the linebacker so he couldn't drop back in front of Taylor.

Caught up in the excitement, Craig lined up on the wrong side, but it made no difference because the linebacker still followed him. The safety bit on Taylor's fake, leaving him in single coverage. Montana hit him in the end zone, and the 49ers had a thrilling 20-16 victory.

Rice, who showed no signs of a sprained ankle

Roger Craig rushed for 190 yards—the second-best single-game performance in club history—in a victory over the Rams in 1988.

suffered in practice earlier in the week, caught 11 passes for a Super Bowl–record 215 yards and was named the game's most valuable player.

WALSH'S SUCCESSOR

There was more drama to come in the next three days. Walsh had talks with DeBartolo and Carmen Policy, the club's vice president, and made his retirement official. DeBartolo considered hiring Jimmy Johnson, at that time coaching at the University of Miami, but Walsh, who always valued continuity, wanted George Seifert to be the next coach. Walsh would stay on as director of football operations and be responsible for trades and masterminding the draft.

First, Walsh had to make sure Seifert wasn't hired by somebody else. Seifert was ready to be a

head coach. He'd interviewed in San Diego, and he had an interview scheduled in Cleveland. It appeared he might be hired by Browns' owner Art Modell. "I flew out of San Francisco and was supposed to change planes in Dallas to go to Cleveland," Seifert said. "We were stacked up over Dallas because of a storm, so to pass the time I made a call on an airplane phone to my wife, Linda. She said that Carmen Policy had called and said not to make any commitment without talking to him first. Well, I knew what that meant, so when I got to Dallas, I called Carmen, and he told me to come to San Francisco, which I did."

The next day, in Carmel, California, the 49ers held an emotional press conference to announce that Walsh was stepping down as head coach and Seifert would replace him. It was the moment Seifert had been waiting for, and it didn't faze him that he was following a legend.

"I grew up in San Francisco," he said, "and I worked for Bill at Stanford and with the 49ers. I had kind of grown up in the organization. If I'd gotten a head-coaching job with another team, sure, I'd have been elated with that, but there was never any question that if I got a chance to coach the 49ers, that was what I wanted. When I got the job, my wife told me, 'Now, don't screw it up,' and that's the way I've approached it ever since."

CONTINUITY UNDER SEIFERT

Repeating as champions had been an insurmountable challenge for the 49ers after their first two Super Bowls. In 1989, though, they had a special incentive: proving they could win without Bill Walsh. "We started talking about repeating from the time Bill left," Ronnie Lott said. "We knew we had to step up and beat the odds. It was another challenge."

Though the 49ers had players the caliber of Montana and Rice, who were considered among the best ever to play their positions, it definitely was Bill Walsh's team, and some players chafed at that, most notably Lott. After Walsh announced his retirement, Lott publicly criticized his coach for not telling the players earlier, but there also were players who were sorry that Walsh retired.

"I really miss him," Steve Young said six seasons

after Walsh retired. "He was so far ahead of everybody. I just enjoyed being in the meetings because he had so many ideas. Now a lot of teams are trying to copy what we've done, but I don't see anybody his equal."

Roger Craig, too, was concerned because Walsh left. "He knew exactly how to use me," Craig said. "He always seemed to have the best play selected, whether I was running the ball or catching a pass. He

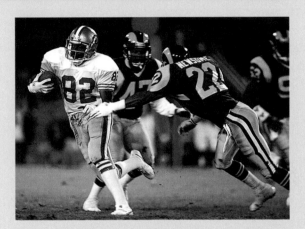

TWO TIMES NINETY

When executed properly, Bill Walsh's offense is profoundly efficient.

And when the 49ers drafted wide receivers Jerry Rice (1985) and John Taylor (1986), they added big-play potential that made the offense almost unstoppable.

The best demonstration of that came on December 11, 1989, in a game in Anaheim against the Los Angeles Rams.

The Rams seemed to have everything going their way when they scored 17 unanswered points in the first quarter. Even after Mike Cofer kicked a field goal 49 seconds into the second quarter, the Rams still seemed to have the game under control, especially when a punt backed the 49ers to their 1-yard line on what figured to be their last series of the half.

Two runs moved the ball to the 8-yard line, but the 49ers still needed a first down to avoid having to punt (thus giving the Rams the ball in good field position). Quarterback Joe Montana completed a pass to Taylor, who found himself in

the clear when the defender fell down. Taylor sprinted upfield and turned a short gain into a 92-yard touchdown that pulled the 49ers to within 17-10 at halftime.

Still, the Rams were in control, and a third-quarter touchdown and a field goal early in the fourth quarter reinstated their 17 point lead. Even after a 7-yard touchdown pass from Montana to Mike Wilson, the 49ers trailed 27-17. The Rams threatened to put the game away with another touchdown, but lost a fumble at the 49ers' 5-yard line.

On the next play, Montana hit Taylor on a short slant pattern. Taylor burst upfield and outran the Rams' defenders, this time for a 95-yard touchdown. It was the first time in NFL history that a player scored two touchdowns covering more than 90 yards in a game.

The flustered Rams fumbled the ensuing kickoff. The 49ers recovered on Los Angeles's 27-yard line and scored on a 1-yard plunge by Roger Craig to win the game 30-27.

really made me what I was. I worship the ground the man walks on."

Jerry Rice felt much the same as Craig. "Bill was like a father to me," he said. "He saw something nobody else did. When he left, it hurt me. I wanted to play my whole career for this guy."

There were some veterans, however, who were glad Walsh was gone and eager to prove what they could do without him. There would be no complacency in the 1989 season. There would be no Walsh, either—in any capacity.

Walsh had moved into the front office, in theory, to make trades and oversee the draft, but he was obviously uncomfortable in his new role. Walsh always said that the coach should be the focal point of the operation. Now he no longer was the coach, and he was trying very hard to avoid anything that would lessen Seifert's authority. It got to the point where he felt he was little more than a figurehead. "Now I'm a typical general manager," he said. "My most important job is figuring out the best restaurants around the league." When NBC-TV offered Walsh a job as its top analyst on AFC games, he left the 49ers.

Walsh's system and operational methods were still being used by the 49ers, though, and the key coaches, including Seifert, had been long-time Walsh assistants. "It was business as usual," tight end Brent Jones said. "George didn't make any big changes. We pretty much did things the way we'd always done them."

Walsh brought in the significant players, and the most important one, Montana, had his best season statistically in 1989. Montana completed 70.2 percent of his passes for 3,521 yards, with 26 touchdowns and only 8 interceptions. He set an NFL record (since broken by Young) with a quarterback rating of 112.4 and was an easy choice as the league's most valuable player. Montana had more weapons than ever, including Jones, who caught 40 passes for 500 yards in 1989.

The tight end was important, though he was seldom the primary receiver in Walsh's system, and the 49ers had some good ones, including Charle Young, Russ Francis, and John Frank. It took some time before Jones improved his

OFF THE DECK

The Philadelphia Eagles had the 49ers on the ropes on September 24, 1989, in a game at Philadelphia. It was not only that the Eagles had a 21-10 lead ten seconds into the fourth quarter, but that they had sacked Joe Montana 8 times.

The 49ers threatened to get back in the game when John Taylor took a pass from Montana and ran 70 yards for a touchdown, but Randall Cunningham came right back with a touchdown pass for the Eagles.

But Montana was just getting warmed up. First, he took the 49ers on a 75-yard drive, throwing 8 yards to running back Tom Rathman for a score that brought the 49ers within 28-24. Then he hit tight end Brent Jones for a 24-yard touchdown that put the 49ers ahead.

Finally, Montana teamed with Jerry Rice on a 33-yard touchdown pass, and the 49ers completed an improbable 38-28 victory over the Eagles.

blocking enough to start for the 49ers, but as a pass catcher he is perhaps the best tight end the 49ers have ever had.

Jones's success came as a surprise even to close observers of the 49ers because he followed such an unusual route to stardom. Jones, who played his college ball at Santa Clara, just a few miles from the 49ers' current practice facility, was drafted by the Pittsburgh Steelers in 1986 but released because a back injury suffered in an automobile accident was slow to heal. He came home and signed with the 49ers, not realizing that Walsh, knowing there could be a strike in 1987, was signing many players who could be used on a replacement team. "When I got to camp," he said, "I was eighth on the depth chart at tight end."

He injured his neck in the opening preseason game in 1987, but Walsh recognized his potential and kept him on the squad. He blossomed in 1989 after starting tight end John Frank, who planned to become a doctor, quit football because he feared he would damage his hands.

Just as important as Jones's development for the 49ers was the emergence of wide receiver John Taylor, who developed into the perfect complement to Jerry Rice. Taylor, an even better open-field runner than Rice, was another of Walsh's remarkable draft picks. An unknown when he was drafted in the third round in 1986, Taylor missed his first season with a back injury and caught only 23 passes the next two years, but he came into his own in 1989 with 60 catches for 1,077 yards.

Eventually, the 1989 team would be compared to the 1984 champions because it was so dominant, but in the beginning of the season it seemed the comparison might be with the 1981 team, when Montana's heroics made the difference in so many close games.

In the second game of the season, for instance, the 49ers beat the Buccaneers 20-16 when Montana ran 4 yards for a touchdown with only 40 seconds left. The next week, Montana threw 4 touchdown passes in the fourth quarter to rally the 49ers past the Eagles, 38-28.

By the end of the season the 49ers were breezing. They closed the year with five consecutive

Joe Montana and Jerry Rice teamed on 55 touchdown passes between 1985 and 1990.

victories—the only close one a 30-27 win over the Rams in which Taylor set a club record with 286 receiving yards and Montana set another with 458 passing yards—and finished 14-2.

That kind of finish was typical of the 49ers in the eighties. In 1981 (five games), 1984 (nine games), and 1987 (six games), San Francisco finished the regular season with long winning streaks. In 1983 they won their last three. In 1985, 1986, and 1988, they won four of their last five. The 49ers' formula—more mental preparation and less head-butting on the practice field—was a major factor in their success.

"We've always been fresher, mentally and physically, than other teams late in the season because we don't do so much hitting on the practice field," Jones said. "Football is a very tough game, and it's impossible to recover by Tuesday from a Sunday game. Yet there are still many coaches who don't get that message. When players come to our team, they're usually surprised by how little hitting we do on the practice field."

In 1984, 49ers were dominant from start to finish. The 1989 team had more ups and downs, and more games when it took extraordinary individual performances to pull out victories, but when the postseason arrived, the 1989 team was more dominating than the '84 champions.

CRUISING THROUGH THE PLAYOFFS

The divisional playoff game against Minnesota at Candlestick Park would pose no problem because the 49ers discovered the way to block the Vikings' pass rushers the year before. Given the time he needed, Montana threw 4 touchdown passes, one of 72 yards to Rice only five minutes into the game, and the 49ers breezed to a 41-13 victory.

Significantly, Roger Craig rushed for 125 yards on 18 carries, the best single-game performance against Minnesota that season and Craig's best outing since he rushed for 131 yards in the season opener against Indianapolis. He never used injuries as an excuse during the season, and his performance

The 49ers routed the Broncos 55-10 in a record-setting offensive performance in Super Bowl XXIV. Joe Montana threw 5 touchdown passes in the game, 3 of them to Jerry Rice.

in this game showed that he was still a top-notch running back.

That set up the NFC Championship Game against the Los Angeles Rams, who were playing very well. The Rams won five of their last six games to finish the regular season 11-5, losing only to the 49ers down the stretch. They beat the Eastern Division–champion Eagles 21-7 in a wild-card game in Philadelphia and then defeated the Giants 19-13 in an overtime thriller.

The Rams led 3-0 in the title game when Ronnie Lott made one of those plays that turn a game around, knocking down a long pass from Jim Everett to Willie Anderson at San Francisco's 10-yard line. Had Lott not made that play, Anderson probably would have scored, and a 10-0 lead would have given Los Angeles a considerable boost of confidence. As it was, that was the Rams' last gasp. Everett could be pressured into making bad throws,

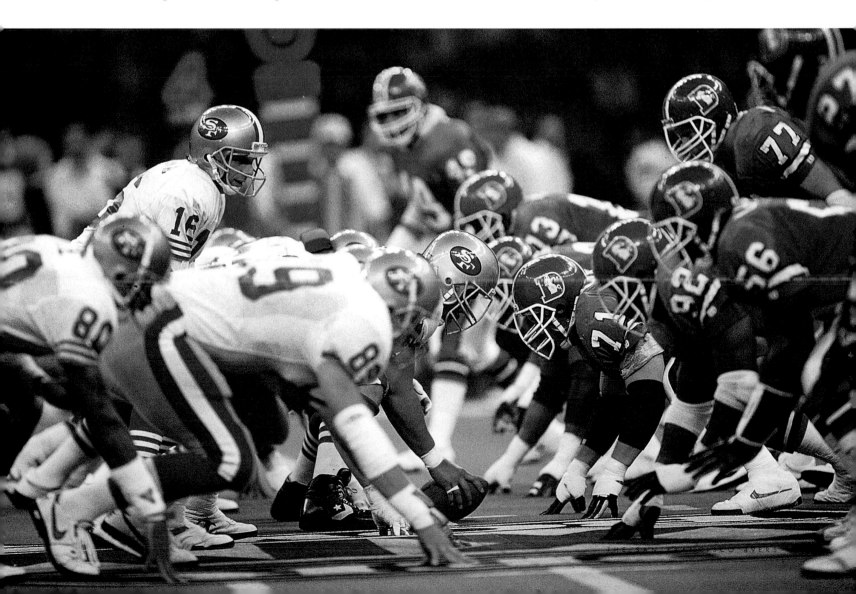

and the 49ers' defense harassed him the rest of the game. The Rams' quarterback completed only 16 of 36 passes and threw 3 interceptions; the Rams didn't advance beyond midfield in the second half.

Meanwhile, Montana was having a near-perfect game, completing 26 of 30 attempts for 262 yards and 2 touchdowns. The 49ers posted a lopsided 30-3 victory.

BACK-TO-BACK

By this time, the NFC was clearly the dominant conference, having won five consecutive Super Bowls. The 49ers were favored over the Denver Broncos by nearly 2 touchdowns in Super Bowl XXIV. Almost everybody in the media predicted a lopsided 49ers victory.

The 49ers could easily have become overconfident, too, except that they had only to look back one year to see what could happen. They were heavily favored to beat Cincinnati, too, yet came perilously close to losing.

In private interviews, Bill Walsh said he expected the game to be a rout. "With their defensive alignment," he said, "they can't put pressure on Joe and they can't cover Rice, Taylor, and Jones. I'd expect the 49ers to score at least five touchdowns, and I can't see the Broncos getting more than two or three against the 49ers' defense."

Walsh was conservative. The 49ers led 7-3 until Montana threw a 7-yard touchdown pass to Jones with three seconds left in the first quarter. The rout was on. The 49ers scored 2 touchdowns in each of the next three quarters, while the Broncos registered only a third-quarter touchdown.

Denver's John Elway, one of the finest quarterbacks in NFL history, had a miserable day as the 49ers' pass rushers teed off, aware that he had to throw in a futile effort to catch up. Elway completed only 10 of 26 passes for 108 yards. He was intercepted twice.

In the third quarter, Randy Cross, who had done television reports during the week, came into the press box. "If this were a boxing match, the referee would end it," he said. The Broncos had no such hope. The final score was 55-10.

Montana, who completed 22 of 29 passes for 297 yards and a record 5 touchdowns, became the first

Owner Edward DeBartolo, Jr., gets a celebratory bath from Keena Turner (far right) in the victors' locker room following Super Bowl XXIV.

player to earn the Super Bowl's MVP award three times. He also set Super Bowl career records for pass attempts (122), completions (83), yards (1,142), and touchdowns (11). In four Super Bowls, he never threw an interception.

A LOFTY GOAL

For 1990, the 49ers adopted an awkward slogan, "Three-peat," as they tried to become the first team to win three consecutive Super Bowls. They came within one play of getting back to the Super Bowl, but it was an agonizing year that ended with the departures of Lott and Craig.

"There was a feeling of invincibility throughout the organization," said Carmen Policy, the team's current president, and its executive vice president at that time. "The players thought they were part of a dynasty. The pundits thought we were poised to win another one.

"Our payroll was terribly high. The DeBartolos were funding losses of $10 million or more. It should have been a year of rebuilding, bringing in youth, cutting our payroll, and getting ourselves back to financial reality. But we saw the opportunity to become the first team to win three straight Super Bowls and five total. So we made a conscious decision to go for it. Eddie [DeBartolo, Jr.] committed a lot of capital. We not only took care of our veterans but went out and got expensive backups."

Montana began the season as if he were going to break every club record. He broke two in a memorable performance against Atlanta in the fifth game, throwing for 476 yards and 6 touchdowns in a 45-35 victory.

Three weeks later, Montana passed for 411 yards against Green Bay. He also had games of 398, 390, and 318 yards in the first half of the season. Some observers thought he'd never been better, but in the second half of the season, Montana's statistics declined dramatically. He failed to throw for 300 yards in any of the final eight games. He fell below 200 three times and had 88 yards when he played only the first half of the regular season finale.

What made the difference? Roger Craig was injured, and Montana no longer had an effective running threat to complement his passing.

LOST OPPORTUNITY

To some fans, running back Roger Craig (33) will always be associated with the fumble that set up the Giants' winning field goal in the 1990 NFC Championship Game, thus ending the 49ers' chance to become the first team to win three consecutive Super Bowls.

That's a bitter reality for Craig, and an ironic one. "I was never a fumbler," he said. "I had a clause in my contract that I'd get a bonus if I fumbled fewer than three times in a season, and I always reached that goal."

For Craig, the fumble was devastating. "That put a black cloud over me for months," he said. "I always felt that if I did something wrong, I had to do something right to make up for it right away, but I didn't have a chance this time. That's the last thing 49er fans had to remember about me."

Craig tore a ligament in his knee in the fourth game of the season, against Houston. He had his poorest season as a 49er, rushing for only 439 yards and averaging just 3.1 yards per carry. He didn't even lead the team in rushing (rookie Dexter Carter ran for 460 yards). Overall, the entire team gained only 1,718 yards rushing in 1990. By contrast, in 1981 when no one thought they had a running attack, they gained 1,941.

Incredibly, though, they kept winning. By the eleventh week of the season, the 49ers and the New York Giants were 10-0. The next week, the 49ers lost to the Rams, but the Giants also lost. In what was either a brilliant bit of scheduling or a terrific piece of luck, the 49ers and Giants were scheduled to meet in a Monday-night game on December 3 at Candlestick.

The 49ers won a great defensive battle 7-3. All the scoring came in the second quarter: a field goal by the Giants, and a 4-yard touchdown pass from Montana to Taylor. "That game was by far the best football game I've ever played in," Lott said. "The emotion, the whole dynamics of what had happened during the year, the hype. That game lived up to the hype. It was the most physical, 1960s-type game I've ever been associated with."

The win put the 49ers ahead of the Giants in the battle for home-field advantage in the playoffs. The 49ers lost to New Orleans late in the year, but finished the regular season 14-2 and upheld their lead.

The 49ers easily beat the Redskins 28-10 in the divisional playoffs. The most memorable moment of that game was supplied by nose tackle Michael Carter, who intercepted a tipped pass and lumbered 61 yards for a touchdown, looking as if he might fall down at any moment. That brought up the rematch everybody expected—the 49ers and Giants in the NFC Championship Game.

There may never have been two more evenly-matched teams in a title game. Montana's passing gave the 49ers an edge on offense, but that was offset because the Giants' fierce defense yielded yards and points grudgingly.

Montana and Taylor teamed for one big play, a 61-yard touchdown pass in the third quarter. Otherwise, it was all field goals, 2 by the 49ers'

Mike Cofer and 3 by the Giants' Matt Bahr, as the 49ers took a 13-9 lead into the fourth quarter.

Bahr kicked another field goal to close the gap to 13-12. Then, as the 49ers tried desperately to widen their lead, Giants defensive end Leonard Marshall burst through blockers to flatten Montana from the blind side, breaking Montana's hand, bruising his sternum, and giving him a concussion. Effectively, that momentarily symbolized the close of Montana's great 49ers' career because he would never again play in a meaningful situation for them.

Steve Young relieved Montana and completed

Brent Jones gives the 49ers a formidable pass-catching threat at tight end. By the end of the 1994 season, he'd moved into the franchise's top ten for career receptions.

a key 25-yard pass to Brent Jones, but with 2:36 left in the game, Craig fumbled and linebacker Lawrence Taylor recovered for the Giants at their 43-yard line. New York drove 33 yards in six plays, and Bahr's 42-yard field goal on the last play of the game gave the Giants a 15-13 victory. New York didn't score a touchdown in two games against the 49ers, but the Giants were in the Super Bowl. The fallout from that game was almost as devastating as the game itself.

"Everybody was really, really hurting when that was over," Policy said. "There was a hostility that

Linebacker Matt Millen (opposite) and fullback Tom Rathman (above) were two of the most rugged players in 49ers history. (Left) special consultant Harry Edwards and linebacker Keena Turner talk in the locker room.

seemed to develop that was most uncharacteristic of the people who make up this organization."

The decision was made to do what had been postponed the year before: reduce the payroll by releasing veteran players such as Eric Wright, Keena Turner, and Mike Wilson. The 49ers decided to let Craig and Lott become unprotected free agents under the NFL's Plan B. They wanted to keep both players, but at reduced salaries. In addition, they assumed each player had only one year left in his career.

A man of fierce pride, Lott was determined to play more than one year, and he was galled by being put subjected to Plan B. He signed with the Raiders, played two years there, and then moved on to the New York Jets.

The issue with Craig was purely financial—he got a better offer from the Raiders. He played one year in Los Angeles and two seasons with Minnesota before retiring. "If I had it to do all over again," Craig said, "I'd have kept my butt right here [San Francisco]. At the time, I thought it was important to do the best thing for my family, but playing for the Raiders and the Vikings was just a blur for me. My memories are all here. I'm a 49er."

But in 1991, Craig and Lott were Raiders. It was the end of an era.

STEVE YOUNG TAKES OVER

It was August 23, 1991. The 49ers were scheduled to play an exhibition game against the Seattle Seahawks. Bill Walsh told NBC's national television audience that Joe Montana felt a twinge in his right elbow and would not play that night.

It was assumed that Montana would miss the first couple of games in the regular season—at most—but four days later, he was put on injured reserve.

Enter Steve Young.

Young came to the 49ers in 1987 expecting to be the starter in a relatively short time, but his chief duty the next few seasons was signaling plays from the sideline.

(Opposite) Ray Rhodes tutors the defensive backs in 1990; (above) defensive end Pierce Holt.

"When George Seifert came in, he basically told me to sit down," Young said. "He didn't want to hear me complaining. Now, looking at it from his perspective, I can understand what George was thinking. At the time, though, it was pretty hard.

"But I didn't want to go in and say, 'Trade me,' because who knows where I would have gone. Maybe I'd have gotten into another situation like Tampa Bay, and I sure didn't want that."

Young became a starter when Montana went on injured reserve, but it was assumed he was just keeping the position warm—until Montana had elbow surgery on October 9.

It was a crazy season, starting with the opener against the Giants, which New York won 16-14 in a virtual replay of the 1990 championship game. The Giants won when Matt Bahr kicked a field goal with just five seconds remaining. Young played reasonably well against the Giants' tough defense (he completed 12 of 22 passes for 162 yards and 1 touchdown, with 1 interception), but to no avail.

Young had only one bad game in his first nine, throwing 2 interceptions in a 12-6 loss to the Raiders. He had some excellent games also: 26 of 36 for 348 yards and 3 touchdowns against the Chargers; 19 of 27 for 275 yards and 2 touchdowns against the Vikings; 21 of 31 for 288 yards and 2 touchdowns against the Rams; 22 of 38 for 348 yards and 2 touchdowns (plus 68 yards and 2 touchdowns rushing) against Atlanta; and 18 of 20 for 237 yards and 2 touchdowns against Detroit.

Unfortunately, Young's individual success didn't always translate into team success. The 49ers were 4-5 after nine games, and there were various problems. The drafts since the great one in 1986 had been disappointing. From subsequent drafts, only tackle Harris Barton (1987) and defensive tackle Pierce Holt (1988) were significant players on the 1991 team. Defensively, Ronnie Lott's leadership and ability were missed. Offensively, the 49ers had no running back capable of replacing Roger Craig.

They often played just well enough to lose, but to the media and many of their fans, there was only one explanation for the 49ers' poor start: Steve Young.

Young was quite different from Montana. On the plus side, he was a better runner than Montana ever was—as fast or faster than most running backs and elusive enough to escape from pass rushers. He also was a better passer than Montana, going deep.

Young could not, however, make the quick passing decisions that Montana could (no other quarterback could, either), nor did he have the same kind of accuracy. Young was a very accurate passer, but Montana was able to hit receivers at exactly the

Wide receiver John Taylor proved to be the perfect complement to Jerry Rice.

right spot so they didn't have to break stride. Young got the ball to his receivers, but often just a little high or low, causing them to delay a fraction of a second. In the 49ers' intricate "timing" offense, that could make the difference between a short-yardage play and a big gainer.

At first, Young and Jerry Rice weren't comfortable together. "Our timing was off a little," Rice said, "and we didn't have the same chemistry I'd had with Joe. I don't think Steve was used to some of the things I did. I didn't really start getting comfortable with him until the 1993 season."

The 49ers' players had great confidence in Montana, not just in his ability but also in his leadership. When they got into tight situations, they were certain he would bring them victory. They had neither the same experience nor confidence with Young at quarterback—which he understood. "You don't just step up and say you're a leader," Young said. "People have to decide to follow you, and that's what makes you a leader. It wasn't easy here because I was following one of the game's all-time great leaders."

Young's teammates just were starting to get comfortable with him when he injured his knee against Atlanta in the ninth game of the season. Steve Bono came in for the second half of the game (Atlanta came from behind to win 17-14), and he started against New Orleans a week later. That 10-3 loss dropped San Francisco's record to 4-6.

But then the 49ers' rallied to win five consecutive games with Bono at quarterback. Young was healthy for the final game of the season against Chicago. Seifert put him back in the starting lineup even though there was considerable public support for Bono.

Young delivered his best game yet, completing 21 of 32 passes for 338 yards and 3 touchdowns and running for 63 yards and another touchdown in a 52-14 rout. It was the sixth consecutive victory for the 49ers, who finished the regular season 10-6 and may have been the best team in the league at that point.

Statistically, Young had an excellent season, completing 65 percent of his passes for 2,517 yards and 17 touchdowns, with only 8 interceptions. He led the NFL with a quarterback rating of 101.8. Despite the 49ers' late rush, however, they missed the playoffs for the first time since 1982, and

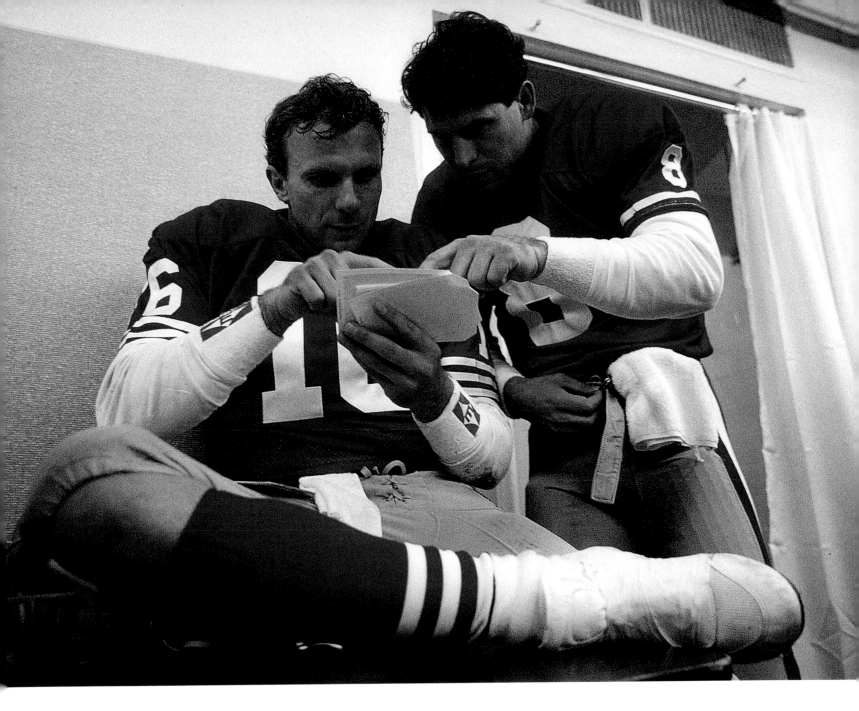

the fans could hardly wait for the return of Joe Montana in 1992.

MORE ELBOW PROBLEMS

Montana threw passes in the 49ers' mini-camp in the spring and, according to Seifert, "looked better than he'd ever looked." Seifert figured he'd be the starting quarterback, and Montana's picture adorned the club's media guide. He had minor elbow surgery on May 14, 1992, to remove scar tissue.

But Montana's elbow flared up on him again in training camp. The elbow didn't respond to treatment. "There was a point in August where there was

(Above) Joe Montana and Steve Young, two masters at reading opposing defenses, compare notes at half-time; (page 200) Jesse Sapolu is a versatile offensive lineman who has played twelve seasons with the 49ers and made the Pro Bowl at both center and guard; (page 201) strong-legged Mike Cofer led the 49ers in scoring each year from 1988 to 1993. His 56-yard field goal against Atlanta in 1990 is the longest in club history.

serious consideration simply to put Joe on injured reserve for the season," Policy said. "Our thinking was this way everybody would know who the quarterback was. We wouldn't be waiting for somebody to come out of right field. Then we got to thinking that it wouldn't be fair to Joe—and what would happen if at midseason he was throwing great, especially if Steve got hurt."

On September 12, Montana had another operation on his elbow, his third in eleven months, to remove more scar tissue. After that there were almost daily reports throughout the season on the condition of Montana's arm—even stories of Montana playing catch with his kids in the backyard.

Meanwhile, Seifert tried to keep the team focused. When Montana was able to throw, he did it apart from the regular team practice so that it wouldn't be a distraction. By the season's twelfth game or so, Montana was probably able to play again, but Seifert did not activate him until the final week.

For his part, Young was having one of the best seasons of any quarterback in NFL history. He completed 66.7 percent of his passes for 3,465 yards, averaged more than 8.6 yards per pass attempt, and threw for 25 touchdowns with only 7 interceptions, compiling a league-leading quarterback rating of 107.0. He was voted the league's most valuable player.

A NEW APPROACH

To an extent, Young's success was due to a change in offensive coordinators. Mike Holmgren had departed to become head coach at Green Bay, and Mike Shanahan brought a slightly different approach to the 49ers' offense. Shanahan changed the order in which the quarterback looked for receivers on certain patterns. "Just a little change like that made it easier for us to move the ball against a team like New Orleans, which had played us so much and knew us so well," Young said.

Shanahan helped Young in other ways, too. "He made me think more about the mental approach," Young said. "I just wanted to go out there and play, but he made me see that if I look at films just a little longer, I can learn something that will help me on the field. He really has a knack for thinking like a defensive coach. He'll take game films home and then he'll come to me and say, 'This is what the defensive coordinator is going to try to do, and this is what we can do.'"

Young suffered a concussion in the first game of the 1992 season, a 31-14 victory over the Giants, but he came back the next week against Buffalo and not only passed for 449 yards and 3 touchdowns but also ran for 50 yards on 7 carries.

Steve Young (left), George Seifert, and Joe Montana talk things over during a Monday night game against the Giants in 1990. The 10-1 49ers beat the 10-1 Giants 7-3 in a fierce defensive struggle.

Unfortunately, the 49ers' defense couldn't stop
Buffalo, either (neither team punted that day, an
NFL first), and the 49ers lost 34-31. It was all too
reminiscent of 1991, but that would be the last sim-
ilarity. The 49ers won their next five games (including a 56-17 rout of the Falcons, the most points the
49ers ever scored in an NFL game), and later reeled
off eight consecutive victories to finish the regular
season 14-2.

The season was hardly all Steve Young. Rice,
who caught 84 passes, had 10 touchdown receptions
to break Steve Largent's NFL career record of 100
(he finished the season at 103).

Rice, though, had been a constant for years. What
really made the difference in the 49ers' offense in
1992 was Ricky Watters, who took the pressure off
Young with the kind of running the 49ers hadn't
seen since Roger Craig was in his prime. Watters,
who spent his rookie season in 1991 on injured reserve, ran for 100 yards (on only 13 carries) in the
opener against the Giants and had three more 100-
yard games, including 163 yards in a 27-10 victory
over the Rams. He finished the season with 1,013
yards rushing even though he missed two games
with injuries.

More than his ability, though, it was Watters's
exuberant personality that excited the fans. The
49ers did not have demonstrative players or ones
who bragged about their feats. "I let my playing do
my talking," said Rice, who had more to brag about
than anybody else in the league. Watters was quite
different. He flipped himself up from the ground
after tackles without putting his hands down. He
ran back to the huddle instead of trotting and
chattered constantly, telling his quarterback, "Give
me the ball."

"I've always been like that," he said. "From day
one, when I started playing football, baseball,
basketball. It was the same with all sports. If I
did something super, I wanted to celebrate it. Now,
if I make a play, why shouldn't I be happy? I've

(Opposite) Forty-Niners fans were happy to have him back, but Joe Montana—
welcoming Jerry Rice in pregame introductions—was relegated to observer
for most of 1992; (right) Montana's last meaningful game for the 49ers came in
the NFC title game in 1990. He was knocked out in the fourth quarter by a
thundering hit from the Giants' Leonard Marshall.

just gone through some of the best athletes in the world." Watters's emergence as a star was an exciting story, as was Young's MVP season, but those seemed to be only subplots to the main story line for many 49ers fans: When would Joe Montana return?

MONTANA'S 49ER FINALE

Montana returned for the final game of the season, a Monday night game against Detroit.

The game was meaningless to the overall standings because the 49ers had already clinched home-field advantage throughout the playoffs and the Lions, who finished 5-11, were out of contention. It was pouring down rain through most of the game, but none of that mattered to 49ers fans, who went crazy at the appearance of the legendary Montana in a league game for the first time in two years. Montana came on to start the second half with the 49ers leading 7-6. He did little in the third quarter, but in the final stanza he showed the touch that made him famous, throwing 2 touchdown passes. He finished with 15 completions in 21 attempts for 126 yards, and the 49ers won the game 24-6.

The reaction to Montana's appearance showed Seifert's wisdom in withholding him from earlier games. The pressure to play Montana—even though Young was having a great season—would have been almost unbearable if Montana had been activated earlier.

Indeed, there was considerable talk among fans that Montana should start the divisional playoff game against the Washington Redskins. He didn't, and in fact, he would not play a down in the postseason.

HEADING FOR A SHOWDOWN WITH DALLAS

Meanwhile, on another rainy day that turned the Candlestick field to mud, Young had an alternately terrific and terrible day against the Redskins. In the first half, he threw 2 touchdown passes as the 49ers took a 17-3 lead, seemingly on their way to an

FROM BENGALS WIDE RECEIVER CRIS COLLINSWORTH, AFTER THE 49ERS' 20-16 VICTORY OVER CINCINNATI IN SUPER BOWL XXIII:

"JOE MONTANA IS NOT HUMAN. I DON'T WANT TO CALL HIM A GOD, BUT HE'S DEFINITELY SOMEWHERE IN BETWEEN."

(Opposite) Montana is destined to be elected to the Pro Football Hall of Fame when he first becomes eligible, in the year 2000.

easy victory. In the second half, though, Young fumbled twice and threw an interception, and the Redskins closed the gap to 17-13 early in the fourth quarter. The defense, led by Pierce Holt's 3 sacks, shut down the Redskins the rest of the way, and Mike Cofer's 33-yard field goal with 2:22 left made the final score 20-13.

The NFC Championship Game the following week matched the two best teams in the NFL, San Francisco and Dallas. The 49ers were favored slightly because the game was played at Candlestick Park.

The 49ers struck quickly. On the third play of the game, Young spotted a blitz and hit wide-open Jerry Rice on a 63-yard touchdown play. Or so it seemed. An official caught guard Guy McIntyre holding, and the play was called back. The 49ers did not score on that possession. The Cowboys, in fact, scored first on a field goal before Young climaxed a 48-yard drive with a 1-yard run to give the 49ers a 7-3 lead after one quarter.

The 49ers were not able to build on their four-point lead, however, and the Cowboys were able to control the ball with Emmitt Smith's running and Troy Aikman's pin-point passing. At halftime it was 10-10, but the Cowboys took the lead with a 78-yard touchdown drive to begin the second half. Darryl Johnston's 3-yard run made it 17-10.

Cofer cut the 49ers' deficit to 17-13 with a 42-yard field goal, but the Cowboys went on a 79-yard scoring drive capped by Aikman's 16-yard touchdown pass to Smith that not only boosted their lead to 24-13 but also took nine minutes off the clock.

On the 49ers' next series, Young threw a terrible pass that was intercepted by Dallas linebacker Ken Norton, and the Cowboys had another chance to score. Even a field goal would have put them ahead by 2 touchdowns, but aggressive Cowboys coach Jimmy Johnson passed up a short field goal on fourth down and went for a first down. The Cowboys failed, and the 49ers took possession on their 7-yard line.

Young then put together his best series of the game, moving his team 93 yards in nine plays, the

last a 5-yard touchdown pass to Rice to bring his team within 24-20 with 4:22 left. The 49ers were still in the game.

But not for long. With the ball on Dallas's 21-yard line, Aikman hit Alvin Harper on what should have been a short slant pass, but safety Dana Hall came up at the wrong angle and was out of position to make the tackle. Hall didn't catch Harper until he reached the 49ers' 9-yard line, and three plays later Aikman threw a 6-yard touchdown pass to Kelvin Martin. The kick failed, but it didn't matter. The Cowboys were ahead 30-20 and that's how it ended. Desperate for a quick score, Young threw an interception on the 49ers' final drive.

Aikman had a great game, completing 24 of 34

Steve Young (opposite, with Jerry Rice, and below) has taken over the reins at quarterback in the post-Montana era.

passes for 322 yards and 2 touchdowns. He was being called a "young Joe Montana," a comparison that didn't help Young, who already was being compared to the old Joe Montana. In fact, Young had virtually the same statistics as Aikman in the title game, completing 25 of 35 passes for 313 yards and 1 touchdown. The difference between the teams was their defense, not their quarterbacks.

AN EVENTFUL OFFSEASON

It would be a long and contentious offseason for the 49ers. In the first year of true "free agency," teams that reached the conference championship games were restricted in their pursuit of free agents. The clause, known as the Rooney Rule

because it was proposed by Pittsburgh owner Dan Rooney, may have been aimed at the 49ers because many NFL owners had resented the fact that Eddie DeBartolo, Jr., spent money so freely to keep his team at the top.

The 49ers designated Holt as a "transition player," which gave them the right to match any offer, but when the Atlanta Falcons made an offer that was guaranteed, they did not match it and lost their most valuable defensive player. They also lost Tim Harris, who had led the team with 17 sacks in 1992. To strengthen their defense, they picked up safety Tim McDonald, but their efforts to sign free-agent defensive end Reggie White, the NFL's career sacks leader, failed because, limited by provisions of the Rooney Rule, they could not match Green Bay's offer to White.

All of this paled in comparison to The Joe Montana Story. Would Montana be traded? Would he return as the starting quarterback? What did he want to do? Were the 49ers' being fair to him? Those questions dominated newspaper columns, radio talk shows, and television. The controversy almost tore apart the 49ers' organization.

"That whole offseason was a nightmare," Policy said. "The guys in this organization who eat, drink, and sleep 49ers were thinking, 'Are we being fair to Joe?' There was a division of loyalty. That's not the way we've operated, but there were people who felt we should go one way, while people who worked right next door felt we should go the other way. It was a tremendous distraction.

"You had the fan reaction and then you had Eddie [DeBartolo, Jr.], who grew up with Joe. Eddie will never forget the defining moments of 1981, everything that went with that year. I think the thought of Joe in another uniform caused him to distance himself from the club."

The 49ers were inundated with calls and letters

ROAD WARRIORS

When the 49ers defeated the Washington Redskins 30-17 at RFK Stadium early in the 1981 season, it marked a dramatic change in their fortunes away from home. Prior to that victory, San Francisco had dropped 26 of its previous 28 road games. Since then, the 49ers have won on the road at an astonishing clip of better than 75 percent. From late in 1988 through the 1990 season, the 49ers won an NFL-record 18 consecutive road games— no other team has won more than 11 in a row away from home. Each NFL team's road record from 1981 to 1994:

Team	W- L- T	Pct.
San Francisco	81-26-1	.755
Miami	60-49-0	.550
Washington	60-49-0	.550
L.A. Raiders	57-51-0	.528
Dallas	56-52-0	.519
N.Y. Giants	54-52-1	.509
Chicago	54-54-0	.500
New Orleans	53-55-0	.491
Philadelphia	50-56-1	.472
N.Y. Jets	48-59-1	.449
Cleveland	47-62-0	.431
Minnesota	46-61-0	.430
Denver	45-61-1	.425
Pittsburgh	45-64-0	.413
San Diego	45-64-0	.413
Buffalo	44-63-0	.411
L.A. Rams	44-64-0	.407
Green Bay	40-67-1	.375
Seattle	40-67-0	.374
Kansas City	38-69-2	.358
Cincinnati	38-70-0	.352
Detroit	38-70-0	.352
New England	38-70-0	.352
Arizona	36-72-1	.335
Indianapolis	35-73-0	.324
Houston	32-76-0	.296
Atlanta	30-77-0	.280
Tampa Bay	21-87-0	.194

from fans demanding that Montana be named the starting quarterback. Policy got calls from team executives around the league wondering what was happening. The 49ers left it up to Montana to decide whether to stay or be traded. If he had to make a choice, Seifert wanted Young as his quarterback. Seifert was being realistic. He knew Montana's football health was precarious and that, because of his elbow problems, he was not the quarterback he had been.

But Seifert also knew that it never would work to have Montana on the bench, so he told DeBartolo that if Montana stayed, he would bring him to training camp as the starting quarterback—though Young would have a chance to beat him out.

That announcement was interpreted as a decision made by DeBartolo, with Seifert falling in line as the good soldier. But Seifert, DeBartolo, and Policy all insist that it was Seifert's decision. "Eddie was very pumped up, because he thought that was all that had to be done," Policy said.

Then Montana flew to Youngstown, Ohio, to meet with DeBartolo and tell him that he wanted to go to Kansas City. Policy worked out a deal for Montana that included a first-round draft pick from the Chiefs (which turned out to be Dana Stubblefield, a very good defensive lineman), defensive back David Whitmore, and a third-round draft choice. It was a surprisingly good trade. In preliminary discussions with other clubs, Policy had no offer higher than a third-round draft pick until Phoenix owner Bill Bidwill said he'd give up a first-round choice. Montana wanted to go to Kansas City, not Phoenix, so Policy made the deal with the Chiefs.

Before the press conference announcing the trade, Policy remembers Montana telling him, "This is the best thing for everybody. I can understand Eddie not seeing it, but next year you

Offensive coordinator Mike Shanahan (left) brought new twists to the 49ers' offense in 1992. Shanahan was named the Broncos' head coach in 1995.

guys are going to have a salary cap. I'm going to be a big noose around your neck. If I go to Kansas City, I'm the man. If I get hurt, they're going to be praying I get healthy. If I stay here and get hurt, I'll be pushed out."

Montana's assessment was right on target, and the trade worked out well for both teams. Montana was hurt frequently in Kansas City, but played well enough when healthy to lead the Chiefs to the AFC Championship Game. Young had another strong season for the 49ers and he, too, led his team to the conference championship game.

LIFE AFTER MONTANA

The 1993 season did not start well for the 49ers. In a freak accident in a preseason game against the Raiders, Young hit his left thumb on the helmet of a defensive lineman and broke a couple of small bones. He returned to the lineup for the regular-season opener in Pittsburgh but obviously was still bothered by the injury. Uncharacteristically, he threw 6 interceptions in the first two games as the 49ers beat the Steelers and lost to the Cleveland Browns.

Young's passing improved—5 touchdowns and 3 interceptions in the next four games—as his thumb began to heal. The 49ers split those four games, however, and the nature of the two losses seemed to indicate that the 49ers had slipped from their lofty NFL perch.

The first loss was at New Orleans. Theretofore, it was a given that, in a key game, the 49ers would always find a way to beat the Saints. This time, it was the Saints who made the big plays.

Trailing 13-10 late in the fourth quarter, the 49ers seemed on their way to a touchdown when Young was sacked on third down. Mike Cofer's 30-yard field goal tied the score with 1:14 left. The objective for the 49ers' defense was clear: stop the Saints before they got in position for a Morten Andersen field goal. But New Orleans quarterback Wade Wilson moved the Saints to San Francisco's 32-yard line, and Andersen's 49-yard field goal with five seconds left won the game.

Two weeks later, the 49ers lost 26-17 at Dallas. Again, it was not just the loss but the way it happened. The 49ers always played offense aggressively.

(Opposite) Even the pros need some help now and then; (above) nose tackle Michael Carter looks over photos taken from the press box high above the field.

They didn't subscribe to the "take what the defense gives you" theory; when they had the ball they dictated to the opposing defense. This time, though, the 49ers tried to finesse the Cowboys. They used Watters more as a flanker than a running back; he ran the ball only 8 times. They used Rice more as a decoy than a receiver; though he caught 7 passes, most were long after the issue was decided. The 49ers, in fact, scored only 1 offensive touchdown, on a 12-yard pass from Young to tight end Brent Jones. Their other touchdown came on a 47-yard fumble return by cornerback Eric Davis.

At 3-3, the 49ers trailed the Saints by two games in the NFC West and seemed to be going nowhere. But the Dallas game was a wakeup call for them. They would win their next six games.

(Above) players await the outcome of the coin toss prior to an important regular-season game against the Cowboys in 1994; team president Carmen Policy chats with cornerback Deion Sanders (right); (opposite) full-back William Floyd enjoys some solitude.

The streak started with a 28-14 victory over Phoenix that was sparked by a 9-catch, 155-yard, 2-touchdown performance by Rice. It continued with three consecutive victories in which the 49ers scored at least 40 points: 40-17 over the Rams, 45-21 over Tampa Bay, and a crushing 42-7 win over the slumping Saints, which put the 49ers in first place in the NFC West to stay. Relatively modest victories of 35-10 over the Rams and 21-8 over the Bengals improved the 49ers' record to 9-3. Young set a club record during the winning streak by throwing 183 consecutive passes without an interception, breaking Montana's mark of 154.

There was one more offensive explosion. In the fourteenth game, at Detroit, the 49ers amassed 565 total yards in a 55-17 romp. Young passed for 354 yards and 4 touchdowns in just three quarters before giving way to Steve Bono. For Young, it was a satisfying season. Despite the early injury, he set a club record with 4,023 passing yards, and with a rating of 101.5, became the first quarterback to lead the league in passing three consecutive years.

Just as important personally, Young felt he was becoming more effective within the 49ers' system. "I'm making better decisions because I understand the system better," he said, "and I'm running less every season. I've always said I don't want the play to end with the ball in my hand. I'm taking that extra look now, to see if there's a receiver I can dump it off to. I'd rather dump it off and get seven yards than run for ten, because when I pass the ball, I'm involving others in the offense, and that keeps everybody happy."

The 49ers had nothing to prove in their final two games (having clinched the NFC West), so Seifert rested his star players, including Young. They lost both games and finished 10-6.

That made some people think the Giants might

CENTURY MARKS

The NFL rates its passers through a complex formula that considers a quarterback's touchdown passes, completions, interceptions, and yards per attempt. Steve Young led the NFL four years in a row by compiling a passing rating of more than 100 from 1991 to 1994. No other quarterback has led the league in passing more than two consecutive years, and none have posted back-to-back seasons with a rating exceeding 100. In fact, there have been only twenty instances where quarterbacks have exceeded a rating of 100, and 49ers' quarterbacks have accounted for seven of them:

Player, Team	Season	Rating
Steve Young, San Francisco	1994	112.8
Joe Montana, San Francisco	1989	112.4
Milt Plum, Cleveland	1960	110.4
Sammy Baugh, Washington	1945	109.9
Dan Marino, Miami	1984	108.9
Sid Luckman, Chicago	1943	107.5
Steve Young, San Francisco	1992	107.0
Bart Starr, Green Bay	1966	105.0
Roger Staubach, Dallas	1971	104.8
Y. A. Tittle, N.Y. Giants	1963	104.8
Bart Starr, Green Bay	1968	104.3
Ken Stabler, Oakland	1976	103.4
Joe Montana, San Francisco	1984	102.9
Charlie Conerly, N.Y. Giants	1959	102.7
Bert Jones, Baltimore	1976	102.5
Joe Montana, San Francisco	1987	102.1
Steve Young, San Francisco	1991	101.8
Len Dawson, Kansas City	1966	101.7
Steve Young, San Francisco	1993	101.5
Jim Kelly, Buffalo	1990	101.2

(Opposite) Steve Young has been remarkably proficient since taking over as the 49ers' quarterback full time in 1991. He's now the highest rated passer in NFL history.

pose a problem for the 49ers in a divisional playoff game at Candlestick Park. The 49ers, though, matched up well against the Giants' two-deep zone. Before the game, Bill Walsh said that because the Giants' safeties played so deep, they would be unable to support against the run or to stop the 49ers' crossing patterns. He was right on both counts. Young had a flawless day, completing 17 of 22 passes for 226 yards, and Watters scored a postseason-record 5 touchdowns as the 49ers cruised to a 44-3 victory.

That was the good news. The bad news was that the 49ers would have to travel to Dallas to play the Cowboys again in the NFC Championship Game. It was a game for little more than a quarter only. The 49ers' tied the score at 7-7 when Young threw a 7-yard touchdown pass to running back Tom Rathman on the first play of the second quarter, but the Cowboys scored 3 touchdowns before halftime to break open the game. Dallas won 38-21, and it wasn't that close.

The year before, the 49ers had played the "What-if?" game: What if that first touchdown pass hadn't been called back? What if they'd stopped Alvin Harper for a short gain instead of giving up a 70-yard play? There was no speculation this time. The 49ers were beaten soundly. There would have to be some big changes before the next season if they were to get back to the Super Bowl.

CHANGES FOR THE BETTER

The devastating whipping by Dallas in the 1993 NFC Championship Game forced the 49ers to face a bitter reality: though they might be the second-best team in the league, the gap between them and the Cowboys was large and widening. Something drastic had to be done.

"We were all terribly embarrassed after the championship game," club president Carmen Policy said. "It hurt pretty bad. Some people were saying

The Best Ever?

When the 49ers drafted wide receiver Jerry Rice in 1985, they knew they were getting a good player. What they didn't know was that they were getting a perfectionist in everything from running routes to tucking in his uniform.

"I was a very neat person in high school," Rice said. "If I had a pair of jeans, they had to be starched. When I went to college, I had a roommate who just threw things around. I can't live like that. I have to have a clean environment.

"In college, I would take my uniform home every day and wash it in the sink. We [the wide receivers] took a lot of pride in how we practiced and how we wore our uniforms. The socks and the shoes had to be just right. I have to have a new pair of shoes every game. My socks have to fit just right. I have to be comfortable. If you notice me on the field, I'm always tucking something in."

Rice also is superstitious. "When we played [a divisional playoff game against the Giants] in the Meadowlands in 1987, I was wearing long sleeves and

Rice and San Francisco mayor Frank Jordan (right) celebrate Jerry Rice Day in 1994.

I fumbled the ball [on the way to what would have been a touchdown]. I've never worn them since."

The pride that drives Rice to wear a perfect uniform also drives him in practices and games. He's always striving for something better. When he came into the NFL, he weighed 200 pounds, but after five years in the game, he decided that was too much, so he started an incredibly rigorous physical workout routine and diet in the offseason.

Rice leaves nothing to chance. When the rest of the team takes a break during practice, he has assistant equipment manager Ted Walsh throw passes to him — because Walsh is left-handed, as is 49ers quarterback Steve Young.

Rice doesn't mind admitting that he's aware of his competition. "During the season, I keep up with other receivers. If Michael Irvin goes out and catches eight to ten balls, yeah, it's going to tick me off because I'm a competitor. I'm sure they're the same way. If they see me catching five touchdowns, it's going to tick them off."

The Super Bowl victories have been the sweetest for Rice, especially Super Bowl XXIII, when he caught 11 passes for 215 yards and was named the game's most

Once quiet and reserved, Rice emerged as a vocal team leader in 1994.

valuable player. He also has a vivid memory of a 1990 game against Atlanta, when the Falcons inexplicably left cornerback Charles Dimry in single coverage against him the whole game.

"It was like being in some type of zone," Rice said. "The weirdest thing was they kept bringing the house [blitzing]. Every time I came to the line of scrimmage, I looked at the defense and saw the same thing [quarterback] Joe Montana saw. It was just up to me to get open."

Which he did, for a club record 5 touchdown receptions.

There's more to Rice, though, than just catching the ball. He runs out his patterns even when he doesn't think he's getting the ball, to keep the defense honest, and he even relishes blocking, which few receivers like to do. "If I can really stick a guy early, that helps me get in the game," he said.

By almost any standard, Rice is one of the best — if not the best — receivers in NFL history.

From 1992 to 1994, Ricky Watters gave the 49ers their best rushing-receiving threat since the heyday of Roger Craig.

we did better than we deserved to given the defense we had, and that all things considered, we did very well. But if you start thinking like that, the next year you don't make the playoffs.

"It was our opinion that we were better off doing things that would change us and give us the chance of getting to another level—even if we took the risk that we'd fall on our faces and miss the playoffs—than to stand relatively pat, win the division, and fall short again in the playoffs."

The big changes had to come on defense because the offense was the best in the league. Policy and Seifert sat down to list the free agents who could help the team the most. "[Linebacker] Ken Norton, [linebacker] Gary Plummer, and [defensive end] Richard Dent were all on the list," Seifert said. "We liked Norton from the start because we coached him in the Pro Bowl, and we thought he'd provide leadership, as well as his ability. He has a great work ethic. So we made an offer for him first, and then for Plummer." The 49ers got all three—plus linebacker/defensive end Rickey Jackson, center Bart Oates, and (after the second regular-season game) cornerback Deion Sanders. Combined, the six free agents had been to seventeen Pro Bowls.

Around the league, other teams were accusing the 49ers of breaking the salary-cap rules. Policy denied that, pointing out that the 49ers' payroll actually was in the middle of the league. Many of the new contracts had incentive bonuses based on the 49ers reaching the Super Bowl, but even those were not much beyond the norm. "If we win the Super Bowl, we'll pay about $2.7 million in incentives," Policy said. "We're normally in the $2.3 to 2.4 million range."

For most of the free agents, the big incentive was the chance to play on a Super Bowl team. Jackson (previously with the Saints), Plummer (Chargers), and Sanders (Falcons) had never played on one. Oates (Giants) and Dent (Bears) had, but they figured they wouldn't make it back with their old teams. To sign all these players under the salary cap, though, the 49ers had to let some well-paid veterans go elsewhere.

The first player to go was a Seifert favorite, linebacker Bill Romanowski, who was traded to

QUICK WORK

Wide receiver Jerry Rice had 124 career touchdowns when the 1994 season began, only two behind Jim Brown's NFL record of 126. It was a foregone conclusion that Rice would break Brown's record; the only question was when. Rice wanted to do it immediately, against the Los Angeles Raiders in the season opener on Monday night at Candlestick Park.

On the 49ers' first series, Steve Young teamed with Rice on a 69-yard touchdown pass. Rice also scored a touchdown on a 23-yard reverse early in the fourth quarter, tying Brown's record and giving the 49ers an insurmountable 37-14 lead.

With 4:05 left in the game, the 49ers took over on downs at the Raiders' 38-yard line. It seemed time for the regulars to rest, but coach George Seifert sent the first unit out, including Young and Rice. Everybody saw why when, on the first play from scrimmage, Young lofted a pass toward the end zone and Rice leaped high to grab it. The record was his.

the Eagles on draft day. Defensive lineman Ted Washington signed with Denver. Reserve quarterback Steve Bono was traded to Kansas City, leaving the 49ers with only untested reserves Elvis Grbac and Bill Musgrave behind Steve Young. Cornerback Don Griffin and fullback Tom Rathman, both significant players in the past who were on the downhill slope of their careers, were not re-signed.

"We had to have people on the team to make significant plays, to make the difference between reaching the Super Bowl and not reaching the Super Bowl," Policy said. "We wanted to make two or three good moves on defense that would significantly upgrade its talent level and personality. We needed an attitude."

Meanwhile, the 49ers upgraded their scouting, putting rising star Vinny Cerrato in charge, and it resulted in their best draft since 1986. First, they traded up to the number-seven spot in the first round where they selected defensive tackle Bryant Young of Notre Dame. Young and second-year tackle Dana Stubblefield would become the anchors of the defensive line. Then they got fullback William Floyd with a late first-round pick. It was no coincidence that Floyd's first game as a starter would be the first game of a ten-game winning streak. They got kicker Doug Brien in the fourth round and a real surprise in the sixth round—Lee Woodall of West Chester (Pennsylvania). Woodall played defensive back at the NCAA Division II school but became a starting linebacker for the 49ers and played effectively enough to earn all-rookie honors.

The 49ers opened the season with emotional games against the Los Angeles Raiders and on the road at Kansas City. Both opponents were considered Super Bowl contenders, and the Chiefs had the added appeal of Joe Montana. So when the 49ers routed the Raiders 44-14 and lost 24-17 to the Chiefs, the games were given more significance than they deserved. The truly significant games came later: the fifth and sixth games of the season against Philadelphia and Detroit, and the tenth game against Dallas.

The 49ers were hurting, literally, entering the game against the Eagles. Injuries had destroyed the offensive line. At one point early in the season, center Bart Oates was the only healthy lineman who had been projected as a starter — and Oates hadn't been with the team the year before.

Defensively, the 49ers seemed to be standing around. "I think there was a feeling that we'd brought in all these stars and they'd just go out there and do the job," Seifert said, "but it didn't work that way. Everybody was looking at somebody else to do the job, and nobody knew exactly what was expected as far as leadership was concerned."

Even with those problems the 49ers beat two division opponents, the Rams (34-19) and Saints (24-13). But the Eagles' game would be different. The 49ers were destroyed 40-8 as every part of the team broke down.

Late in the third quarter, Seifert lifted Young from the game because he didn't want the Eagles' defense teeing off on his quarterback. Young was enraged. His competitive spirit didn't want to acknowledge the inevitable defeat, and he thought because he was relieved in the middle of a series he was being singled out for blame. He screamed profanities at his coach.

That show of emotion by Young, who was not normally demonstrative in public, was the first step in the 49ers' turnaround. An even more important step came the next week. The 49ers fell behind 14-0 at Detroit, and Young was sacked brutally by the Lions on a third-down play. He had to crawl off the field and, he admitted later, he didn't think he'd return. But he did, and his teammates rallied behind him on the next series. The 49ers came back to beat the Lions 27-21—the start of a ten-game winning streak.

The most important victory in the string came against Dallas in the tenth game of the season. The game didn't start out well for the 49ers: Young was overwhelmed by Dallas's pass rush in the early going, and the Cowboys scored on a touchdown set up by a 90-yard pass from Troy Aikman to Alvin Harper. It was all too reminiscent of the 49ers' breakdowns in the championship games against the Cowboys.

But the 49ers neutralized the Cowboys' pass rush by having Young run naked bootlegs, and they scored the tying touchdown on a drive manufactured solely on the ground.

LOOKING GOOD

When the NFL went to "throwback" uniforms to celebrate the league's seventy-fifth anniversary in 1994, the 49ers chose the 1955 uniforms because they were the only ones that had shaded numbers.

The NFL's plan was to use the uniforms only early in the season, but when the 49ers embarked on a winning streak that eventually tied the franchise's single-season record of ten, coach George Seifert wanted to stay with them. So the 49ers got league permission to keep wearing them.

Did the uniforms bring good luck to the 49ers? They hadn't done much for the players who originally wore them— the 1955 team was 4-8. Of course, that team didn't have Steve Young throwing to Jerry Rice, or Deion Sanders making 3 long interception returns for touchdowns.

At halftime, though, they'd managed a mere 1 yard passing, they were tied 7-7.

For the first time in three years, the 49ers' defense was asserting itself against the Cowboys. Given that kind of help, Young was patient. The threat of his running slowed the pass rushers, particularly defensive end Charles Haley, and Young put the 49ers ahead for the first time with a 57-yard touchdown pass to Jerry Rice in the third quarter. When Rice reached the end zone, Young raced down the field to celebrate with his favorite target.

The 49ers went on to win 21-14, a victory that put them ahead of the Cowboys in the race for home-field advantage in the playoffs. They maintained that edge by winning their next five games before losing a meaningless finale to Minnesota, when Seifert rested his starters as early as the second quarter.

Young, who set an NFL single-season record with a passer rating of 112.8, was named the league's most valuable player for the second time. His teammates honored him with the Len Eshmont Award as the 49ers' most inspirational player.

Deion Sanders was named the NFL's defensive player of the year. George Seifert was the NFC coach of the year. Carmen Policy was named one of the nation's one hundred most influential sports figures by *The Sporting News*.

All the free agent acquisitions made an impact except for Dent, who tore knee ligaments in his second game and missed the rest of the season (except for a brief appearance in the first playoff game).

The twelve-year NFL veteran contributed, however, by tutoring his teammates on the defensive line. "He's our highest-paid coach," Seifert quipped. In the second Atlanta game, Dent rushed out on the field with a water pail during a time out, as if he were an assistant trainer, to give advice. "I told Rickey [Jackson] he'd been beating on his man, so now was the time to give him a fake and go around him. I told Todd [Kelly] he needed to make an inside move. I told Dana [Stubblefield] just to keep doing what he was doing."

This 49ers team was very different than the 49ers of the past. They had demonstrative

Linebacker Gary Plummer (50) was one of a handful of free agents who helped revamp the 49ers' defense in 1994.

(Opposite) Eric Davis set the tone for the victory over Dallas in the 1994 NFC title game with an interception return for a touchdown one minute into the game; (left) Vinny Cerrato, formerly the director of college scouting, was promoted to head of football operations following the 1994 season; (below) Steve Young ran for a touchdown in a rout of the Bears in the '94 divisional playoffs.

players such as Sanders, Watters, and Floyd. That bothered Seifert at first, but he loosened up as the season went along. "We brought in so many diverse personalities that we wondered at first how they'd get along," he said, "but there's great harmony in the clubhouse. We've always had teams that are close, but this one was the closest of all."

The 49ers' first playoff game was against a much-outclassed Chicago Bears' team. The final score was 44-15. The 49ers led 30-3 at halftime, and Seifert took out Young when it reached 37-3 midway through the third quarter.

It was time to play the Cowboys in the NFC Championship Game for the third consecutive year.

THIRD TIME A CHARM

The week was reminiscent of thirteen years before when the 49ers beat the Cowboys for their first conference championship: torrential rains hit the Bay Area, making the Candlestick Park field soggy and slippery, and the 49ers were forced to fly to Phoenix, Arizona, to utilize a dry practice field.

The Latest Legend

As befits a man intelligent enough to finish law school during his playing career, quarterback Steve Young helped to engineer the trade that brought him to the 49ers in 1987.

Young's career had been chaotic. He would have been the first pick in the 1984 NFL draft, but his agent, Leigh Steinberg, could not come to terms with the Cincinnati Bengals so Steinberg worked out a $40 million deal (including annuities) for Young with the Los Angeles Express of the USFL.

That was the last good news for Young for three years. In 1985, injuries reduced Los Angeles's active squad to twenty-four players and forced Young to move to running back at times. He bought his way out of his contract after the season and signed with Tampa Bay, who had obtained his rights by selecting him with the first pick of the 1984 supplemental draft.

At Tampa Bay, owner Hugh Culverhouse told Young, "You're my quarterback." But when Ray Perkins was hired as coach in 1987, he decided to draft Vinny Testaverde, then regarded as a franchise quarterback.

Perkins had a deal worked out for Young to go to St. Louis. Young called Culverhouse and said, "If I'm going to be traded, at least trade me somewhere I want to go."

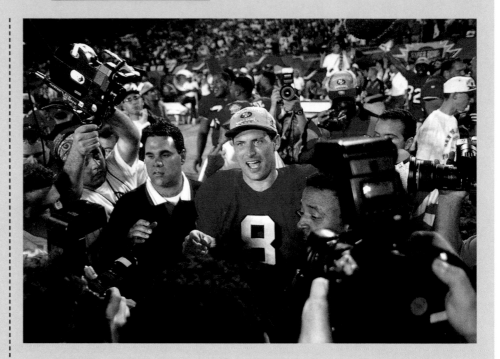

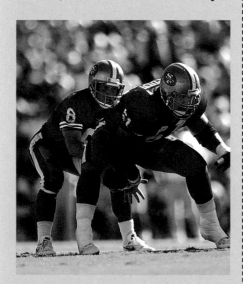

Young led the NFL in passing a record four consecutive seasons, from 1991 to 1994.

Young had heard that Bill Walsh was interested, so he told Culverhouse he wanted to go to the 49ers. A deal was worked out, and Young was traded to the 49ers in exchange for second- and fourth-round draft choices in 1987 and cash. Though many doubted it at the time, Young was a bargain.

"I couldn't believe it when I got here," he said. "At Tampa Bay there was so much going on—racial fights in the dressing room, guys stabbing each other in the back. The football was still fun, but the rest of it—well, if I hadn't been traded, I might have decided it wasn't worth it and just gone to law school.

"When I got here, there was none of that. Everybody was just focused on winning. I think that was the greatest thing Bill did as a coach. I've been around long enough now that I think that's the biggest part of winning. I know Bill passed up some players who were more talented because they didn't have the right attitude."

Once again, Walsh was exercising his independent judgment. At the time, few people in the NFL thought Young would ever be a good quarterback because his play was so unpredictable.

Young was a happy man after leading the 49ers to victory in Super Bowl XXIX.

"I had to unlearn a lot of bad habits," Young said. "At Tampa Bay, we didn't have much of an offensive line, so I was expected to be a wild and crazy guy, just running around and trying to make something happen."

Young played much the same way at first with the 49ers, mixing great and terrible plays. But with the right coaching and the right system, he blossomed into a record-setting quarterback.

Walsh got Young because he feared Joe Montana's career might be nearing an end—Montana missed half of the 1986 season because of back surgery—and Young anticipated moving into the starting lineup much sooner than he did, in 1991.

"If I'd known it would be five years," he said during the 1994 season, "I might have gone somewhere else. Still, I had the best coach and the best system, and I got to watch the master [Montana]—plus, I love the Bay Area. So it all worked out."

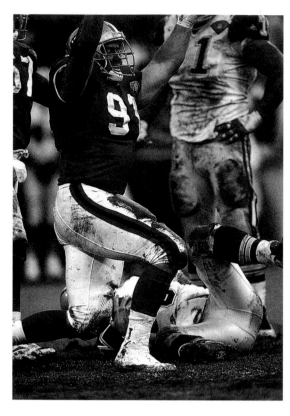

(Left) Defensive tackle Rhett Hall celebrates a sack late in the '94 title-game victory over Dallas; (below) following the game, a jubilant Steve Young took a victory lap around Candlestick, then addressed the crowd and a national television audience.

The Cowboys were talking tough. Charles Haley threatened Steve Young if he tried to run around him again. Michael Irvin guaranteed a Dallas win.

This time, though, the Cowboys' boasts had a hollow ring. The 49ers had shaken them with their regular season victory, and the Cowboys were not the same team they were in the 1993 championship game. Erik Williams, perhaps the best tackle in the game, had been sidelined since midseason from injuries suffered in an automobile accident. Running back Emmitt Smith, the key to Dallas's offense, had a pulled hamstring, and it was questionable how much he would play.

As it happened, Smith was effectively neutralized and taken out of the game when the 49ers jumped to a 21-0 lead midway through the first quarter.

On the game's third play, wide receiver Kevin Williams appeared open to quarterback Troy Aikman, but the 49ers had disguised their coverage and Eric Davis read the play perfectly, putting on a

quick burst to step in front of Williams and intercept at the Cowboys' 44-yard line. He raced into the end zone for a touchdown and a 7-0 lead.

The 49ers switched their pass coverages for this game, putting Deion Sanders on Alvin Harper and Davis on Michael Irvin. The switch paid off on the next series. Aikman hit Irvin for a 16-yard gain, but Davis stripped the ball and Tim McDonald recovered for the 49ers at Dallas's 39.

Five plays later, from the 29, Young looked for Jerry Rice down the middle, then switched to Ricky Watters running down the right sideline, lofting a beautiful pass that Watters caught in stride. Ricky was hit at the 5-yard line, but powered his way into the end zone. "No defensive back is going to keep me out of the end zone," he said later.

On the ensuing kickoff, Williams fumbled at the 35, and 49ers kicker Doug Brien recovered. It was the first time in his career—high school, college, or pro—that Brien recovered a fumble.

It took the 49ers seven plays to get in the end zone. Young's pass to John Taylor resulted in a first down at the 10. On the next play, the 49ers put a back in motion to clear a Dallas linebacker out of the middle. Young ran that gap for 9 yards, and William Floyd ran 1 yard for a touchdown on the next play.

It looked like a rout at that point, but the Cowboys were too good to roll over. They kept coming back on Aikman's passing (380 yards), but the 49ers always had an answer, usually from Young.

After the Cowboys closed the gap to 24-14, for instance, Young lofted a picture-perfect pass to Rice for a 28-yard touchdown eight seconds before halftime. When the Cowboys closed within 10 points again early in the third quarter, Young capped a 70-yard drive by bulling his way into the end zone on a 3-yard touchdown run.

The defense also made enough plays in the fourth quarter—2 sacks by midseason pickup Tim Harris and another by reserve defensive tackle Rhett Hall were the biggest—to keep the game out of reach, and the 49ers won 38-28. They were Super Bowl–bound for the first time in five years—and for the first time without Joe Montana.

It was not a great statistical game for Young, who completed only 13 of 29 passes for 155 yards,

Tackle Harris Barton has been a mainstay on the 49ers' offensive line since being selected in the first round of the 1987 draft.

but he made the big plays when he had to and did not throw an interception. Young also played with great courage. In practice the day before the game, he was knocked over inadvertently by Dent and twisted his neck. He could hardly move his head when he woke up the next morning, but he ignored the pain to play the game. When the game was finally won, Young took a victory lap around the field, and the fans cheered in a way it once seemed they never would.

FIVE-TIME CHAMPIONS

The 49ers played the San Diego Chargers, who upset Pittsburgh in the AFC Championship Game, in Super Bowl XXIX at Miami's Joe Robbie Stadium. Nobody gave the Chargers much chance. "If football is sex," one writer wrote, "the Chargers are the cigarette."

The 49ers were loose and confident. "It's not a matter of whether we respect the Chargers," said center Bart Oates, who had been to two Super Bowls with the Giants. "We just know that if we do the things we can do, we'll win. It's as simple as that."

It wasn't only the seasoned players who were confident. "When I was in my first couple of years with the Redskins," defensive end Charles Mann said, "I followed the veterans around like a puppy dog. I knew I had so much to learn. But these kids [defensive linemen Dana Stubblefield and Bryant Young] don't do that. They feel they already know how to play—and they're right."

The 49ers were so sharp in practice that even tackle Harris Barton, the team's designated worrier, was confident. "Our practices have been unbelievable," Barton said. "This is a fabulous team."

The 49ers' confidence worried former wide receiver Dwight Clark, now a team executive. "Are we okay for this game?" Clark asked a writer the day before the Super Bowl. "I can hardly sleep. I'm afraid the guys are too loose." Clark was too close to the team. Others who had no connections with either team were confident the 49ers would win big.

"It's no advantage to be an underdog in this game," said Fran Tarkenton, the quarterback on three Vikings teams in the Super Bowl. "The Chargers will be coming into this game wondering if they're good enough. The 49ers aren't wondering. They know they're good. Steve Young is a great quarterback, and he's running the best offense the NFL has ever seen."

Hank Stram, who coached the Kansas City Chiefs to victory in Super Bowl IV and who would broadcast the game for CBS radio, also predicted a lopsided 49ers victory. Stram broke the teams down into seventy-four separate categories. "For the NFC Championship Game," he said, "I gave Dallas the advantage by three points, which is basically a pick

FOUR-EVER YOUNG

The final game of the 1994 season was meaningless for the 49ers, but Coach Seifert wanted to give quarterback Steve Young a chance to break the NFL's single-season mark for passing efficiency. Young's predecessor, Joe Montana, set the mark with a rating of 112.4 in 1989, and Young entered the season finale against the Minnesota Vikings at 112.2.

When Young completed a touchdown pass to Jerry Rice early in the second quarter, it increased his rating to 112.8, and Seifert took him out of the game.

Young finished the season as the league's top passer for the fourth consecutive year, and his passer rating topped 100 for the fourth straight year. Both are league records.

'em game. This time, I give the 49ers a thirty-two-point advantage."

Clark and some 49ers fans might have worried about the team being overconfident, but too many players had something to prove for there to be any letdown.

Young, of course, was getting his first chance to start in a Super Bowl, and to prove himself to those who still clung to the memory of Joe Montana and his four Super Bowl championships.

The 49ers had attracted free agents who wanted a shot at a Super Bowl ring. For some, such as Rickey Jackson, it might be the last shot. "Rickey might have been as good an outside linebacker as [former Giants star] Lawrence Taylor," said 49ers defensive back Toi Cook, who played with Jackson at New Orleans, "but LT was in the playoffs, with everybody watching, so he got the attention. I know Rickey's frustration. I was very well paid for several years with the Saints, but I was unhappy. I was especially unhappy when the playoffs came, because we weren't in them."

Asked to compare this team to the 1984 and 1989 editions of the 49ers Seifert said, "Those teams won championships. This team has played very well, but until it wins a championship, I'm not making any comparisons."

The Chargers' pass defense was their vulnerable spot, ranking twenty-second among the twenty-eight NFL teams in the regular season. The 49ers attacked the "soft middle" of San Diego's defense when the teams met in the regular season, and the result was a 38-15 rout. In that game, Chargers defensive coordinator Bill Arnsparger had his linebackers drop deeper than normal, so Young completed pass after pass underneath the coverage. This time, Arnsparger would play his linebackers in a normal position, and the result was even more disastrous. But it wasn't Arnsparger's fault—the Chargers didn't have the players to stop the 49ers no matter what defensive scheme they used.

When the 49ers won the coin toss, analyst Dan Dierdorf told ABC's television audience that it might work to the Chargers' advantage because their defense needed to "make a statement." But on the third play of the game, Rice faked to the outside and then went down the middle of the field.

Cornerback Deion Sanders (above, left) had his own pregame ritual; George Seifert's quiet time (left) was a bit less orchestrated.

Chargers safeties Stanley Richards and Darren Carrington were supposed to cover him, but Carrington did not come over and Richards got left behind as Rice gathered in the pass for a 44-yard touchdown. The 49ers had scored just 1:24 into the game, the quickest touchdown in Super Bowl history.

"Well, the Chargers certainly made a statement," Dierdorf said.

The next time the 49ers got the ball they took only four plays to score. Young's 51-yard touchdown pass to Ricky Watters made it 14-0. The Chargers came back with a touchdown drive of their own, but that would be their last gasp. The 49ers just kept

(Above) Offensive line coach Bobb McKittrick meets with his troops at halftime of the 1994 NFC title game against the Cowboys; (left) Ricky Watters's 9-yard touchdown run against the Chargers in Super Bowl XXIX put the 49ers ahead 35-10 en route to their 49-26 triumph; (pages 234–35) Jerry Rice quickly put the 49ers on top against the Chargers in Super Bowl XXIX, catching a 44-yard touchdown pass from Steve Young just 1:24 into the game.

rolling, scoring touchdowns on their first three possessions and four of their first five.

Offensive coordinator Mike Shanahan had followed the example set by Bill Walsh by scripting the offense's first fifteen plays. Shanahan's game plan counted on the Chargers' linebackers to play aggressively. The first two series started with runs to get the Chargers thinking run instead of pass, and on the second touchdown, Young's play fake was so good that the Chargers actually tackled fullback William Floyd as the touchdown pass was in the air to Watters.

Young gave Shanahan much of the credit, not just for this game but also for the season. "Mike learned from Bill Walsh," Young said, "but he also understood a player's desire to attack and put away another team. Mike kept attacking when we had a lead. We didn't get conservative and allow teams to sneak back into contention. It always began with the script. We were always confident of those plays going in."

The 49ers led 28-10 at halftime and built their lead to 32 points in the third quarter. It could have been much more lopsided than the 49-26 final score, but Seifert pulled most of his starters on offense, including Young and Rice, in the fourth quarter, and the Chargers scored a meaningless touchdown just before the two-minute warning.

There was no suspense in the final outcome, but

mediately. "If he retires, so will I," Young joked after the game.

As good as Rice was, though, this game belonged to Young. He completed 24 of 36 passes for 325 yards and a Super Bowl–record 6 touchdown passes. He went through the postseason without throwing an interception. Since the lopsided loss to Philadelphia in the fifth game of the season, Young had thrown 35 touchdown passes with only 3 interceptions.

Young was also the game's leading rusher with 49 yards on 5 carries. He kept 2 touchdown drives alive with his feet, scrambling for 21 yards on one third-down play and running for 15 yards on second-and-11 on another drive.

During the week following the game, the 49ers lost both of their coordinators. They attempted to keep Shanahan with an unusual deal that would give him a hefty pay raise and guarantee that he would become the head coach in 1997, but Shanahan chose to go to Denver as their head coach. Defensive coordinator Ray Rhodes left to become head coach in Philadelphia. Quarterbacks coach Gary Kubiak also left, joining Shanahan in Denver.

But the 49ers were able to keep defensive line coach John Marshall, who turned down an offer from Houston, and they moved quickly to replace their coordinators, signing former Jets coach Pete Carroll as defensive coordinator and Marc Trestman as offensive coordinator. They also made front office changes. Vice president/general manager John McVay, who intended to retire, was persuaded to stay on as a consultant. Dwight Clark moved into McVay's position. Vinny Cerrato, the director of college scouting, was promoted to head of football operations.

Most important, the 49ers still have Steve Young and Jerry Rice at the heart of their great offense.

The 49ers have had great quarterbacks throughout their history, starting with Frankie Albert in 1946, but they were especially blessed in the 1980s and 1990s, first with Joe Montana and then with Young. At thirty-three, Young clearly is in his prime, his body that of a younger player because of his relative inactivity in his first four seasons as a 49er.

Tony Morabito's dream had come true in spectacular fashion.

for anybody who enjoyed perfection, it was a beautiful spectacle: one of the best offenses in NFL history operating at peak efficiency.

Rice separated a shoulder in the second quarter and came out of the game for a few minutes, but he returned and caught 3 touchdown passes, tying his own Super Bowl record. "Jerry Rice with one arm is better than anybody else with two," an appreciative Young said.

During the week, Rice said that he might retire if the 49ers won, a remark he recanted almost im-

(Above) Steve Young passed for 325 yards and a game-record 6 touchdowns to earn MVP honors in Super Bowl XXIX; (opposite) the 49ers' defense shut down San Diego's potent rushing game in Super Bowl XXIX, limiting the Chargers to 67 rushing yards; (page 240) Steve Young (left) and Jerry Rice savor the 49ers' record fifth Super Bowl victory.

APPENDIX

49ERS' SUPER BOWL STATISTICS

SUPER BOWL XXIX

Joe Robbie Stadium, Miami, Florida
January 29, 1995
Attendance: 74,107

San Diego	7	3	8	8	—	26
San Francisco	14	14	14	7	—	49

SF   Rice 44 pass from S.Young (Brien kick)
SF   Watters 51 pass from S.Young (Brien kick)
SD   Means 1 run (Carney kick)
SF   Floyd 5 pass from S.Young (Brien kick)
SF   Watters 8 pass from S.Young (Brien kick)
SD   FG Carney 31
SF   Watters 9 run (Brien kick)
SF   Rice 15 pass from S.Young (Brien kick)
SD   Coleman 98 kickoff return (Seay pass from Humphries)
SF   Rice 7 pass from S.Young (Brien kick)
SD   Martin 30 pass from Humphries (Pupunu pass from Humphries)

TEAM STATISTICS	SD	SF
First downs	20	28
Net rushing yards	67	133
Net passing yards	287	316
Total yards	354	449
PA-PC-HI	55-27-3	38-25-0
Fumbles-lost	1-0	2-0
Penalties-yards	6-63	3-18
Time of possession	28:29	31:31

RUSHING

SD   Means, 13 for 33, 1 TD; Harmon, 2 for 10; Jefferson, 1 for 10; Gilbert, 1 for 8; Bieniemy, 1 for 3; Humphries, 1 for 3.

SF   S. Young, 5 for 49; Watters, 15 for 47, 1 TD; Floyd, 9 for 32; Rice, 1 for 10; Carter, 2 for 5.

PASSING

SD   Humphries, 24 of 49 for 275, 1 TD, 2 int; Gilbert, 3 of 6 for 30, 1 int.

SF   S. Young, 24 of 36 for 325, 6 TD; Musgrave, 1 of 1 for 6; Grbac, 0 of 1.

RECEIVING

SD   Harmon, 8 for 68; Seay, 7 for 75; Pupunu, 4 for 48; Martin, 3 for 59, 1 TD; Jefferson, 2 for 15; Bieniemy, 1 for 33; Means, 1 for 4; D.Young, 1 for 3.

SF   Rice, 10 for 149, 3 TD; Taylor, 4 for 43; Floyd, 4 for 26, 1 TD; Watters, 3 for 61, 2 TD; Jones, 2 for 41; Popson, 1 for 6; McCaffrey, 1 for 5.

SUPER BOWL XXIV

Louisiana Superdome, New Orleans, Louisiana
January 28, 1990
Attendance: 72,919

San Francisco	13	14	14	14	—	55
Denver	3	0	7	0	—	10

SF   Rice 20 pass from Montana (Cofer kick)
Den FG Treadwell 42
SF   Jones 7 pass from Montana (kick failed)
SF   Rathman 1 run (Cofer kick)
SF   Rice 38 pass from Montana (Cofer kick)
SF   Rice 28 pass from Montana (Cofer kick)
SF   Taylor 35 pass from Montana (Cofer kick)
Den Elway 3 run (Treadwell kick)
SF   Rathman 3 run (Cofer kick)
SF   Craig 1 run (Cofer kick)

TEAM STATISTICS	SF	Den
First downs	28	12
Net rushing yards	144	64
Net passing yards	317	103
Total yards	461	167
PA-PC-HI	32-24-0	29-11-2
Fumbles-lost	0-0	3-2
Penalties-yards	4-38	0-0
Time of possession	39:31	20:29

RUSHING

SF   Craig 20 for 69, 1 TD; Rathman, 11 for 38, 2 TD; Montana, 2 for 15; Flagler, 6 for 14; Young, 4 for 6; Sydney, 1 for 2.

Den Humphrey, 12 for 61; Elway, 4 for 8, 1 TD; Winder, 1 for 5.

PASSING

SF   Montana, 22 of 29 for 297, 5 TD; Young, 2 of 3 for 20.

Den Elway, 10 of 26 for 108, 2 int.; Kubiak, 1 of 3 for 28.

RECEIVING

SF   Rice, 7 for 148, 3 TD; Craig, 5 for 34; Rathman, 4 for 43; Taylor, 3 for 49, 1 TD; Sherrard, 1 for 13; Walls, 1 for 9; Jones, 1 for 7, 1 TD; Sydney, 1 for 7; Williams, 1 for 7.

Den Humphrey, 3 for 38; Sewell, 2 for 22; Johnson, 2 for 21; Nattiel, 1 for 28; Bratton, 1 for 14; Winder, 1 for 7; Kay, 1 for 6.

49ERS' SUPER BOWL STATISTICS

SUPER BOWL XXIII

Joe Robbie Stadium, Miami, Florida
January 22, 1989
Attendance: 75,129

Cincinnati	0	3	10	3 —	16
San Francisco	3	0	3	14 —	20

SF   FG Cofer 41
Cin   FG Breech 34
Cin   FG Breech 43
SF   FG Cofer 32
Cin   Jennings 93 kickoff return (Breech kick)
SF   Rice 14 pass from Montana (Cofer kick)
Cin   FG Breech 40
SF   Taylor 10 pass from Montana (Cofer kick)

TEAM STATISTICS

	Cin	SF
First downs	13	23
Net rushing yards	106	112
Net passing yards	123	339
Total yards	229	451
PA-PC-HI	25-11-1	36-23-0
Fumbles-lost	1-0	4-1
Penalties-yards	7-65	4-32
Time of possession	32:43	27:17

RUSHING

Cin   Woods, 20 for 79; Brooks, 6 for 24; Jennings, 1 for 3; Esiason, 1 for 0.

SF   Craig, 17 for 71; Rathman, 5 for 23; Montana, 4 for 13; Rice, 1 for 5.

PASSING

Cin   Esiason, 11 of 25 for 144, 1 int.

SF   Montana, 23 of 36 for 357, 2 TD.

RECEIVING

Cin   Brown, 4 for 44; Collinsworth, 3 for 40; McGee, 2 for 23; Brooks, 1 for 20; Hillary, 1 for 17.

SF   Rice, 11 for 215, 1 TD; Craig, 8 for 101; Frank, 2 for 15; Rathman, 1 for 16; Taylor, 1 for 10, 1 TD.

SUPER BOWL XIX

Stanford Stadium, Stanford, California
January 20, 1985
Attendance: 84,059

Miami	10	6	0	0 —	16
San Francisco	7	21	10	0 —	38

Mia   FG von Schamann 37
SF   Monroe 33 pass from Montana (Wersching kick)
Mia   D. Johnson 2 pass from Marino (von Schamann kick)
SF   Craig 8 pass from Montana (Wersching kick)
SF   Montana 6 run (Wersching kick)
SF   Craig 2 run (Wersching kick)
Mia   FG von Schamann 31
Mia   FG von Schamann 30
SF   FG Wersching 27
SF   Craig 16 pass from Montana (Wersching kick)

TEAM STATISTICS

	Mia	SF
First downs	19	31
Net rushing yards	25	211
Net passing yards	289	326
Total yards	314	537
PA-PC-HI	50-29-2	35-24-0
Fumbles-lost	1-0	2-2
Penalties yards	1-10	2-10
Time of possession	22:49	37:11

RUSHING

Mia   Nathan, 5 for 18; Bennett, 3 for 7; Marino 1 for 0.

SF   Tyler, 13 for 65; Montana, 5 for 59, 1 TD; Craig, 15 for 58, 1 TD; Harmon, 5 for 20; Solomon, 1 for 5; Cooper, 1 for 4.

PASSING

Mia   Marino, 29 of 50 for 318, 1 TD, 2 int.
SF   Montana, 24 of 35 for 331, 3 TD.

RECEIVING

Mia   Nathan, 10 for 83; Clayton, 6 for 92; Rose, 6 for 73; D. Johnson, 3 for 28, 1 TD; Moore, 2 for 17; Cefalo, 1 for 14; Duper, 1 for 11.

SF   Craig, 7 for 77, 2 TD; D. Clark, 6 for 77; Francis, 5 for 60; Tyler, 4 for 70; Monroe, 1 for 33, 1 TD; Solomon, 1 for 14.

49ERS' SUPER BOWL STATISTICS

SUPER BOWL XVI

Pontiac Silverdome, Pontiac, Michigan
January 24, 1982
Attendance: 81,270

San Francisco	7	13	0	6	—	26
Cincinnati	0	0	7	14	—	21

SF   Montana 1 run (Wersching kick)
SF   Cooper 11 pass from Montana (Wersching kick)
SF   FG Wersching 22
SF   FG Wersching 26
Cin   Anderson 5 run (Breech kick)
Cin   Ross 4 pass from Anderson (Breech kick)
SF   FG Wersching 40
SF   FG Wersching 23
Cin   Ross 3 pass from Anderson (Breech kick)

TEAM STATISTICS	SF	Cin
First downs	20	24
Net rushing yards	127	72
Net passing yards	148	284
Total yards	275	356
PA-PC-HI	22-14-0	34-25-2
Fumbles-lost	2-1	2-2
Penalties-yards	8-65	8-57
Time of possession	32:13	27:47

RUSHING

SF   Patton, 17 for 55; Cooper, 9 for 34; Montana, 6 for 18, 1 TD; Ring, 5 for 17; J. Davis, 2 for 5; Clark, 1 for 2.

Cin   Johnson, 14 for 36; Alexander, 5 for 17; Anderson, 4 for 15, 1 TD; A. Griffin, 1 for 4.

PASSING

SF   Montana, 14 of 22 for 157, 1 TD.
Cin   Anderson, 25 of 34 for 300, 2 TD, 2 int.

RECEIVING

SF   Solomon, 4 for 52; Clark, 4 for 45; Cooper, 2 for 15, 1 TD; Wilson, 1 for 22; Young, 1 for 14; Patton, 1 for 6; Ring, 1 for 3.

Cin   Ross, 11 for 104, 2 TD; Collinsworth, 5 for 107; Curtis, 3 for 42; Kreider, 2 for 36; Johnson, 2 for 8; Alexander, 2 for 3.

49ERS' CAREER STATISTICAL LEADERS

SCORING

	TD	PAT	FG	Pts
Ray Wersching (1977–87)	0	409-425	190-261	979
Jerry Rice (1985–)	139	0	0	836*
Tommy Davis (1959–69)	0	348-350	130-276	738
Mike Cofer (1988–93)	0	289-297	128-194	673
Gordy Soltau (1950–58)	25	284-302	70-138	644
Bruce Gossett (1970–74)	0	163-168	99-153	460
Roger Craig (1983–90)	66	0	0	396
Ken Willard (1965–73)	61	0	0	366
Gene Washington (1969–77)	59	0	0	354
Joe Perry (1950–60, 1963)	57	6-7	1-6	351

Rice's total includes 1 two-point conversion.

RECEIVING

	No.	Yards	Avg	Long	TD
Jerry Rice (1985–)	820	13,275	16.2	96	131
Roger Craig (1983–90)	508	4,442	8.7	73	16
Dwight Clark (1979–87)	506	6,750	13.3	80	48
Billy Wilson (1951–60)	407	5,902	14.5	77	49
Gene Washington (1969–77)	371	6,664	17.9	79	59
John Taylor (1986–)	318	5,211	16.4	97	41
Freddie Solomon (1978–85)	310	4,873	15.7	93	43
Brent Jones (1987–)	295	3,789	12.8	69	27
Tom Rathman (1986–93)	294	2,490	8.5	36	8
Bernie Casey (1961–66)	277	4,008	14.5	68	27

RUSHING

	No.	Yards	Avg	Long	TD
Joe Perry (1950–60, 1963)	1,475	7,344	4.9	78	50
Roger Craig (1983–90)	1,686	7,064	4.2	71	50
Ken Willard (1965–73)	1,582	5,930	3.7	69	45
J. D. Smith (1956–64)	1,007	4,370	4.3	80	37
Hugh McElhenny (1952–60)	877	4,288	4.9	89	35
Wendell Tyler (1983–86)	624	3,112	4.9	40	16
Delvin Williams (1974–77)	669	2,966	4.4	80	20
Wilbur Jackson (1974–79)	745	2,955	3.9	80	10
Ricky Watters (1991–)	653	2,840	4.3	43	25
Steve Young (1987–)	376	2,307	6.1	49	21

INTERCEPTIONS

	No.	Yards	Avg	Long	TD
Ronnie Lott (1981–90)	51	643	12.6	83	5
Jimmy Johnson (1961–76)	47	615	13.1	63	2
Kermit Alexander (1963–69)	36	499	13.9	66	1
Dwight Hicks (1979–85)	30	586	19.5	72	3
Lowell Wagner (1950–53, 1955)	25	331	13.2	40	0
Rex Berry (1951–56)	22	404	18.4	44	3
Don Griffin (1986–93)	22	49	2.2	23	0
Dave Baker (1959–61)	21	294	14.0	40	0
Dick Moegle (1955–59)	20	232	11.6	40	1
Eric Wright (1981–90)	18	256	14.2	60	2
Bruce Taylor (1970–77)	18	201	11.2	70	0

PASSING (YARDS)

	Att	Comp	Pct	Yards	TD	Int	Long	Rating
Joe Montana (1979–92)	4,600	2,929	63.7	35,124	244	123	96	93.5
John Brodie (1957–73)	4,491	2,469	55.0	31,548	214	224	83	70.4
Steve Young (1987–)	1,928	1,279	66.3	16,652	129	47	97	105.5
Y. A. Tittle (1951–60)	2,194	1,226	55.9	16,016	108	134	78	70.0
Steve DeBerg (1977–80)	1,201	670	55.8	7,220	37	60	93	63.1
Steve Spurrier (1967–75)	840	441	52.5	5,250	33	48	81	61.2
Frankie Albert (1950–52)	601	316	52.6	3,847	27	43	60	57.7
Jim Plunkett (1976–77)	491	254	51.7	3,285	22	30	85	62.5
Steve Bono (1989–93)	359	220	61.2	2,558	14	7	78	87.7
George Mira (1964–68)	240	112	46.7	1,711	17	14	79	70.0

49ERS' CAREER STATISTICAL LEADERS

PUNT RETURNS (YARDS)

	No.	Yards	Avg	Long	TD
Dana McLemore (1982–87)	142	1,531	10.8	93	4
John Taylor (1986–)	138	1,461	10.6	95	2
Bruce Taylor (1970–77)	142	1,323	9.3	76	0
Ralph McGill (1972–76)	105	964	9.2	54	1
Abe Woodson (1958–64)	105	949	9.0	85	2
Freddie Solomon (1978–85)	106	804	7.6	57	2
Kermit Alexander (1963–69)	120	782	6.5	70	2
Joe Arenas (1951–57)	124	774	6.2	67	1
Dexter Carter (1990–)	72	732	10.2	72	1
Don Griffin (1986–93)	74	667	9.0	76	1

PUNTING (YARDS)

	No.	Yards	Avg	Long
Tommy Davis (1959–69)	511	22,841	44.7	82
Tom Wittum (1973–77)	380	15,494	40.8	68
Max Runager (1984–88)	281	11,370	40.5	62
Steve Spurrier (1967–75)	230	8,882	38.6	61
Jim Miller (1980–82)	214	8,686	40.6	80
Barry Helton (1988–90)	202	7,832	38.8	56
Klaus Wilmsmeyer (1992–)	145	5,871	40.5	61
Frankie Albert (1950–52)	139	5,828	41.9	70
Jim McCann (1971–72)	113	4,439	39.3	63
Mike Connell (1978)	96	3,583	37.3	59

KICKOFF RETURNS (YARDS)

	No.	Yards	Avg	Long	TD
Abe Woodson (1958–64)	166	4,873	29.4	105	5
Joe Arenas (1951–57)	139	3,798	27.3	96	1
Dexter Carter (1990–)	153	3,276	21.4	98	2
Kermit Alexander (1963–69)	137	3,271	23.9	56	0
Vic Washington (1971–73)	84	2,178	25.9	98	1
James Owens (1979–80)	72	1,728	24.0	101	2
Carl Monroe (1983–87)	76	1,660	21.8	95	1
Doug Cunningham (1967–73)	68	1,613	23.7	94	0
Hugh McElhenny (1952–60)	65	1,494	23.0	55	0
Paul Hofer (1976–81)	68	1,466	21.6	48	0

YARDS FROM SCRIMMAGE

	Total Yards	Rushing	Receiving
Jerry Rice (1985–)	13,786	511	13,275
Roger Craig (1983–90)	11,506	7,064	4,442
Joe Perry (1950–60, 1963)	8,624	7,344	1,280
Ken Willard (1965–73)	8,086	5,930	2,156
Hugh McElhenny (1952–60)	6,954	4,069	2,666
Dwight Clark (1979–87)	6,800	50	6,750
Gene Washington (1969–77)	6,667	3	6,664
Billy Wilson (1951–60)	5,902	0	5,902
J. D. Smith (1956–64)	5,479	4,370	1,109
John Taylor (1986–)	5,242	31	5,211

49ERS' TEAM vs. TEAM RESULTS

(since 1950)

49ERS vs. ARIZONA*

49ers lead series, 10-9

1951	Cardinals, 27-21 (SF)
1957	Cardinals, 20-10 (SF)
1962	49ers, 24-17 (StL)
1964	Cardinals, 23-13 (SF)
1968	49ers, 35-17 (SF)
1971	49ers, 26-14 (StL)
1974	Cardinals, 34-9 (SF)
1976	Cardinals, 23-20 (StL) OT
1978	Cardinals, 16-10 (SF)
1979	Cardinals, 13-10 (StL)
1980	49ers, 24-21 (SF) OT
1982	49ers, 31-20 (StL)
1983	49ers, 42-27 (StL)
1986	49ers, 43-17 (SF)
1987	49ers, 34-28 (SF)
1988	Cardinals, 24-23 (P)
1991	49ers, 14-10 (SF)
1992	Cardinals, 24-14 (P)
1993	49ers, 28-14 (SF)

Franchise known as Phoenix prior to 1994, in St. Louis prior to 1988, and in Chicago prior to 1960

49ERS vs. ATLANTA

49ers lead series, 34-21-1

1966	49ers, 44-7 (A)
1967	49ers, 38-7 (SF)
	49ers, 34-28 (A)
1968	49ers, 28-13 (SF)
	49ers, 14-12 (A)
1969	Falcons, 24-12 (A)
	Falcons, 21-7 (SF)
1970	Falcons, 21-20 (A)
	49ers, 24-20 (SF)
1971	Falcons, 20-17 (A)
	49ers, 24-3 (SF)
1972	49ers, 49-14 (A)
	49ers, 20-0 (SF)
1973	49ers, 13-9 (A)
	Falcons, 17-3 (SF)

1974	49ers, 16-10 (A)
	49ers, 27-0 (SF)
1975	Falcons, 17-3 (SF)
	Falcons, 31-9 (A)
1976	49ers, 15-0 (SF)
	Falcons, 21-16 (A)
1977	Falcons, 7-0 (SF)
	49ers, 10-3 (A)
1978	Falcons, 20-17 (SF)
	Falcons, 21-10 (A)
1979	49ers, 20-15 (SF)
	Falcons, 31-21 (A)
1980	Falcons, 20-17 (SF)
	Falcons, 35-10 (A)
1981	Falcons, 34-17 (A)
	49ers, 17-14 (SF)
1982	Falcons, 17-7 (SF)
1983	49ers, 24-20 (SF)
	Falcons, 28-24 (A)
1984	49ers, 14-5 (SF)
	49ers, 35-17 (A)
1985	49ers, 35-16 (SF)
	49ers, 38-17 (A)
1986	Tie, 10-10 (A) OT
	49ers, 20-0 (SF)
1987	49ers, 25-17 (A)
	49ers, 35-7 (SF)
1988	Falcons, 34-17 (SF)
	49ers, 13-3 (A)
1989	49ers, 45-3 (SF)
	49ers, 23-10 (A)
1990	49ers, 19-13 (SF)
	49ers, 45-35 (A)
1991	Falcons, 39-34 (SF)
	Falcons, 17-14 (A)
1992	49ers, 56-17 (SF)
	49ers, 41-3 (A)
1993	49ers, 37-30 (SF)
	Falcons, 27-24 (A)
1994	49ers, 42-3 (A)
	49ers, 50-14 (SF)

49ERS vs. BUFFALO

Bills lead series 3-2

1972	Bills, 27-20 (B)
1980	Bills, 18-13 (SF)
1983	49ers, 23-10 (B)
1989	49ers, 21-10 (SF)
1992	Bills, 34-31 (SF)

49ERS vs. CHICAGO

49ers lead series, 28-25-1

1950	Bears, 32-20 (SF)
	Bears, 17-0 (C)
1951	Bears, 13-7 (C)
1952	49ers, 40-16 (C)
	Bears, 20-17 (SF)
1953	49ers, 35-28 (C)
	49ers, 24-14 (SF)
1954	49ers, 31-24 (C)
	Bears, 31-27 (SF)
1955	49ers, 20-19 (C)
	Bears, 34-23 (SF)
1956	Bears, 31-7 (C)
	Bears, 38-21 (SF)
1957	49ers, 21-17 (C)
	49ers, 21-17 (SF)
1958	Bears, 28-6 (C)
	Bears, 27-14 (SF)
1959	49ers, 20-17 (SF)
	Bears, 14-3 (C)
1960	Bears, 27-10 (C)
	49ers, 25-7 (SF)
1961	Bears, 31-0 (C)
	49ers, 41-31 (SF)
1962	Bears, 30-14 (SF)
	49ers, 34-27 (C)
1963	49ers, 20-14 (SF)
	Bears, 27-7 (C)
1964	49ers, 31-21 (SF)
	Bears, 23-21 (C)
1965	49ers, 52-24 (SF)
	Bears, 61-20 (C)
1966	Tie, 30-30 (C)
	49ers, 41-14 (SF)

1967	Bears, 28-14 (SF)
1968	Bears, 27-19 (C)
1969	49ers, 42-21 (SF)
1970	49ers, 37-16 (C)
1971	49ers, 13-0 (SF)
1972	49ers, 34-21 (C)
1974	49ers, 34-0 (C)
1975	49ers, 31-3 (SF)
1976	Bears, 19-12 (SF)
1978	Bears, 16-13 (SF)
1979	Bears, 28-27 (SF)
1981	49ers, 28-17 (SF)
1983	Bears, 13-3 (C)
1984	49ers, 23-0 (SF)*
1985	Bears, 26-10 (SF)
1987	49ers, 41-0 (SF)
1988	Bears, 10-9 (C)
	49ers, 28-3 (C)*
1989	49ers, 26-0 (SF)
1991	49ers, 52-14 (SF)
1994	49ers, 44-15 (SF)**

NFC Championship
**NFC Divisional Playoff*

49ERS vs. CINCINNATI

49ers lead series, 8-1

1974	Bengals, 21-3 (SF)
1978	49ers, 28-12 (SF)
1981	49ers, 21-3 (C)
	49ers, 26-21 (Detroit)*
1984	49ers, 23-17 (SF)
1987	49ers, 27-26 (C)
1988	49ers, 20-16 (Miami)**
1990	49ers, 20-17 (C)
1993	49ers, 21-8 (SF)

Super Bowl XVI
**Super Bowl XXIII*

49ERS vs. CLEVELAND

Browns lead series, 9-6

1950	Browns, 34-14 (C)
1951	49ers, 24-10 (SF)
1953	Browns, 23-21 (C)
1955	Browns, 38-3 (SF)
1959	49ers, 21-20 (C)
1962	Browns, 13-10 (SF)
1968	Browns, 33-21 (SF)
1970	49ers, 34-31 (SF)
1974	Browns, 7-0 (C)
1978	Browns, 24-7 (C)
1981	Browns, 15-12 (SF)
1984	49ers, 41-7 (C)
1987	49ers, 38-24 (SF)
1990	49ers, 20-17 (SF)
1993	Browns, 23-13 (C)

49ERS vs. DALLAS

49ers lead series, 12-11-1

1960	49ers, 26-14 (D)
1963	49ers, 31-24 (SF)
1965	Cowboys, 39-31 (D)
1967	49ers, 24-16 (SF)
1969	Tie, 24-24 (D)
1970	Cowboys, 17-10 (SF)*
1971	Cowboys, 14-3 (D)*
1972	49ers, 31-10 (D)
	Cowboys, 30-28 (SF)**
1974	Cowboys, 20-14 (D)
1977	Cowboys, 42-35 (SF)
1979	Cowboys, 21-13 (SF)
1980	Cowboys, 59-14 (D)
1981	49ers, 45-14 (SF)
	49ers, 28-27 (SF)*
1983	49ers, 42-17 (SF)
1985	49ers, 31-16 (SF)
1989	49ers, 31-14 (D)
1990	49ers, 24-6 (D)
1992	Cowboys, 30-20 (SF)*
1993	Cowboys, 26-17 (D)
	Cowboys, 38-21 (D)*
1994	49ers, 21-14 (SF)
	49ers, 38-28 (SF)*

NFC Championship
**NFC Divisional Playoff*

49ERS' TEAM vs. TEAM RESULTS

49ERS vs. DENVER

Series tied, 4-4

1970   49ers, 19-14 (SF)
1973   49ers, 36-34 (D)
1979   Broncos, 38-28 (SF)
1982   Broncos, 24-21 (D)
1985   Broncos, 17-16 (D)
1988   Broncos, 16-13 (SF) OT
1989   49ers, 55-10
        (New Orleans)*
1994   49ers, 42-19 (SF)

Super Bowl XXIV

49ERS vs. DETROIT

49ers lead series, 28-26-1

1950   Lions, 24-7 (D)
        49ers, 28-27 (SF)
1951   49ers, 20-10 (D)
        49ers, 21-17 (SF)
1952   49ers, 17-3 (SF)
        49ers, 28-0 (D)
1953   Lions, 24-21 (D)
        Lions, 14-10 (SF)
1954   49ers, 37-31 (SF)
        Lions, 48-7 (D)
1955   49ers, 27-24 (D)
        49ers, 38-21 (SF)
1956   Lions, 20-17 (D)
        Lions, 17-13 (SF)
1957   49ers, 35-31 (SF)
        Lions, 31-10 (D)
        Lions, 31-27 (SF)*
1958   49ers, 24-21 (SF)
        Lions, 35-21 (D)
1959   49ers, 34-13 (D)
        49ers, 33-7 (SF)
1960   49ers, 14-10 (D)
        Lions, 24-0 (SF)
1961   49ers, 49-0 (D)
        Tie, 20-20 (SF)
1962   Lions, 45-24 (D)
        Lions, 38-24 (SF)
1963   Lions, 26-3 (D)
        Lions, 45-7 (SF)

1964   Lions, 26-17 (SF)
        Lions, 24-7 (D)
1965   49ers, 27-21 (D)
        49ers, 17-14 (SF)
1966   49ers, 27-24 (SF)
        49ers, 41-14 (D)
1967   Lions, 45-3 (SF)
1968   49ers, 14-7 (D)
1969   Lions, 26-14 (SF)
1970   Lions, 28-7 (D)
1971   49ers, 31-27 (SF)
1973   Lions, 30-20 (D)
1974   Lions, 17-13 (D)
1975   Lions, 28-17 (SF)
1977   49ers, 28-7 (SF)
1978   Lions, 33-14 (D)
1980   Lions, 17-13 (D)
1981   Lions, 24-17 (D)
1983   49ers, 24-23 (SF)**
1984   49ers, 30-27 (D)
1985   Lions, 23-21 (D)
1988   49ers, 20-13 (SF)
1991   49ers, 35-3 (SF)
1992   49ers, 24-6 (SF)
1993   49ers, 55-17 (D)
1994   49ers, 27-21 (D)

Conference Playoff
**NFC Divisional Playoff*

49ERS vs. GREEN BAY

49ers lead series, 25-21-1

1950   Packers, 25-21 (GB)
        49ers, 30-14 (SF)
1951   49ers, 31-19 (SF)
1952   49ers, 24-14 (SF)
1953   49ers, 37-7 (Mil)
        49ers, 48-14 (SF)
1954   49ers, 23-17 (Mil)
        49ers, 35-0 (SF)
1955   Packers, 27-21 (Mil)
        Packers, 28-7 (SF)
1956   49ers, 17-16 (GB)
        49ers, 38-20 (SF)
1957   49ers, 24-14 (Mil)
        49ers, 27-20 (SF)

1958   49ers, 33-12 (Mil)
        49ers, 48-21 (SF)
1959   Packers, 21-20 (GB)
        Packers, 36-14 (SF)
1960   Packers, 41-14 (Mil)
        Packers, 13-0 (SF)
1961   Packers, 30-10 (GB)
        49ers, 22-21 (SF)
1962   Packers, 31-13 (Mil)
        Packers, 31-21 (SF)
1963   Packers, 28-10 (Mil)
        Packers, 21-17 (SF)
1964   Packers, 24-14 (Mil)
        49ers, 24-14 (SF)
1965   Packers, 27-10 (GB)
        Tie, 24-24 (SF)
1966   49ers, 21-20 (SF)
        Packers, 20-7 (Mil)
1967   Packers, 13-0 (GB)
1968   49ers, 27-20 (SF)
1969   Packers, 14-7 (Mil)
1970   49ers, 26-10 (SF)
1972   Packers, 34-24 (Mil)
1973   49ers, 20-6 (SF)
1974   49ers, 7-6 (SF)
1976   49ers, 26-14 (GB)
1977   Packers, 16-14 (Mil)
1980   Packers, 23-16 (Mil)
1981   49ers, 13-3 (Mil)
1986   49ers, 31-17 (Mil)
1987   49ers, 23-12 (GB)
1989   Packers, 21-17 (SF)
1990   49ers, 24-20 (GB)

49ERS vs. HOUSTON

49ers lead series, 5-3

1970   49ers, 30-20 (H)
1975   Oilers, 27-13 (SF)
1978   Oilers, 20-19 (H)
1981   49ers, 28-6 (SF)
1984   49ers, 34-21 (H)
1987   49ers, 27-20 (SF)
1990   49ers, 24-21 (H)
1993   Oilers, 10-7 (SF)

49ERS vs. INDIANAPOLIS*

Colts lead series, 21-16

1953   49ers, 38-21 (B)
        49ers, 45-14 (SF)
1954   Colts, 17-13 (B)
        49ers, 10-7 (SF)
1955   Colts, 26-14 (B)
        49ers, 35-24 (SF)
1956   49ers, 20-17 (B)
        49ers, 30-17 (SF)
1957   Colts, 27-21 (B)
        49ers, 17-13 (SF)
1958   Colts, 35-27 (B)
        49ers, 21-12 (SF)
1959   Colts, 45-14 (B)
        Colts, 34-14 (SF)
1960   49ers, 30-22 (B)
        49ers, 34-10 (SF)
1961   Colts, 20-17 (B)
        Colts, 27-24 (SF)
1962   49ers, 21-13 (B)
        Colts, 22-3 (SF)
1963   Colts, 20-14 (SF)
        Colts, 20-3 (B)
1964   Colts, 37-7 (B)
        Colts, 14-3 (SF)
1965   Colts, 27-24 (B)
        Colts, 34-28 (SF)
1966   Colts, 36-14 (B)
        Colts, 30-14 (SF)

1967   Colts, 41-7 (B)
        Colts, 26-9 (SF)
1968   Colts, 27-10 (B)
        Colts, 42-14 (SF)
1969   49ers, 24-21 (B)
        49ers, 20-17 (SF)
1972   49ers, 24-21 (SF)
1986   49ers, 35-14 (SF)
1989   49ers, 30-24 (I)

*Franchise in Baltimore
prior to 1984*

49ERS vs. KANSAS CITY

49ers lead series, 4-2

1971   Chiefs, 26-17 (SF)
1975   49ers, 20-3 (KC)
1982   49ers, 26-13 (KC)
1985   49ers, 31-3 (SF)
1991   49ers, 28-14 (SF)
1994   Chiefs, 24-17 (KC)

49ERS vs. L.A. RAIDERS*

Raiders lead series, 5-3

1970   49ers, 38-7 (O)
1974   Raiders, 35-24 (SF)
1979   Raiders, 23-10 (O)
1982   Raiders, 23-17 (SF)
1985   49ers, 34-10 (LA)
1988   Raiders, 9-3 (SF)
1991   Raiders, 12-6 (LA)
1994   49ers, 44-14 (SF)

*Franchise in Oakland
prior to 1982*

49ERS' TEAM VS. TEAM RESULTS

49ERS vs. L.A. RAMS*
Rams lead series, 48-41-2
1950 Rams, 35-14 (SF)
     Rams, 28-21 (LA)
1951 49ers, 44-17 (SF)
     Rams, 23-16 (LA)
1952 Rams, 35-9 (LA)
     Rams, 34-21 (SF)
1953 49ers, 31-30 (SF)
     49ers, 31-27 (LA)
1954 Tie, 24-24 (LA)
     Rams, 42-34 (SF)
1955 Rams, 23-14 (SF)
     Rams, 27-14 (LA)
1956 49ers, 33-30 (SF)
     Rams, 30-6 (LA)
1957 49ers, 23-20 (SF)
     Rams, 37-24 (LA)
1958 Rams, 33-3 (SF)
     Rams, 56-7 (LA)
1959 49ers, 34-0 (SF)
     49ers, 24-16 (LA)
1960 49ers, 13-9 (SF)
     49ers, 23-7 (LA)
1961 49ers, 35-0 (SF)
     Rams, 17-7 (LA)
1962 Rams, 28-14 (SF)
     49ers, 24-17 (LA)
1963 Rams, 28-21 (LA)
     Rams, 21-17 (SF)
1964 Rams, 42-14 (LA)
     49ers, 28-7 (SF)
1965 49ers, 45-21 (LA)
     49ers, 30-27 (SF)
1966 Rams, 34-3 (LA)
     49ers, 21-13 (SF)
1967 49ers, 27-24 (LA)
     Rams, 17-7 (SF)
1968 Rams, 24-10 (LA)
     Tie, 20-20 (SF)

1969 Rams, 27-21 (SF)
     Rams, 41-30 (LA)
1970 49ers, 20-6 (LA)
     Rams, 30-13 (SF)
1971 Rams, 20-13 (SF)
     Rams, 17-6 (LA)
1972 Rams, 31-7 (LA)
     Rams, 26-16 (SF)
1973 Rams, 40-20 (SF)
     Rams, 31-13 (LA)
1974 Rams, 37-14 (LA)
     Rams, 15-13 (SF)
1975 Rams, 23-14 (SF)
     49ers, 24-23 (LA)
1976 49ers, 16-0 (LA)
     Rams, 23-3 (SF)
1977 Rams, 34-14 (LA)
     Rams, 23-10 (SF)
1978 Rams, 27-10 (LA)
     Rams, 31-28 (SF)
1979 Rams, 27-24 (LA)
     Rams, 26-20 (SF)
1980 Rams, 48-26 (LA)
     Rams, 31-17 (SF)
1981 49ers, 20-17 (SF)
     49ers, 33-31 (LA)
1982 49ers, 30-24 (LA)
     Rams, 21-20 (SF)
1983 Rams, 10-7 (SF)
     49ers, 45-35 (LA)
1984 49ers, 33-0 (LA)
     49ers, 19-16 (SF)
1985 49ers, 28-14 (LA)
     Rams, 27-20 (SF)
1986 Rams, 16-13 (LA)
     49ers, 24-14 (SF)
1987 49ers, 31-10 (LA)
     49ers, 48-0 (SF)
1988 49ers, 24-21 (LA)
     Rams, 38-16 (SF)

1989 Rams, 13-12 (SF)
     49ers, 30-27 (LA)
     49ers, 30-3 (SF)**
1990 Rams, 28-17 (SF)
     49ers, 26-10 (LA)
1991 49ers, 27-10 (SF)
     49ers, 33-10 (LA)
1992 49ers, 27-24 (SF)
     49ers, 27-10 (LA)
1993 49ers, 40-17 (SF)
     49ers, 35-10 (LA)
1994 49ers, 34-19 (LA)
     49ers, 31-27 (SF)

*Franchise moved to St. Louis
following the 1994 season.
**NFC Championship

49ERS vs. MIAMI
Dolphins lead series, 4-3
1973 Dolphins, 21-13 (M)
1977 Dolphins, 19-15 (SF)
1980 Dolphins, 17-13 (M)
1983 Dolphins, 20-17 (SF)
1984 49ers, 38-16 (Stanford)*
1986 49ers, 31-16 (M)
1992 49ers, 27-3 (SF)
*Super Bowl XIX

49ERS vs. MINNESOTA
49ers lead series, 18-17-1
1961 49ers, 38-24 (M)
     49ers, 38-28 (SF)
1962 49ers, 21-7 (SF)
     49ers, 35-12 (M)
1963 Vikings, 24-20 (SF)
     Vikings, 45-14 (M)
1964 Vikings, 27-22 (SF)
     Vikings, 24-7 (M)
1965 Vikings, 42-41 (SF)
     49ers, 45-24 (M)
1966 Tie, 20-20 (SF)
     Vikings, 28-3 (SF)
1967 49ers, 27-21 (M)
1968 Vikings, 30-20 (SF)
1969 Vikings, 10-7 (M)
1970 49ers, 17-14 (M)*
1971 49ers, 13-9 (M)
1972 49ers, 20-17 (SF)
1973 Vikings, 17-13 (SF)
1975 Vikings, 27-17 (M)
1976 49ers, 20-16 (SF)
1977 Vikings, 28-27 (M)
1979 Vikings, 28-22 (M)
1983 49ers, 48-17 (M)
1984 49ers, 51-7 (SF)
1985 Vikings, 28-21 (M)
1986 Vikings, 27-24 (SF) OT
1987 Vikings, 36-24 (SF)*
1988 49ers, 24-21 (SF)
     49ers, 34-9 (SF)*
1989 49ers, 41-13 (SF)*
1990 49ers, 20-17 (M)
1991 Vikings, 17-14 (M)
1992 49ers, 20-17 (M)
1993 49ers, 38-19 (SF)
1994 Vikings, 21-14 (M)
*NFC Divisional Playoff

49ERS vs. NEW ENGLAND
49ers lead series, 6-1
1971 49ers, 27-10 (SF)
1975 Patriots, 24-16 (NE)
1980 49ers, 21-17 (SF)
1983 49ers, 33-13 (NE)
1986 49ers, 29-24 (NE)
1989 49ers, 37-20 (SF)
1992 49ers, 24-12 (NE)

49ERS vs. NEW ORLEANS
49ers lead series, 35-14-2
1967 49ers, 27-13 (SF)
1969 Saints, 43-38 (NO)
1970 Tie, 20-20 (SF)
     49ers, 38-27 (NO)
1971 49ers, 38-20 (NO)
     Saints, 26-20 (SF)
1972 49ers, 37-2 (NO)
     Tie, 20-20 (SF)
1973 49ers, 40-0 (SF)
     Saints, 16-10 (NO)
1974 49ers, 17-13 (NO)
     49ers, 35-21 (SF)
1975 49ers, 35-21 (SF)
     49ers, 16-6 (NO)
1976 49ers, 33-3 (SF)
     49ers, 27-7 (NO)
1977 49ers, 10-7 (NO) OT
     49ers, 20-17 (SF)
1978 Saints, 14-7 (SF)
     Saints, 24-13 (NO)
1979 Saints, 30-21 (SF)
     Saints, 31-20 (NO)
1980 49ers, 26-23 (NO)
     49ers, 38-35 (SF) OT
1981 49ers, 21-14 (SF)
     49ers, 21-17 (NO)
1982 Saints, 23-20 (SF)
1983 49ers, 32-13 (NO)
     49ers, 27-0 (SF)

49ERS' TEAM vs. TEAM RESULTS

49ERS vs. New Orleans (cont.)

1984	49ers, 30-20 (SF)	
	49ers, 35-3 (NO)	
1985	Saints, 20-17 (SF)	
	49ers, 31-19 (NO)	
1986	49ers, 26-17 (SF)	
	Saints, 23-10 (NO)	
1987	49ers, 24-22 (NO)	
	Saints, 26-24 (SF)	
1988	49ers, 34-33 (NO)	
	49ers, 30-17 (SF)	
1989	49ers, 24-20 (NO)	
	49ers, 31-13 (SF)	
1990	49ers, 13-12 (NO)	
	Saints, 13-10 (SF)	
1991	Saints, 10-3 (NO)	
	49ers, 38-24 (SF)	
1992	49ers, 16-10 (NO)	
	49ers, 21-20 (SF)	
1993	Saints, 16-13 (NO)	
	49ers, 42-7 (SF)	
1994	49ers, 24-13 (SF)	
	49ers, 35-14 (NO)	

49ERS vs. N.Y. GIANTS

Giants lead series, 14-13

1952	Giants, 23-14 (NY)
1956	Giants, 38-21 (SF)
1957	49ers, 27-17 (NY)
1960	Giants, 21-19 (SF)
1963	Giants, 48-14 (NY)
1968	49ers, 26-10 (NY)
1972	Giants, 23-17 (SF)
1975	Giants, 26-23 (SF)
1977	Giants, 20-17 (NY)
1978	Giants, 27-10 (NY)
1979	Giants, 32-16 (NY)
1980	49ers, 12-0 (SF)
1981	49ers, 17-10 (SF)
	49ers, 38-24 (SF)*
1984	49ers, 31-10 (NY)
	49ers, 21-10 (SF)*
1985	Giants, 17-3 (NY)**
1986	Giants, 21-17 (SF)
	Giants, 49-3 (NY)*
1987	49ers, 41-21 (NY)
1988	49ers, 20-17 (NY)
1989	49ers, 34-24 (SF)
1990	49ers, 7-3 (SF)
	Giants, 15-13 (SF)***
1991	Giants, 16-14 (NY)
1992	49ers, 31-14 (NY)
1993	49ers, 44-3 (SF)*

*NFC Divisional Playoff
**NFC Wild Card Playoff
***NFC Championship

49ERS vs. N.Y. JETS

49ers lead series, 6-1

1971	49ers 24-21 (NY)
1976	49ers 17-6 (SF)
1980	49ers 32-27 (NY)
1983	Jets 27-13 (SF)
1986	49ers 24-10 (SF)
1989	49ers 23-10 (NY)
1992	49ers 31-14 (NY)

49ERS vs. PHILADELPHIA

49ers lead series, 13-6-1

1951	Eagles, 21-14 (P)
1953	49ers, 31-21 (SF)
1956	Tie, 10-10 (P)
1958	49ers, 30-24 (P)
1959	49ers, 24-14 (SF)
1964	49ers, 28-24 (P)
1966	Eagles, 35-34 (SF)
1967	49ers, 28-27 (P)
1969	49ers, 14-13 (SF)
1971	49ers, 31-3 (P)
1973	49ers, 38-28 (SF)
1975	Eagles, 27-17 (P)
1983	Eagles, 22-17 (SF)
1984	49ers, 21-9 (P)
1985	49ers, 24-13 (SF)
1989	49ers, 38-28 (P)
1991	49ers, 23-7 (P)
1992	49ers, 20-14 (SF)
1993	Eagles, 37-34 (SF) OT
1994	Eagles, 40-8 (SF)

49ERS vs. PITTSBURGH

49ers lead series, 8-7

1951	49ers, 28-24 (P)
1952	Steelers, 24-7 (SF)
1954	49ers, 31-3 (SF)
1958	49ers, 23-20 (SF)
1961	Steelers, 20-10 (P)
1965	49ers, 27-17 (SF)
1968	49ers, 45-28 (P)
1973	Steelers, 37-14 (SF)
1977	Steelers, 27-0 (P)
1978	Steelers, 24-7 (SF)
1981	49ers, 17-14 (P)
1984	Steelers, 20-17 (SF)
1987	Steelers, 30-17 (P)
1990	49ers, 27-7 (SF)
1993	49ers, 24-13 (P)

49ERS vs. SAN DIEGO

49ers lead series, 5-3

1972	49ers, 34-3 (SF)
1976	Chargers, 13-7 (SD) OT
1979	Chargers, 31-9 (SD)
1982	Chargers, 41-37 (SF)
1988	49ers, 48-10 (SD)
1991	49ers, 34-14 (SF)
1994	49ers, 38-15 (SD)
	49ers, 49-26 (Miami)*

*Super Bowl XXIX

49ERS vs. SEATTLE

49ers lead series, 4-1

1976	49ers, 37-21 (S)
1979	Seahawks, 35-24 (SF)
1985	49ers, 19-6 (SF)
1988	49ers, 38-7 (S)
1991	49ers, 24-22 (S)

49ERS vs. TAMPA BAY

49ers lead series, 12-1

1977	49ers, 20-10 (SF)
1978	49ers, 6-3 (SF)
1979	49ers, 23-7 (SF)
1980	Buccaneers, 24-23 (SF)
1983	49ers, 35-21 (SF)
1984	49ers, 24-17 (SF)
1986	49ers, 31-7 (TB)
1987	49ers, 24-10 (TB)
1989	49ers, 20-16 (TB)
1990	49ers, 31-7 (SF)
1992	49ers, 21-14 (SF)
1993	49ers, 45-21 (TB)
1994	49ers, 41-16 (SF)

49ERS vs. WASHINGTON

49ers lead series, 13-7-1

1952	49ers, 23-17 (W)
1954	49ers, 41-7 (SF)
1955	Redskins, 7-0 (W)
1961	49ers, 35-3 (SF)
1967	Redskins, 31-28 (W)
1969	Tie, 17-17 (SF)
1970	49ers, 26-17 (SF)
1971	49ers, 24-20 (SF)*
1973	Redskins, 33-9 (W)
1976	Redskins, 24-21 (SF)
1978	Redskins, 38-20 (W)
1981	49ers, 30-17 (W)
1983	Redskins, 24-21 (W)**
1984	49ers, 37-31 (SF)
1985	49ers, 35-8 (W)
1986	Redskins, 14-6 (W)
1988	49ers, 37-21 (SF)
1990	49ers, 26-13 (SF)
	49ers, 28-10 (SF)*
1992	49ers, 20-13 (SF)*
1994	49ers, 37-22 (W)

*NFC Divisional Playoff
**NFC Championship

49ERS' YEAR BY YEAR SCORES

ALL-AMERICA FOOTBALL CONFERENCE

1946 (9-5)
Lawrence T. (Buck) Shaw, Coach

L	7	N.Y. Yankees	21
W	21	Miami	14
W	32	Brooklyn	13
L	7	at Chi. Rockets	21
W	34	at Miami	7
W	23	at L.A. Dons	14
L	14	at Buffalo	17
W	34	at Cleveland	20
W	27	Buffalo	14
L	7	Cleveland	14
L	9	at N.Y. Yankees	10
W	30	at Brooklyn	14
W	14	Chi. Rockets	0
W	48	L.A. Dons	7

1947 (8-4-2)
Lawrence T. (Buck) Shaw, Coach

W	23	Brooklyn	7
W	17	L.A. Dons	14
W	14	Baltimore	7
L	16	N.Y. Yankees	21
W	41	at Buffalo	24
T	28	at Baltimore	28
W	42	Chi. Rockets	28
L	7	Cleveland	14
W	26	at L.A. Dons	16
L	16	at N.Y. Yankees	24
L	14	at Cleveland	37
W	41	at Chi. Rockets	16
W	21	at Brooklyn	7
T	21	Buffalo	21

1948 (12-2)
Lawrence T. (Buck) Shaw, Coach

W	35	Buffalo	14
W	36	Brooklyn	20
W	41	N.Y. Yankees	0
W	36	L.A. Dons	14
W	38	at Buffalo	28
W	31	at Chi. Rockets	14
W	56	at Baltimore	14
W	21	at N.Y. Yankees	7
W	21	Baltimore	10
W	44	Chi. Rockets	21
L	7	at Cleveland	14
W	63	at Brooklyn	40
L	28	Cleveland	31
W	38	at L.A. Dons	21

1949 (9-3/10-4)
Lawrence T. (Buck) Shaw, Coach

W	31	Baltimore	17
W	42	Chi. Hornets	7
W	42	L.A. Dons	14
L	17	at Buffalo	28
W	42	at Chi. Hornets	24
W	56	Cleveland	28
W	51	Buffalo	7
L	3	at N.Y. Yankees	24
L	28	at Cleveland	30
W	28	at Baltimore	10
W	41	at L.A. Dons	24
W	35	N.Y. Yankees	14

Playoff Game

W	17	N.Y. Yankees	7

Championship Game

L	7	at Cleveland	21

NATIONAL FOOTBALL LEAGUE

1950 (3-9)
Lawrence T. (Buck) Shaw, Coach

L	17	N.Y. Yankees	21
L	20	Chi. Bears	32
L	14	L.A. Rams	35
L	7	at Detroit	24
L	24	at N.Y. Yankees	29
W	28	Detroit	27
W	17	Baltimore	14
L	21	at L.A. Rams	28
L	14	at Cleveland	34
L	0	at Chi. Bears	17
L	21	at Green Bay	25
W	30	Green Bay	14

1951 (7-4-1)
Lawrence T. (Buck) Shaw, Coach

W	24	Cleveland	10
L	14	at Philadelphia	21
W	28	at Pittsburgh	24
L	7	at Chi. Bears	13
W	44	L.A. Rams	17
L	16	at L.A. Rams	23
W	19	N.Y. Yankees	14
L	21	Chi. Cardinals	27
T	10	at N.Y. Yankees	10
W	20	at Detroit	10
W	31	Green Bay	19
W	21	Detroit	17

1952 (7-5)
Lawrence T. (Buck) Shaw, Coach

W	17	Detroit	3
W	37	at Dallas	14
W	28	at Detroit	0
W	40	at Chi. Bears	16
W	48	Dallas	21
L	17	Chi. Bears	20
L	14	at N.Y. Giants	23
W	23	at Washington	17
L	9	at L.A. Rams	35
L	21	L.A. Rams	34
L	7	Pittsburgh	24
W	24	Green Bay	14

1953 (9-3)
Lawrence T. (Buck) Shaw, Coach

W	31	Philadelphia	21
W	31	L.A. Rams	30
L	21	at Detroit	24
W	35	at Chi. Bears	28
L	10	Detroit	14
W	24	Chi. Bears	14
W	31	at L.A. Rams	27
L	21	at Cleveland	23
W	37	at Green Bay (Milw.)	7
W	38	at Baltimore	21
W	48	Green Bay	14
W	45	Baltimore	14

1954 (7-4-1)
Lawrence T. (Buck) Shaw, Coach

W	41	Washington	7
T	24	at L.A. Rams	24
W	23	at Green Bay (Milw.)	17
W	31	at Chi. Bears	24
W	37	Detroit	31
L	27	Chi. Bears	31
L	34	L.A. Rams	42
L	7	at Detroit	48
W	31	at Pittsburgh	3
L	13	at Baltimore	17
W	35	Green Bay	0
W	10	Baltimore	7

1955 (4-8)
Norman (Red) Strader, Coach

L	14	L.A. Rams	23
L	3	Cleveland	38
W	20	at Chi. Bears	19
W	27	at Detroit	24
L	23	Chi. Bears	34
W	38	Detroit	21
L	14	at L.A. Rams	27
L	0	at Washington	7
L	21	at Green Bay (Milw.)	27
L	14	at Baltimore	26
L	7	Green Bay	28
W	35	Baltimore	24

1956 (5-6-1)
Frankie Albert, Coach

L	21	N.Y. Giants	38
W	33	L.A. Rams	30
L	7	at Chi. Bears	31
L	17	at Detroit	20
L	21	Chi. Bears	38
L	13	Detroit	17
L	6	at L.A. Rams	30
W	17	at Green Bay	16
T	10	at Philadelphia	10
W	20	at Baltimore	17
W	38	Green Bay	20
W	30	Baltimore	17

1957 (8-4/8-5)
Frankie Albert, Coach

L	10	Chi. Cardinals	20
W	23	L.A. Rams	20
W	21	at Chi. Bears	17
W	24	at Green Bay (Milw.)	14
W	21	Chi. Bears	17
W	35	Detroit	31
L	24	at L.A. Rams	37
L	10	at Detroit	31
L	21	at Baltimore	27
W	27	at N.Y. Giants	17
W	17	Baltimore	13
W	27	Green Bay	20

Divisional Playoff Game

L	27	Detroit	31

49ERS' YEAR BY YEAR SCORES

1958 (6-6)
Frankie Albert, Coach

W	23	Pittsburgh	20
L	3	L.A. Rams	33
L	6	at Chi. Bears	28
W	30	at Philadelphia	24
L	14	Chi. Bears	27
W	24	Detroit	21
L	7	at L.A. Rams	56
L	21	at Detroit	35
W	33	at Green Bay (Milw.)	12
L	27	at Baltimore	35
W	48	Green Bay	21
W	21	Baltimore	12

1959 (7-5)
Howard (Red) Hickey, Coach

W	24	Philadelphia	14
W	34	L.A. Rams	0
L	20	at Green Bay	21
W	34	at Detroit	13
W	20	Chi. Bears	17
W	33	Detroit	7
W	24	at L.A. Rams	16
L	3	at Chi. Bears	14
L	14	at Baltimore	45
W	21	at Cleveland	20
L	14	Baltimore	34
L	14	Green Bay	36

1960 (7-5)
Howard (Red) Hickey, Coach

L	19	N.Y. Giants	21
W	13	L.A. Rams	9
W	14	at Detroit	10
L	10	at Chicago	27
L	14	at Green Bay (Milw.)	41
W	25	Chicago	7
L	0	Detroit	24
W	26	at Dallas	14
W	30	at Baltimore	22
W	23	at L.A. Rams	7
L	0	Green Bay	13
W	34	Baltimore	10

1961 (7-6-1)
Howard (Red) Hickey, Coach

W	35	Washington	3
L	10	at Green Bay	30
W	49	at Detroit	0
W	35	L.A. Rams	0
W	38	at Minnesota	24
L	0	at Chicago	31
L	10	at Pittsburgh	20
T	20	Detroit	20
L	7	at L.A. Rams	17
W	41	Chicago	31
W	38	Minnesota	28
L	17	at Baltimore	20
W	22	Green Bay	21
L	24	Baltimore	27

1962 (6-8)
Howard (Red) Hickey, Coach

L	14	Chicago	30
L	24	at Detroit	45
W	21	Minnesota	7
W	21	at Baltimore	13
W	34	at Chicago	27
L	13	at Green Bay (Milw.)	31
L	14	L.A. Rams	28
L	3	Baltimore	22
L	24	Detroit	38
W	24	at L.A. Rams	17
W	24	at St. Louis	17
W	35	at Minnesota	12
L	21	Green Bay	31
L	10	Cleveland	13

1963 (2-12)
Coach*

L	20	Minnesota	24
L	14	Baltimore	20
L	14	at Minnesota	45
L	3	at Detroit	26
L	3	at Baltimore	20
W	20	Chicago	14
L	21	at L.A. Rams	28
L	7	Detroit	45
W	31	Dallas	24
L	14	at N.Y. Giants	48
L	10	at Green Bay (Milw.)	28
L	17	L.A. Rams	21
L	7	at Chicago	27
L	17	Green Bay	21

*Coach Red Hickey resigned after the
third game; Jack Christiansen
was appointed his successor.

1964 (4-10)
Jack Christiansen, Coach

L	17	Detroit	26
W	28	at Philadelphia	24
L	13	St. Louis	23
W	31	Chicago	21
L	14	at Green Bay (Milw.)	24
L	14	at L.A. Rams	42
L	22	Minnesota	27
L	7	at Baltimore	37
L	7	at Minnesota	24
W	24	Green Bay	14
L	21	at Chicago	23
L	3	Baltimore	14
W	28	L.A. Rams	7
L	7	at Detroit	24

1965 (7-6-1)
Jack Christiansen, Coach

W	52	Chicago	24
W	27	Pittsburgh	17
L	24	at Baltimore	27
L	10	at Green Bay	27
W	45	at L.A. Rams	21
L	41	Minnesota	42
L	28	Baltimore	34
L	31	at Dallas	39
W	27	at Detroit	21
W	30	L.A. Rams	27
W	45	at Minnesota	24
W	17	Detroit	14
L	20	at Chicago	61
T	24	Green Bay	24

1966 (6-6-2)
Jack Christiansen, Coach

T	20	Minnesota	20
L	14	at Baltimore	36
L	3	at L.A. Rams	34
W	21	Green Bay	20
W	44	at Atlanta	7
W	27	Detroit	24
L	3	at Minnesota	28
W	21	L.A. Rams	13
T	30	at Chicago	30
L	34	Philadelphia	35
W	41	at Detroit	14
L	7	at Green Bay (Milw.)	20
W	41	Chicago	14
L	14	Baltimore	30

1967 (7-7)
Jack Christiansen, Coach

W	27	at Minnesota	21
W	38	Atlanta	7
L	7	at Baltimore	41
W	27	at L.A. Rams	24
W	28	at Philadelphia	27
W	27	New Orleans	13
L	3	Detroit	45
L	7	L.A. Rams	17
L	28	at Washington	31
L	0	at Green Bay	13
L	9	Baltimore	26
L	14	Chicago	28
W	34	at Atlanta	28
W	24	Dallas	16

1968 (7-6-1)
Dick Nolan, Coach

L	10	at Baltimore	27
W	35	St. Louis	17
W	28	Atlanta	13
L	10	at L.A. Rams	24
L	14	Baltimore	42
W	26	at N.Y. Giants	10
W	14	at Detroit	7
L	21	Cleveland	33
L	19	at Chicago	27
T	20	L.A. Rams	20
W	45	at Pittsburgh	28
W	27	Green Bay	20
L	20	Minnesota	30
W	14	at Atlanta	12

1969 (4-8-2)
Dick Nolan, Coach

L	12	at Atlanta	24
L	7	at Green Bay (Milw.)	14
T	17	Washington	17
L	21	L.A. Rams	27
L	7	Atlanta	21
W	24	at Baltimore	21
L	14	Detroit	26
L	30	at L.A. Rams	41
W	20	Baltimore	17
L	38	at New Orleans	43
T	24	at Dallas	24
W	42	Chicago	21
L	7	at Minnesota	10
W	14	Philadelphia	13

4 9 E R S ' Y E A R B Y Y E A R S C O R E S

1970 (10-3-1/11-4-1)
Dick Nolan, Coach

W	26	Washington	17
W	34	Cleveland	31
L	20	at Atlanta	21
W	20	at L.A. Rams	6
T	20	New Orleans	20
W	19	Denver	14
W	26	Green Bay	10
W	37	at Chicago	16
W	30	at Houston	20
L	7	at Detroit	28
L	13	L.A. Rams	30
W	24	Atlanta	20
W	38	at New Orleans	27
W	38	at Oakland	7

NFC Divisional Playoff Game

W	17	at Minnesota	14

NFC Championship Game

L	10	Dallas	17

1971 (9-5/10-6)
Dick Nolan, Coach

L	17	at Atlanta	20
W	38	at New Orleans	20
W	31	at Philadelphia	3
L	13	*L.A. Rams	20
W	13	Chicago	0
W	26	at St. Louis	14
W	27	New England	10
W	13	at Minnesota	9
L	20	New Orleans	26
L	6	at L.A. Rams	17
W	24	at N.Y. Jets	21
L	17	Kansas City	26
W	24	Atlanta	3
W	31	Detroit	27

NFC Divisional Playoff Game

W	24	Washington	20

NFC Championship Game

L	3	at Dallas	14

49ers' first regular-season game at Candlestick Park

1972 (8-5-1/8-6-1)
Dick Nolan, Coach

W	34	San Diego	3
L	20	at Buffalo	27
W	37	at New Orleans	2
L	7	at L.A. Rams	31
L	17	N.Y. Giants	23
T	20	New Orleans	20
W	49	at Atlanta	14
L	24	at Green Bay (Milw.)	34
W	24	Baltimore	21
W	34	at Chicago	21
W	31	at Dallas	10
L	16	L.A. Rams	26
W	20	Atlanta	0
W	20	Minnesota	17

NFC Divisional Playoff Game

L	28	Dallas	30

1973 (5-9)
Dick Nolan, Coach

L	13	at Miami	21
W	36	at Denver	34
L	20	L.A. Rams	40
W	13	at Atlanta	9
L	13	Minnesota	17
W	40	New Orleans	0
L	3	Atlanta	17
L	20	at Detroit	30
L	9	at Washington	33
L	13	at L.A. Rams	31
W	20	Green Bay	6
W	38	Philadelphia	28
L	10	at New Orleans	16
L	14	Pittsburgh	37

1974 (6-8)
Dick Nolan, Coach

W	17	at New Orleans	13
W	17	at Atlanta	10
L	3	Cincinnati	21
L	9	St. Louis	34
L	13	at Detroit	17
L	14	at L.A. Rams	37
L	24	Oakland	35
L	13	L.A. Rams	15
L	14	at Dallas	20
W	34	at Chicago	0
W	27	Atlanta	0
L	0	at Cleveland	7
W	7	Green Bay	6
W	35	New Orleans	21

1975 (5-9)
Dick Nolan, Coach

L	17	at Minnesota	27
L	14	L.A. Rams	23
W	20	at Kansas City	3
L	3	Atlanta	17
W	35	New Orleans	21
L	16	at New England	24
L	17	Detroit	28
W	24	at L.A. Rams	23
W	31	Chicago	3
W	16	at New Orleans	6
L	17	at Philadelphia	27
L	13	Houston	27
L	9	at Atlanta	31
L	23	N.Y. Giants	26

1976 (8-6)
Monte Clark, Coach

W	26	at Green Bay	14
L	12	Chicago	19
W	37	at Seattle	21
W	17	N.Y. Jets	6
W	16	at L.A. Rams	0
W	33	New Orleans	3
W	15	Atlanta	0
L	20	at St. Louis	23 (OT)
L	21	Washington	24
L	16	at Atlanta	21
L	3	L.A. Rams	23
W	20	Minnesota	16
L	7	at San Diego	13 (OT)
W	27	at New Orleans	7

1977 (5-9)
Ken Meyer, Coach

L	0	at Pittsburgh	27
L	15	Miami	19
L	14	at L.A. Rams	34
L	0	Atlanta	7
L	17	at N.Y. Giants	20
W	28	Detroit	7
W	20	Tampa Bay	10
W	10	at Atlanta	3
W	10	at New Orleans	7 (OT)
L	10	L.A. Rams	23
W	20	New Orleans	17
L	27	at Minnesota	28
L	35	Dallas	42
L	14	at Green Bay (Milw.)	16

1978 (2-14)
Coach*

L	7	at Cleveland	24
L	14	Chicago	16
L	19	at Houston	20
L	10	at N.Y. Giants	27
W	28	Cincinnati	12
L	10	at L.A. Rams	27
L	7	New Orleans	14
L	17	Atlanta	20
L	20	at Washington	38
L	10	at Atlanta	21
L	10	St. Louis	16
L	28	L.A. Rams	31
L	7	Pittsburgh	24
L	13	at New Orleans	24
W	6	Tampa Bay	3
L	14	at Detroit	33

*Pete McCulley was fired after nine games;
Fred O'Connor was appointed his successor.*

1979 (2-14)
Bill Walsh, Coach

L	22	at Minnesota	28
L	13	Dallas	21
L	24	at L.A. Rams	27
L	21	New Orleans	30
L	9	at San Diego	31
L	24	Seattle	35
L	16	at N.Y. Giants	32
W	20	Atlanta	15
L	27	Chicago	28
L	10	at Oakland	23
L	20	at New Orleans	31
L	28	Denver	38
L	20	L.A. Rams	26
L	10	at St. Louis	13
W	23	Tampa Bay	7
L	21	at Atlanta	31

49ERS' YEAR BY YEAR SCORES

1980 (6-10)
Bill Walsh, Coach

W	26	at New Orleans	23
W	24	St. Louis	21 (OT)
W	37	at N.Y. Jets	27
L	17	Atlanta	20
L	26	at L.A. Rams	48
L	14	at Dallas	59
L	17	L.A. Rams	31
L	23	Tampa Bay	24
L	13	at Detroit	17
L	16	at Green Bay (Milw.)	23
L	13	at Miami	17
W	12	N.Y. Giants	0
W	21	New England	17
W	38	New Orleans	35 (OT)
L	10	at Atlanta	35
L	13	Buffalo	18

1981 (13-3/16-3)
Super Bowl Champions
Bill Walsh, Coach

L	17	at Detroit	24
W	28	Chicago	17
L	17	at Atlanta	34
W	21	New Orleans	14
W	30	at Washington	17
W	45	Dallas	14
W	13	at Green Bay (Milw.)	3
W	20	L.A. Rams	17
W	17	at Pittsburgh	14
W	17	Atlanta	14
L	12	Cleveland	15
W	33	at L.A. Rams	31
W	17	N.Y. Giants	10
W	21	at Cincinnati	3
W	28	Houston	6
W	21	at New Orleans	17

NFC Divisional Playoff Game

W	38	N.Y. Giants	24

NFC Championship Game

W	28	Dallas	27

Super Bowl XVI
(at Pontiac Silverdome, Pontiac, Michigan)

W	26	Cincinnati	21

1982 (3-6)
Bill Walsh, Coach

L	17	L.A. Raiders	23
L	21	at Denver	24
W	31	at St. Louis	20
L	20	New Orleans	23
W	30	at L.A. Rams	24
L	37	San Diego	41
L	7	Atlanta	17
W	26	at Kansas City	13
L	20	L.A. Rams	21

1983 (10-6/11-7)
Bill Walsh, Coach

L	17	Philadelphia	22
W	48	at Minnesota	17
W	42	at St. Louis	27
W	24	Atlanta	20
W	33	at New England	13
L	7	L.A. Rams	10
W	32	at New Orleans	13
W	45	at L.A. Rams	35
L	13	N.Y. Jets	27
L	17	Miami	20
W	27	New Orleans	0
L	24	at Atlanta	28
L	3	at Chicago	13
W	35	Tampa Bay	21
W	23	at Buffalo	10
W	42	Dallas	17

NFC Divisional Playoff Game

W	24	Detroit	23

NFC Championship Game

L	21	at Washington	24

1984 (15-1/18-1)
Super Bowl Champions
Bill Walsh, Coach

W	30	at Detroit	27
W	37	Washington	31
W	30	New Orleans	20
W	21	at Philadelphia	9
W	14	Atlanta	5
W	31	at N.Y. Giants	10
L	17	Pittsburgh	20
W	34	at Houston	21
W	33	at L.A. Rams	0
W	23	Cincinnati	17
W	41	at Cleveland	7
W	24	Tampa Bay	17
W	35	at New Orleans	3
W	35	at Atlanta	17
W	51	Minnesota	7
W	19	L.A. Rams	16

NFC Divisional Playoff Game

W	21	N.Y. Giants	10

NFC Championship Game

W	23	Chicago	0

Super Bowl XIX
(at Stanford Stadium, Stanford, California)

W	38	Miami	16

1985 (10-6/10-7)
Bill Walsh, Coach

L	21	at Minnesota	28
W	35	Atlanta	16
W	34	at L.A. Raiders	10
L	17	New Orleans	20
W	38	at Atlanta	17
L	10	Chicago	26
L	21	at Detroit	23
W	28	at L.A. Rams	14
W	24	Philadelphia	13
L	16	at Denver	17
W	31	Kansas City	3
W	19	Seattle	6
W	35	at Washington	8
L	20	L.A. Rams	27
W	31	at New Orleans	19
W	31	Dallas	16

NFC Wild Card Playoff Game

L	3	at N.Y. Giants	17

1986 (10-5-1/10-6-1)
Bill Walsh, Coach

W	31	at Tampa Bay	7
L	13	at L.A. Rams	16
W	26	New Orleans	17
W	31	at Miami	17
W	35	Indianapolis	14
L	24	Minnesota	27 (OT)
T	10	at Atlanta	10 (OT)
W	31	at Green Bay (Milw.)	17
L	10	at New Orleans	23
W	43	St. Louis	17
L	6	at Washington	14
W	20	Atlanta	0
L	17	N.Y. Giants	21
W	24	N.Y. Jets	10
W	29	at New England	24
W	24	L.A. Rams	14

NFC Divisional Playoff Game

L	3	at N.Y. Giants	49

1987 (13-2/13-3)
Bill Walsh, Coach

L	17	at Pittsburgh	30
W	27	at Cincinnati	26
W	41	at N.Y. Giants	21
W	25	at Atlanta	17
W	34	St. Louis	28
W	24	at New Orleans	22
W	31	at L.A. Rams	10
W	27	Houston	20
L	24	New Orleans	26
W	24	at Tampa Bay	10
W	38	Cleveland	24
W	23	at Green Bay	12
W	41	Chicago	0
W	35	Atlanta	7
W	48	L.A. Rams	0

NFC Divisional Playoff Game

L	24	Minnesota	36

49ERS' YEAR BY YEAR SCORES

1988 (10-6/13-6)
Super Bowl Champions
Bill Walsh, Coach

W	34	at New Orleans	33
W	20	at N.Y. Giants	17
L	17	Atlanta	34
W	38	at Seattle	7
W	20	Detroit	13
L	13	Denver	16 (OT)
W	24	at L.A. Rams	21
L	9	at Chicago	10
W	24	Minnesota	21
L	23	at Phoenix	24
L	3	L.A. Raiders	9
W	37	Washington	21
W	48	at San Diego	10
W	13	at Atlanta	3
W	30	New Orleans	17
L	16	L.A. Rams	38

NFC Divisional Playoff Game

W	34	Minnesota	9

NFC Championship Game

W	28	at Chicago	3

Super Bowl XXIII
(at Joe Robbie Stadium, Miami, Florida)

W	20	Cincinnati	16

1989 (14-2/17-2)
Super Bowl Champions
George Seifert, Coach

W	30	at Indianapolis	24
W	20	at Tampa Bay	16
W	38	at Philadelphia	28
L	12	L.A. Rams	13
W	24	at New Orleans	20
W	31	at Dallas	14
W	37	*New England	20
W	23	at N.Y. Jets	10
W	31	New Orleans	13
W	45	Atlanta	3
L	17	Green Bay	21
W	34	N.Y. Giants	24
W	23	at Atlanta	10
W	30	at L.A. Rams	27
W	21	Buffalo	10
W	26	Chicago	0

*Game played at Stanford Stadium due to Bay Area earthquake

NFC Divisional Playoff Game

W	41	Minnesota	13

NFC Championship Game

W	30	L.A. Rams	3

Super Bowl XXIV
(at Louisiana Superdome, New Orleans, Louisiana)

W	55	Denver	10

1990 (14-2/15-3)
George Seifert, Coach

W	13	at New Orleans	12
W	26	Washington	13
W	19	Atlanta	13
W	24	at Houston	21
W	45	at Atlanta	35
W	27	Pittsburgh	7
W	20	Cleveland	17
W	24	at Green Bay	20
W	24	at Dallas	6
W	31	Tampa Bay	7
L	17	L.A. Rams	28
W	7	N.Y. Giants	3
W	20	at Cincinnati	17 (OT)
W	26	at L.A. Rams	10
L	10	New Orleans	13
W	20	at Minnesota	17

NFC Divisional Playoff Game

W	28	Washington	10

NFC Championship Game

L	13	N.Y. Giants	15

1991 (10-6)
George Seifert, Coach

L	14	at N.Y. Giants	16
W	34	San Diego	14
L	14	at Minnesota	17
W	27	L.A. Rams	10
L	6	at L.A. Raiders	12
L	34	Atlanta	39
W	35	Detroit	3
W	23	at Philadelphia	7
L	14	at Atlanta	17
L	3	at New Orleans	10
W	14	Phoenix	10
W	33	at L.A. Rams	10
W	38	New Orleans	24
W	24	at Seattle	22
W	28	Kansas City	14
W	52	Chicago	14

1992 (14-2/15-3)
George Seifert, Coach

W	31	at N.Y. Giants	14
L	31	Buffalo	34
W	31	at N.Y. Jets	14
W	16	at New Orleans	10
W	27	L.A. Rams	24
W	24	at New England	12
W	56	Atlanta	17
L	14	at Phoenix	24
W	41	at Atlanta	3
W	21	New Orleans	20
W	27	at L.A. Rams	10
W	20	Philadelphia	14
W	27	Miami	3
W	20	at Minnesota	17
W	21	Tampa Bay	14
W	24	Detroit	6

NFC Divisional Playoff Game

W	20	Washington	13

NFC Championship Game

L	20	Dallas	30

1993 (10-6/11-7)
George Seifert, Coach

W	24	at Pittsburgh	13
L	13	at Cleveland	23
W	37	Atlanta	30
L	13	at New Orleans	16
W	38	Minnesota	19
L	17	at Dallas	26
W	28	Phoenix	14
W	40	L.A. Rams	17
W	45	at Tampa Bay	21
W	42	New Orleans	7
W	35	at L.A. Rams	10
W	21	Cincinnati	8
L	24	at Atlanta	27
W	55	at Detroit	17
L	7	Houston	10
L	34	Philadelphia	37 (OT)

NFC Divisional Playoff Game

W	44	N.Y. Giants	3

NFC Championship Game

L	21	at Dallas	38

1994 (13-3/16-3)
Super Bowl Champions
George Seifert, Coach

W	44	L.A. Raiders	14
L	17	at Kansas City	24
W	34	at L.A. Rams	19
W	24	New Orleans	13
L	8	Philadelphia	40
W	27	at Detroit	21
W	42	at Atlanta	3
W	41	Tampa Bay	16
W	37	at Washington	22
W	21	Dallas	14
W	31	L.A. Rams	27
W	35	at New Orleans	14
W	50	Atlanta	14
W	38	at San Diego	15
W	42	Denver	19
L	14	at Minnesota	21

NFC Divisional Playoff Game

W	44	Chicago	15

NFC Championship Game

W	38	Dallas	28

Super Bowl XXIX
(at Joe Robbie Stadium, Miami, Florida)

W	49	San Diego	26

CREDITS

TURNER PUBLISHING, INC.

EDITOR:
Kevin Mulroy

COPY EDITOR:
Lauren Emerson

DESIGN DIRECTOR:
Michael J. Walsh

DESIGNER:
Carol Norton

PICTURE EDITOR:
Marty Moore

PRODUCTION:
Tom Maiellaro

**NFL PROPERTIES
CREATIVE SERVICES**

VICE PRESIDENT,
EDITOR IN CHIEF:
John Wiebusch

GENERAL MANAGER:
Bill Barron

MANAGING EDITOR:
Chuck Garrity, Sr.

PROJECT EDITOR:
Jim Gigliotti

ASSOCIATE EDITORS:
Matt Marini, Jim Perry

PHOTOGRAPHY

(Legend: T=top, B=bottom, L=left, R=right, TL=top left, TR=top right, BL=bottom left, BR=bottom right)

Michael Zagaris: 6, 12, 13, 14, 15, 68, 71, 77, 81, 83, 82, 84, 85, 90–91, 94–95, 96, 97, 98, 100, 101T, 101B, 102, 104–105, 106, 107, 108–109, 110, 111, 112, 113, 114, 115, 116, 117T, 117B, 118T, 118B, 119, 120, 122–123, 124, 125, 126, 127, 128, 129, 131, 132–133, 133T, 134T, 134B, 135, 136, 137, 139, 140, 141, 142–143, 144, 145L, 145R, 146, 147, 148, 149, 150, 151, 152, 153, 154, 155, 156, 157, 158, 159, 160, 161T, 161B, 162–163, 164, 165, 166, 167, 168–169, 170, 171, 172–173, 174, 175, 176T, 176–177, 178, 179, 181, 182, 183, 184, 185, 186, 187, 188–189, 191, 192, 193T, 193B, 194–195, 196, 197, 198, 199, 200, 201, 202–203, 204, 205B, 207, 208, 209, 211, 212, 213, 214–215, 216T, 216B, 217, 218, 220T, 220B, 221, 222, 224, 225, 226, 227T, 227B, 228T, 228B, 229, 230T, 231, 232, 233T, 233B, 237TR; courtesy of Michael Zagaris: programs: 36–37; cards: 28, 43, 55, 77, 89; photos: 42, 44.

NFL Photos: 19, 26B, 26–27, 29, 30–31, 34, 38, 46, 50, 56TR, 59, 69, 74, 78, 87, 138; Clem Albers: 23; Vernon Biever: 20–21; David Boss: 54, 66–67, 72, 73; CAL Pictures: 25, 55B, 61, 62, 76; Lee Hansen: 40; HOF: 18, 60, 75BR; Fred Kaplan: 92; Ross Lewis: 86; Richard Mackson: 190; Fred Matthes: 51BR; Russ Reed: 2–3, 24; Frank Rippon: 16–17, 28, 32, 35, 39, 41, 47, 48–49, 51TL, 51TR, 51BL, 52, 53, 58, 65, 70, 103; George Rose: 205T; *San Francisco Chronicle*: 57; Vic Stein: 45; Chad Surmick: 223; Tony Tomsic: 99.

Sports Illustrated: Walter Iooss, Jr.: 10, 240; J. Lovero: 4–5; John McDonough: 234–235; Peter Read Miller: 236–237; Hy Peskin: 89; Bill Young: 30TR.

AllSport: Jonathan Daniel: 239; Mike Powell: 230B; Rick Stewart: 238.

UPI/**Bettmann Newsphotos:** 22, 75BL.

ILLUSTRATION
Cover illustration by Tom Nikosey.